Eighteenth-Century Women:
An Anthology

Eighteenth-Century Women: An Anthology

Br

ROUTLEDGE

L

First published 1984 by
Unwin Hyman Ltd
First published in paperback 1987

Reprinted 1993
by Routledge
11 New Fetter Lane, London EC4P 4EE
29 West 35th Street, New York, NY 10001

© 1984, 1987 Bridget Hill

Typeset in Times by Alan Sutton Publishing Ltd, Gloucester
Printed and bound in Great Britain by
Biddles Ltd, Guildford and King's Lynn

British Library Cataloguing in Publication Data
A catalogue record for this book is available from the British Library

Library of Congress Cataloging in Publication Data
Also available

ISBN 0-415-10446-7

Contents

Eighteenth-Century Women:
An Anthology

General Introduction

Anthologies need some justification. This one was prompted by the growing realisation of just how little work had been done on women's history in the eighteenth century over the last fifty years. For anyone wanting to know something of women in this century, there remains very little in the way of easily accessible, primary source material and even less in the way of secondary. Yet today we are experiencing a period in which, in the most exciting way, the rise of the feminist movement has concentrated attention on women's history as never before. As a result there has been a re-examination of women's experience, past and present, and a fresh and critical reappraisal of the nature of women's role in society. There is now a great deal of work completed or in progress on many aspects of women's history, but still, for the most part, the eighteenth century in England is ignored. It is not surprising that the initial area on which attention has been focused has been the period of the women's suffrage movement – roughly speaking, the period from the middle of the nineteenth century, for the winning of the vote marked the passing of a major obstacle to women's emancipation. Yet it is surely curious that a period of history like the eighteenth century, which is so generally taught at both school and university, should remain very much male history and so largely ignore women.

It becomes curiouser when one starts to survey the work that has been done on eighteenth-century women. The only major study of working women in agriculture and industry, and covering only the second half of the century, is Ivy Pinchbeck's *Women Workers and the Industrial Revolution* published in 1930 and reprinted by Virago Press in 1981. It is a parallel work to Alice Clark's *Working Life of Women in the 17th Century* written as long ago as 1919. It would be easier to explain the relative absence of further work if these had been bad books. But they were not. Both were extremely thorough, scholarly surveys. Both are works that might have been expected to open up the two periods to further research. (Anyone starting to study eighteenth-century working women ignores Ivy Pinchbeck's book at their cost.) But further research failed to materialise – at least until recently, when after a gap of nearly half a century, work on seventeenth-century women is once more proceeding – in no small part stimulated by historians such as Keith Thomas.

In the case of the eighteenth century very little further work has been done. Why? On the whole, recent historians of the eighteenth century, whether political or economic, have been cautious if not conservative in outlook. Lewis Namier's work on *The Structure of Politics at the Accession of George III*, published in 1929, continued to dominate all work on eighteenth-century politics long after its publication. The debate between optimists and pessimists over whether or not the standard of living rose, fell or remained static in the period between 1770 and 1830 is an old one. In the early years of this century, the cause of the pessimists was perhaps most outstandingly exemplified by the work of the Hammonds, J. L. and B., in *The Village Labourer* (1911), *The Town Labourer* (1917) and *The Skilled Labourer* (1919). Their work came under attack when Professor Clapham (*An Economic History of Modern Britain* (1926), 1950, second preface and passim) queried the reliability of the sources on which the Hammonds had based their work. It was a debate that embraced many other contestants, but the final outcome was not merely to demote the work of the Hammonds but to demote social history in favour of much greater concentration by academic historians on economic history. The work of T. S. Ashton in its cool and dispassionate survey of the eighteenth-century economy is representative of this trend. As a contestant in the debate he concluded that, apart from some short-term dislocations as a result of which some temporary hardships were felt, developments were for the benefit of all.

The last thirty years have seen the production of a vast number of studies of the history of individual industries and trades. In some of these industries women are known to have played a role – on occasion a substantial one – yet not only do the indexes often omit any reference to women, but it would be quite possible to read the work and to conclude that women were in no way involved.

It would be very wrong, however, to leave the impression that no other contribution to the history of women in the eighteenth century had been made before the late 1960s when there was a marked revival of social history as an academically respectable subject. The work of Dorothy Marshall, M. Dorothy George, R. Bayne-Powell, Margaret Hewitt, D. Jarrett and Asa Briggs springs to mind and, in the field of literary studies, the work of such pioneers as Myra Reynolds, R. P. Utter and G. B. Needham. More recently there has been a great deal of work done on the family, on parenthood and childhood, on custom and folklore and, indeed, on women, sex and marriage – but even so relatively little of it has focused attention on the eighteenth century.

If there is now more work in progress on women's part in the social and industrial life of the eighteenth century, the contribution of British as against American historians remains small. Indeed, it is somewhat humiliating to discover the wealth of interest and enthusiasm that is now generated in American universities by the fertile field of women's history on this side of the Atlantic! Why is it that so far our feminist movement has generated so little interest in the eighteenth century? If the purpose of the study of women's history is to establish the ancestry of present-day feminism, then perhaps the eighteenth century has been found wanting. What feminism there was may have been seen as betraying far too many weaknesses and contradictions to be acknowledged. Of course, it all depends on what is seen as the purpose of women's history. It goes without saying that the vast majority of women in the eighteenth century were grossly under-privileged and wickedly exploited. In the face of such exploitation and the intolerable position women were expected to occupy, it is amazing that there were so many who heroically struggled against all their disadvantages to achieve so much. But the history of eighteenth-century women is sometimes anything but heroic. The vast majority of middle-class women unquestioningly conformed to the role assigned to them. If some were aware how restricting and limited was their prescribed role, and longed for more education, expanding employment opportunities and greater free-dom, there were also those who were as brutal and scornful in their reaction to such nonconformity, wherever and whenever it showed itself, as the members of the other sex. If among labouring women, of whom we know all too little, there were those who protested against their exploitation, who pondered on a new and better world for the female poor, the brutalising conditions of many of their lives, and the desperate urgency of making a living ensured that they were but a small minority.

For us it requires an act of imagination to realise that in the eighteenth century by far the majority of the population lived in the countryside and were dependent for their livelihood on the land – if often supplemented by some secondary occupation. Towns were few and, with the exception of London, small. So only a minority of the total population were town-dwellers. The exception was London, already with a population of half a million before our century begins, expanding at a remarkable speed throughout the period and maintaining a dominance in economic, social and cultural life commensurate with its size.

One of the problems confronting any historian of women in the eighteenth century is the difficulty of making a comprehensive study of both 'women' and 'ladies'. In the course of the century, the gulf between the very rich and the very poor which had always existed, was extended by the rapid expansion of a socially con-

scious middle class at pains to distance themselves from those
below them in the social hierarchy. As the process developed,
points of contact between them seemingly diminish. Hence,
perhaps, arises the tendency for recent work to concentrate on
either 'ladies', or working 'women', but rarely on both. Yet this
growing gulf and the reasons for it are of crucial importance for an
understanding of the nature and course of development of the
women's movement in the following century and, indeed, in this.
That gulf was one of the consequences of the rapid changes in
agriculture and industry that are associated with the period of the
Industrial Revolution. Whether one accepts that label or not, the
century certainly saw marked changes in the way of life of many of
the population. The break comes somewhere between 1740 and
1780. By the end of the century, although the majority of the
population were still country-dwellers, there were far more towns
and a much larger degree of urbanisation. For women such
changes had one major consequence. T. S. Ashton (*An Economic
History of England: The 18th Century* (1955), 1972, p. 22) talked
of 'an increased proportion of people' moving into 'the middle
ranges' of society. Among farmers, tradesmen and skilled artisans,
many, in the conditions of a growing population and an expanding
home market, found themselves enjoying a far higher standard of
life than earlier. With such higher standards went aspirations to a
way of life for its womenfolk more in keeping with that of women
of the upper classes. Such aspirations were accompanied by an
increasing awareness of social class and what were regarded as
fitting and seemly occupations for the class to which they aspired.
It became more necessary sharply to differentiate one's own class
from that below. One way to establish membership of the middle
class was by the employment of domestic servants. The number
you employed determined your exact social standing. Such social
aspirations were to lead to a steady withdrawal from labour and a
deliberate cultivation of a life of leisure. As Thomas Day put it,
'When once gentility begins there is an end to industry' (*Sandford
and Merton*, 1786, Vol. 3, p. 303). It affected the wives of
tradesmen who, said Defoe, 'Marry the tradesmen but scorn the
trade' (*The Complete English Tradesman*, Vol. 1, from *The Novels
and Miscellaneous Works*, 1840–1, Vol. 17, p. 216); it affected
shopkeepers' wives who were no longer to be found in the shop; it
transformed the wives of prospering farmers whose important
functions on the farm and in marketing the farm produce, tended
to decline.

It may well be that some middle-class women hated the
drudgery of housework – and let us be under no illusion of just
what drudgery eighteenth-century housework presented. Some

farmers' wives may well have resented the heavy burden of work the life of the farm imposed upon them. Had such increased leisure led to more and better education for women, if it had prompted the opening up of more employments or the use of their new leisure in interesting and fulfilling ways, it might have been different. But, in the majority of cases, the drudgery of housework or work on a farm was exchanged for leisure occupied by time-filling rather than productive pursuits so that many such women found their newly won leisure intolerably boring. It would seem, then, that the main motive, if not the only one behind their withdrawal from work, was aspirations to gentility in the women themselves, their husbands, or both.

Of course, much more was involved than the wishes of the women concerned. In agriculture there were the effects of enclosure and improved farming methods, the trend towards larger farms and more capitalist methods of farming, together with increasing agricultural specialisation, and more sophisticated marketing techniques with the moving in of the middlemen. Farm produce was now sent far greater distances than were involved when the local market was the focus of farms. The result was a steady erosion of those areas of farming – the dairy, butter- and cheese-making, the rearing of pigs and poultry, and the actual marketing of farm produce – in which women had traditionally played so central a role.

As tradesmen and artisans expanded their business they tended to employ more journeymen and apprentices so that the need for their wives' involvement in the business declined. Many such prospering men moved their homes away from their place of work. If it was a consolation for such tradesmen and artisans to have a home and a wife away from all association with their working lives, there were other reasons why they might welcome their wives no longer playing their former role in the business. It served to stress their gentility. It also concealed their financial position from a wife who might well be acquiring rather extravagant 'genteel' tastes.

The changes in agriculture that contributed to making the labour of farmers' wives no longer essential to the economy of the farm worked very differently for women of the labouring class. Many small farms had enjoyed a measure of self-sufficiency only because of the contribution made by their wives. Many could not afford any living-in servants so they were entirely dependent on their own families for labour. The main burden fell on the wife. Even wives of cottagers had been able to contribute significantly to the family economy by work on the cottage garden, by the use of common rights for keeping a few cows or sheep, and by collecting fuel from the forests. The agricultural changes of the century meant that such small farmers, particularly tenant farmers, gradually disappeared, commons and wastes were whittled away by enclosure, many cottages were pulled down to prevent the possibility of their occupants becoming dependent on the parish. All women of the labouring classes suffered, but among those that suffered worst were widows and single women.

As farms got larger and farmers' wives less willing to take on the work involved in housing and feeding servants in husbandry, farmers came to depend on hiring labourers who lived in their own homes but who worked for wages, some few full-time but mostly for certain seasons, for weeks, or even days, of the year. Women could participate in this labour only if they were free from the cares of motherhood, could leave their children with a neighbour, or take their children with them. Even if the amount of such labour had remained the same, it was no longer as easy as earlier for women to carry on productive labour. In fact, for a period from sometime in the second half of the century probably until the early nineteenth century, the amount of agricultural labour open to women declined. Such a decline was not universal throughout the country nor did it happen at the same time in all areas. On the whole, in the east of England, the Home Counties and the Midlands, where there was specialisation on corn production, female labour declined. In the west and south where specialisation was on pastoral farming, women continued to play an important role. There was also a contrast between north and south. In the former, women continued to do farm work which further south was confined to men, and where there was far more restriction on the jobs in agriculture open to women.

Coupled with such developments in agriculture, which led to less productive work being available to women, went a decline in cottage industry, most notably in hand-spinning, the staple employment earlier for women and children throughout the country.

So, on the one hand, the developments of the century led to an increasing number of middle-class women totally divorced from labour – and where their choice of a life of gentility was a major contributory factor. On the other, the female labouring poor found that opportunities for labour were in decline and the consequent unemployment or underemployment was forced on them, not chosen.

Such an almost total alienation from labour among many middle-class women combined with an increasing class-consciousness, led to a polarisation of class differences. No longer were farmers' wives working alongside their milkmaids in the dairies, no longer were they living under the same roof as labourers in husbandry, housing and feeding them as well as working alongside them. If formerly the farmer's family lived and ate in the kitchen alongside the servants employed, they now lived separately, with the family eating alone and living in the newly created parlours. Similarly, in trade and small workshops, no longer were women labouring beside the journeymen and apprentices. Even in the household, there was far less sharing of household tasks between mistress and maid.

One effect of the withdrawal from labour of all classes of women is the end of something approximating to a working partnership between husbands and wives. The implications of this change were different for different social groups, but in all cases what was almost certainly lost was a measure of equality with men. Of course, it was not real equality, but it came far nearer to it than was the experience of most women after the change. In agriculture the loss of women's ability to contribute to the achievement of a degree of self-sufficiency by combining work on a small plot of land – even only a cottage garden – with full use of such common rights as they had, a little seasonal labour on larger neighbouring farms and some spinning or weaving in the home, meant the end of what Professor Malcolmson has called the 'economy of self-reliance' (see *Life and Labour in England 1700–1780*, 1981, p. 24). Whether or not they earned money they were able, by engaging in productive labour, to make their contribution to the household income. Their awareness of their ability to make such a contribution must have had a profound psychological effect and been a source of self-respect and dignity. The loss of that ability meant their only role became that of domestic drudges. The Society for Bettering the Condition and Increasing the Comforts of the Poor was to comment on the problem when, in a report of 1806, it said: 'The wife is no longer able to contribute her share towards the weekly expenses . . . In a kind of despondency she sits down, unable to contribute anything to the general fund of the family and conscious of rendering no other service to her husband except that of the mere care of his family.'

One of the advantages of cottage industry shared by the wives of farmers and smallholders was the compatibility of the work with staying at home, looking after the children, and coping with the housework. It could always be used as a source of supplementing income just as could seasonal work in hay-making and harvest. But, of course, it also suited the employers because the very fact that wages were regarded as supplementary enabled them to pay lower, and sometimes much lower, wages to the women than to the men.

Where mechanisation of industrial processes led to the growth of the factory system, some women were able to move out of domestic industry into factories. Contemporaries are constantly at pains to emphasise that the greater proportion of female labour in factories consisted of young, unmarried girls. It is significant that the Census of 1841 revealed that 75 per cent of female factory labour was under 20 years of age. The assumption that all female labour released from agriculture became available for the factories is just not true. Families tied to the land by the occupation of husbands were in no position for wives to go off to look for employment in factories.

In the early years of the century it had been not only daughters of the labouring poor who went into farm service; daughters of small farmers would also go to neighbouring, larger farms as living-in servants in husbandry. When this source of employment dried up, for many the only source of employment was domestic service. As employment opportunities declined in the countryside, pressure from country girls seeking places created a steady flow into the towns and, more especially, London where demand for servants was growing.

We have no accurate source for the numbers of female domestic servants in the eighteenth century, but contemporaries were in no doubt that the numbers of servants of both sexes were increasing – particularly in the second half of the century. There are constant references to just how numerous they were. All were agreed that by far the greatest concentration was in London. According to Patrick Colquhoun, the magistrate, there were 200,000 servants of both sexes in the metropolitan area in 1796 (in J. J. Hecht, *The Domestic Servant Class in 18th Century England*, 1956, p. 34). For the country as a whole, he estimated that in 1806 there were 800,000 female domestics as compared with 110,000 male. This ratio was not far off that confirmed by the 1851 Census which suggested that the ratio of male to female servants was 13:100. If Colquhoun's figures are correct, female domestic servants must have accounted for a substantial proportion of all the female workforce – perhaps even as much as half. In 1841 the Census revealed that less than 1 per cent of the female workforce was employed in factories. Patricia Branca concludes that 'labour historians have looked for working women in the wrong places' (see 'A new perspective on women's work: a comparative typology', *Journal of Social History*, Vol. 9, no. 2, Winter 1975). Certainly, it seems probable that a considerable increase in the number of female domestic servants occurred in the second half of the eighteenth century. By the early years of the nineteenth, whether purely domestic or, in part, farm servants, they constituted by far the biggest occupational group among working women.

A curious paradox arises from this dominant role of domestic servants. On the one hand, 'ladies' are concerned to distance themselves from their social inferiors, and they rely on their employment of domestic servants as the badge of gentility. It was important not only to employ them in large numbers, but also to dress them (preferably in livery) as well as possible. The strong conventional insistence on the need to distinguish mistresses from maids came into conflict with the equally strong desire to show one's high social status by the clothes worn by one's servants. So domestic service came to bridge the gulf between the upper classes and those below them. As the gulf widened so the bridge had to be extended and broadened.

There is an interesting dialectic here. Whilst domestic service can have offered an opportunity only to a minority and those, most probably, at the upper end of the domestic service hierarchy, nevertheless for parents of the many daughters who entered into domestic service, it must have seemed the only chance of climbing up the social ladder. Paradoxically, contemporary writers are often at pains to explain that the purpose of domestic servants was to protect their mistresses from any contact with tradesmen and other members of the inferior classes, what Leonore Davidoff has called the 'defiling contact with the sordid, or disordered parts of life' (see 'Mastered for life: servant and wife in Victorian and Edwardian England', *Journal of Social History*, vol. 7, no. 4, Summer 1974). Yet by this very function of protection the status of domestic servants was, in fact, upgraded.

The implications of the vast and increasing numbers of domestic servants which must have existed in the later years of the eighteenth century, of the hope of social advancement it offered, the paradoxical relationship between domestic servants and their masters and mistresses, are all areas which deserve further probing.

Leonore Davidoff has suggested that in the ambition for individual advancement through domestic service we may have an explanation of working-class conservatism in the nineteenth century. It certainly was an important contributory factor in the virtual divorce of the early women's suffrage movement from working-class women. Is it significant that only with the decline of domestic service does the women's movement begin to become more militant?

Domestic service, as Leonore Davidoff has pointed out, was regarded as the only fitting destination for lower-class girls in institutions of all kinds – orphanages, charity schools, workhouses, Bridewells and houses for reformed prostitutes. Was it seen as closely comparable with the traditional women's role in the family, and so a link with the known and familiar? Woman's place was in the home – whether her own or someone else's.

A consequence of the increasing numerical and social significance of middle-class women was that middle-class ideas on the woman's role seem to have become widely accepted. It is worth noting that as the possibility of self-respect was withdrawn from many women of the lower classes, no alternative set of viable standards presented themselves. The main principles behind the accepted theory of the role of women were that men and women have entirely different characteristics and capacities; consequently they need totally different educations to prepare them for totally different occupations and employments. For all who could afford it – and, after all, it was they who mattered – woman's place was in the home. Such a view reinforced the traditional double standard between men and women, most notably in attitudes towards chastity and sexual morality. There is abundant evidence of what was seen as the role of upper-class women and the rules of sexual morality they should follow. Are we right, then, in assuming that such standards percolated downwards in the social hierarchy? Many have so argued. Were women of the labouring classes also aspiring to gentility? The popularity of Richardson's novel *Pamela* suggests that this may have been the case. Written in 1740, it is the story of a servant girl who resists the repeated threats of seduction – and rape – from her dead mistress's son and, having against all odds preserved her chastity, ends by marrying him. The story had a riveting interest for those whose daughters formed so large a part of the body of domestic servants. In the village of Slough, where the blacksmith is reputed to have read aloud instalments of the novel, so great was the joy generated by Pamela's lawful marriage, that the church bells were rung in celebration! It serves to underline my earlier point about domestic service being seen as a way of social advancement.

Whether or not the labouring classes had their own independent morality, there can be no doubt that the upper classes believed that different rules and standards applied to the labouring class, and that there should be different punishments for breach of these rules. It was another and more insidious double standard than that between the sexes. The relationship between the two is complex and significant. Women, and more particularly, wives, were seen and treated as servants – if upper servants. You will recall the role assigned to women by Captain Blifil in Fielding's *Tom Jones* who 'looked on a woman as an animal of domestic use, of a somewhat higher consideration than a cat since her offices were of rather more importance, but the difference between the two was in his estimation so small – that . . . it would have been pretty equal which of them he had taken into the bargain' (Everyman's Library edition, Vol. 1, p. 60). Together with apprentices, servants and children, wives belonged to those for whom the master of the household was responsible. A measure of chastisement of them was part of that responsibility. So wives might be beaten – but not, or so went the theory, too excessively. While the relationship between husband and wife parallels that between upper and lower class, the relationship between mistresses and maids assured the former of their essential superiority to the members of the lower classes. Many of the assumptions of the middle-class image of feminine perfection were singularly irrelevant to the experience of working-class women. With the exception of some domestic servants, gentility was something they could not afford. Many upper-class motives for marriage, where property considerations were all-important, had little or no meaning for the labouring poor. Yet they were made abundantly aware of the penalties for breaking the rules for sexual morality laid down by their betters. It is clear, however, that loss of chastity was not seen by them as the worst of sins. If it is still difficult to establish the point, and far more work needs to be done, it seems possible that many of the labouring class had their own and different standards of morality, and did not merely reject those of their betters. Mary Astell, Daniel Defoe and Jonas Hanway are not alone in suggesting that there may have been better chances of equality between the sexes among the lower classes than among their social superiors; it would be interesting to follow up these suggestions. Customs like *charivari* or 'rough music' maintained, in however rough and ready a manner, standards of conduct for men and women acceptable to the community. The concept of a 'moral economy' enforced by limited food riots, the customary rights assumed by many of the labouring poor, both suggest that certain minimum standards were regarded as their due (see E. P. Thompson, 'The moral economy of the English crowd in the 18th century', *Past and Present*, February 1971). Acceptable courtship conditions were very different from those of the upper classes, and the same was true of pre-marital sex. To save enough money to purchase a cottage was a more limiting condition on marriage than questions of pregnancy. Divorce in various forms was probably easier for the labouring class than for all but the very richest of their betters – whether by mutual agreement, by desertion, acceptable bigamy, or wife sale. If female domestic servants seem to warrant special attention because of their numbers, another group deserving close study is spinsters, especially upper-class spinsters. How are we to explain the depths of malice and brutality with which some middle-class writers refer to them? There were some rational reasons for this opprobrium – the decline of hand-spinning meant that they no longer contributed to the household income, so a spinster became a relatively greater burden: there were fewer jobs for them to do around the farm. But what other explanations are there?

Was it because spinsters, like widows, escaped from full male control? Chastity, to which so much importance was attached, becomes in a spinster a frozen asset: no dividends are returned on previous outlay. So far from being a realisable asset, spinsters became a burden in proportion as their market price sank. This must surely be the explanation for the virulence of the hatred of spinsters. At the beginning of the century the well-born Mary Astell spoke up for them; later it is from the impecunious daughters of the middle class who remained single that there came the urgent demand for more employment openings to be made available for spinsters; indeed, it was perhaps from this group that the women's suffrage group sprang a century later. It was no accident that the scorn with which spinsters were treated was linked with that poured upon 'learned ladies'. According to the conventional image 'learned ladies' (whether married or not) were desexed. One reason often given for a girl remaining unmarried was her aspiration to learning unbefitting to her sex.

Many women never questioned their allotted role; there were stupid and silly women as well as stupid and silly men. Such women would themselves be the first to cry out against the failure of members of their own sex to conform. We must realise how exceptionally courageous were women like Mary Astell, Lady Mary Wortley Montagu and Catherine Macaulay. If sometimes their tremendous courage and energy led them to overstep the mark, to become shrill and eccentric, how very natural and understandable that was! We cannot but admire them enormously, the more so because in the eighteenth century, so far as the evidence goes, they seem to have been very few.

As more women began to read, and there was more available for them to read – more books published (especially novels), lending libraries and local newspapers – so their horizons broadened. It began to be possible to conceive of alternatives to their constricted existences. A fantasy world of independence, from their husbands and from the role allotted to them, began to open up. This was one reason for the popularity of novels among women, and a reason for using novels as one of the sources of this anthology.

This anthology starts from the image of womanhood (Part 1) and women's role in society – a middle-class image. It is an important starting-point, since from it derive the rules governing the relations between the sexes, between parents and daughters, attitudes towards woman's role in marriage, ideas of the kind of education suited to women and of the employments and occupations they should pursue; negatively, from it also derive all those things women should avoid – aping men, answering back, being learned or witty or in any way obtrusive. Within this image I see the role of chastity as central (Part 2). Its middle-class origins become clearer directly one appreciates that chastity was woman's only and best-selling economic asset.

This part of the anthology is concerned with views expressed about women's position in and out of marriage. That more of these are by men than women is not surprising. For women to express themselves on such serious topics as marriage was still unusual. Nevertheless, wherever possible, I have included the views of women themselves on education (Part 3) and marriage (Parts 4 and 5). Such writers tend to be limited to women of the upper classes, but this does not prevent them from having very clear ideas on the way in which such women should conduct themselves in marriage.

The image of womanhood reflects their inferior legal position (see Part 6), the 'crimes' committed by women and the way in which they were punished (see Part 8).

Women without husbands have a separate chapter (Part 7), not only because by remaining outside male control they no longer fit into the image of womanhood, but also because the hardships of the century bore particularly severely on such women.

The latter part of the anthology concentrates on women of the labouring class – among the poor (Part 9), among those who worked in agriculture and industry (Parts 10 and 11), and on female domestic servants (Part 12).

Throughout the century the voices of a minority of women are raised in criticism, if not in protest, against the role they are condemned to fill. I end by focusing on the nature of some of that female protest (Part 13).

Eighteenth-century punctuation and spelling is idiosyncratic. Wherever either seemed to obscure meaning I have taken the liberty of modernising it. Inevitably there is some overlapping between sections. Eighteenth-century writers did not have an anthology in mind when they wrote! They are discursive in their style of writing and thus difficult to pin down firmly under one heading. One example of such overlapping is 'infanticide', relevant both to Part 8 *e* and to Part 9 *e*. In such cases, I have made cross-references between them. I have endeavoured to make as rational a division of extracts between sections as possible, but this may not always be obvious to the reader.

Many of the excerpts included here are very short. The very

nature of the source material made this difficult to avoid. In some cases, where one writer returns to the same subject, for example, I have tried to group extracts together. The trouble is that, for so many writers, comments on women are made almost as after-thoughts or asides – not really the subject of the main part of their writing.

For a study of eighteenth-century women the sources are various. What hardly exists at all is the wealth of official reports with which the historians of the nineteenth century are con-fronted. Some such reports there are. The Reports of the Society for Bettering the Condition and Increasing the Comforts of the Poor or the publications of the Board of Agriculture are cases in point, but they tend to be concentrated in the latter years of the century. A greater proportion of the source material is more private and personal than for a social historian of the nineteenth century – diaries, memoirs, reflections and travel journals. There is a wealth of 'courtesy' books – works of advice to parents on the education and upbringing of their daughters, and to daughters on the desirable attributes to cultivate in anticipation of the qualifica-tions thought necessary in the perfect wife.

If women writers other than novelists were rare in the century, there were a number of quite remarkable women, Mary Astell, Lady Mary Wortley Montagu, Catherine Macaulay, Maria Edge-worth, Mary Wollstonecraft and Hannah More – to mention only a few of them – who, in their writings, reflect the deep concern of intelligent women with the nature and inadequacies of feminine education and its aims, the conventions governing the relations between the sexes, and the role of submission in marriage. Admittedly, such women come mostly from the ranks of the upper classes and were more fortunate than most in the education they received.

The works of certain authors may seem to occupy a more than fair share of the excerpts: Daniel Defoe, Jonas Hanway and Arthur Young, for example. They were all prolific writers and it proved impossible not to reflect that fact if one was to do justice to their importance.

Finally, a word about excerpts from novels. It was not accidental that the rise of the novel coincided with the expansion of that body of middle-class women with leisure to read. All contemporary reports suggest that novels were widely read by women – indeed, many were of the opinion that they were too much read. Novelists were not unaware of their readership and the furious debate that was provoked by, for example, Richardson's *Clarissa*, a debate in which women played a major role, suggests a concern, not always so clearly exhibited, with questions of parent/daughter relations, the rights and wrongs of arranged marriages, the role, if any, of love in marriage. In probing such ideas and attitudes eighteenth-century novels are often far more revealing than formal treatises. We glimpse in them something of the conflict between different sexual moralities, and of the tensions set up in individuals by the pressure of economic and social, as well as of moral, aims. Of course, novels must be treated with care by the historian. By themselves they are totally inadequate as source material. Yet often, unwittingly, characters in novels reveal the assumptions of that class or group in society which they represent. Excerpts from novels figure largely in the sections on marriage (see Parts 4 and 5).

I have received help and advice from many more people than I can acknowledge separately. Professor R. W. Malcolmson was particularly generous in making material available to me. Susan Amussen, Maxine Berg, John Gillis, Margaret Hunt, Andrew Lincoln, Peter Linebaugh, Mary Prior, Edward Thompson and Professor Arthur Young gave me useful leads. I owe a particular debt to Penelope Corfield who read the typescript, offered valuable comments and saved me from some of the worst pitfalls. Margaret Golby coped with the bulk of the typing for which I am very grateful. Sue Cannings, Penelope Bide and Shirley Enoch also gave additional assistance. Above all, I thank my husband whose patience is inexhaustible and without whose constant encouragement this book would not have been completed.

Part 1 Ideas of Female Perfection

Such Sweetness and Goodness together combin'd;
So beauteous her Face, and so bright in her Mind;
So loving, yet chaste; and so humble, yet fair;
So comely her Shape, and so decent her Air;
So skilful, that Nature's improv'd by her Art;
So prudent her Head, and so bounteous her Heart;
So wise without Pride, and so modestly neat;
'Tis strange, this agreeable Creature's a Cheat!
For, tho' she to Man, for a Mortal, was giv'n,
These virtues betray her Extraction from Heav'n.
(Stephen Duck, 'On Mrs L——s',
Poems on Several Occasions, 1736)

Introduction

In the eighteenth century the views of middle-class society on the role allotted to women were clearly expounded by a host of writers. In mothers' advice to their daughters (whether real or fictitious), in letters addressed to young ladies, in treatises on the content and objects of female education, and in guides to feminine conduct and deportment, the duties and responsibilities of young women to their parents, and to their future or present husbands, were laid down. It would have been difficult, if not impossible, for a woman of the middle class who could read to remain ignorant of the model to which she was expected to aspire.

Such writings were not new, but they proliferate after 1740 in a concerted attempt to redefine woman's role and sexual ethics.

The authors represented here are mainly, but not solely, of the male sex. Not all of them agree on details. Some of the authors put greater weight on women improving their minds by reading. But what all, except a very small group, have in common is the insistence on the absolute distinction in both mental and physical characteristics between men and women. What follows from that distinction is the totally separate roles allotted to each sex.

Most revealing in all the models of feminine perfection is

what is left out. For example, many authors, including Dr John Gregory (4), condemn wit in a woman. Woman's role was to listen rather than to speak.

The model of feminine perfection created by these writers may have borne little relation to the way women behaved in real life. The biting irony with which Mary Astell writes of wifely submission (7) suggests that at least some women were questioning the role assigned to them. But, by those women anxious to establish their new social status, this role was eagerly accepted as a means to differentiate themselves from women of an inferior social status.

These writings for women's guidance were not merely laying down rules for feminine etiquette. They were seeking to establish an orthodox sexual morality and strict standards of conduct. The vocabulary of this morality – modesty, restraint, passivity, compliance, submission, delicacy and, most important of all, chastity, and the way that vocabulary is used reveals how female virtue was interpreted almost exclusively in sexual terms. 'Masculine' characteristics in a woman were to be avoided because men found them 'forbidding' (14). Women must wear uncomfortable stays, cover their bosoms, never lounge or loll, avoid all suggestion that they were aware of their own bodies, not so much for their own virtue's sake, as not to put temptation in the way of men (2). Elizabeth Montagu, when a young girl, wrote to her mother asking that she be sent her bathing dress as until it arrived she 'must bath in her chemise and jupon'. It was indelicate for women to have to view their own naked bodies, just as all references to bodily functions – and even to pregnancy – were taboo.

There were few writers who attacked such images of feminine perfection. At the very end of the century Hannah More, while arguing that women must develop their minds and their critical faculties, nevertheless saw their role as essentially one of submissive passivity (6).

The eighteenth century opens and closes with a wave of evangelical enthusiasm when fears of social disorder in a period of great moral laxity and dissoluteness led to an urgent need for the middle and upper classes to set an example to those below them in the social hierarchy, and to work for the inculcation of the principles of Christian morality in the labouring class. What was needed were industrious, sober and humble servants and labourers content to endure the sufferings of this life given the certainty of their future rewards in heaven. Women had an important role to play in this process.

So it was that piety was seen as a particularly feminine attribute. It was not just that the idea of woman as the nearest thing to an angel upon earth demanded something of a religious aura (**11**), but that, as an extension of the double standard, women needed the consolations of religion more than men. John Bennett saw it as the 'only true and unfailing resource' for women (**12**) whose lives were otherwise bleak deserts of suffering and endurance.

(a) Restraint and Modesty

1

LUCINDA (an elderly lady): . . . now-a-days, the very virgins, that should be the temples of modesty, go with their bodies half naked, and not only so, but the obscene part of their body.

ANTONIA (her niece): I never knew that one's neck was an obscene part.

LUCINDA: What you call your neck is here, your neck ends at the collarbone, this is your chest, your bosom, this is the pit of your stomach, these are your breasts; you make a strange long neck of it; and are like the sign-painters, who only call it a head, tho' they paint a man or a woman as far as the waist; you may as well call it your chin as your neck.

ANTONIA: Well, let it be call'd bosom, or what part you please, why is it obscene?

LUCINDA: Why, I wonder you should ask that question; can any thing be more obscene than the very marks of your body, by which ye are known to be a woman: all virtuous people think it obscene in either man or woman to show any thing naked that may tempt the other to wickedness; but it is much more so, to prostitute those parts, by which the sexes are distinguished. (Bernard de Mandeville, *The Virgin Unmask'd*, (1714), 1724, pp. 3–4)

2

Never appear in company, without your stays. Make it your general rule, to lace in the morning, before you leave your chamber. The neglect of this, is liable to the censure of indolence, supineness of thought, sluttishness – and very often worse.

> The negligence of loose attire
> May oft' invite to loose desire.

Leaning, and lolling, are often interpreted to various disadvantages. I presume, no lady would be seen to put her hand under her neck-handkerchief in company. (Rev Mr Wettenhall Wilkes, *A Letter of Genteel and Moral Advice to a Young Lady*, (1740), 1766, pp. 211–12, 214)

3

I call heaven to witness, your father was the first man whom I ever made any private assignation with, or even met in a room alone – nor did I take that liberty with him, 'til the most solemn mutual engagement, the matrimonial ceremony, had bound us to each other. (Lady Sarah Pennington, *An Unfortunate Mother's Advice to her Absent Daughters* (1761), 1770, pp. 9–10)

4

One of the chief beauties in a female character is that modest reserve, that retiring delicacy, which avoids the public eye, and is disconcerted even at the gaze of admiration . . .

When a girl ceases to blush, she has lost the most powerful charm of beauty. That extreme sensibility which it indicates, may be a weakness and incumbrance in our sex, as I have too often felt; but in yours it is peculiarly engaging . . .

This modesty, which I think so essential in your sex, will naturally dispose you to be rather silent in company, especially in a large one. People of sense and discernment will never mistake such silence for dullness. One may take a share in conversation without uttering a syllable. The expression in the countenance shows it, and this never escapes an observing eye. (John Gregory, *A Father's Legacy to his Daughters*, 1774, pp. 16–17)

5

JOHNSON: There are ten genteel women for a genteel man, because they are more restrained. A man without some degree of restraint is insufferable; but we are less restrained than women. Were a woman sitting in company to put out her legs before her as most men do, we should be tempted to kick them in. (*Boswell's Life of Johnson* (1776), ed. G. B. Hill and L. F. Powell, 1934–50, pp. 53–4)

6

An early habitual restraint is peculiarly important to the future character and happiness of woman. A judicious, unrelaxing, but steady and gentle curb on their tempers and passions can alone ensure their peace and establish their principles. It is a habit which cannot be adopted too soon, nor persisted in too pertinaciously. They should when very young be enured to contradiction. Instead of hearing their bonmots treasured up and repeated till the guests are tired, and till the children begin to think it dull, when they themselves are not the little heroine of the theme, they should be accustomed to receive but little praise for their vivacity or their wit, though they should receive just commendation for their patience, their industry, their humility, and other qualities which have more worth than splendour. They should be led to distrust their own judgement; they should learn not to murmur at expostulation; they should be accustomed to expect and endure opposition. It is a lesson with which the world will not fail to furnish them; and they will not practise it the worse for having learnt it the sooner. It is of the last importance to their happiness even in this life that they should early acquire a submissive temper and a forbearing spirit. They must even endure to be thought wrong sometimes, when they cannot but feel they are right. (Hannah More, *Strictures on the Modern System of Female Education* (1799), 1800, pp. 105–6)

(b) Submission and Compliance

7

She . . . who marries ought to lay it down for an indisputable maxim, that her husband must govern absolutely and entirely, and that she has nothing else to do but to please and obey. She must not attempt to divide his authority, or so much as dispute it, to struggle with her yoke will only make it gall more, but must believe him wise and good and in all respects the best, at least he must be so to her. She who can't do this is in no way fit to be a wife . . . is not qualify'd to receive that great reward which attends the eminent exercise of humility and self-denial, patience and resignation, the duties that a wife is call'd to. (Mary Astell, *Some Reflections upon Marriage* (1700), 1706, p. 56)

8

I shall, however, without much offence, I hope to the fair sex, advise them not to be so ambitious of power, as but too many of them are, who are fond of having a superiority over their husbands, and by an indecent inversion of original design and order, would govern those over whom they never can exercise a rightful authority. (*Gentleman's Magazine*, 1738, p. 591)

9

That Providence designed women for a state of dependence, and consequently of submission, I cannot doubt, when I consider their timidity of temper, their tenderness of make, the many comforts and even necessaries of life which they are unable to procure without our aid, their evident want of our protection upon a thousand occasions, their incessant study, at every age, in every state, by every means, to engage our attention, and insure our regard. (Dr James Fordyce, *The Character and Conduct of the Female Sex*, 1776, p. 40)

10

A woman can never be seen in a more ridiculous light, than when she appears to govern her husband; – if, unfortunately, the superiority of understanding is on her side, the apparent consciousness of that superiority betrays a weakness that renders her contemptible in the sight of every considerate person – and it may, very probably, fix in his mind a dislike never to be eradicated. In such a case, if it should ever be your own, remember that some degree of dissimulation is commendable – so far as to let your husband's defect appear unobserv'd. When he judges wrong, never flatly contradict, but lead him insensibly into another opinion, in so discreet a manner, that it may seem entirely his own – and, let the whole credit of every prudent determination rest on him, without indulging the foolish vanity of claiming any merit to yourself; – thus a person, of but an indifferent capacity, may be so assisted as, in many instances, to shine with a borrow'd lustre, scarce distinguishable from the native, and, by degrees, he may be brought into a kind of mechanical method of acting properly, in all the common occurrences of life (Lady Sarah Pennington, *An Unfortunate Mother's Advice to her Absent Daughters* (1761), 1770, pp. 112–14)

(c) Piety

11

Never, perhaps, does a fine woman strike more deeply, than

when, composed into pious recollection, and possessed with the noblest considerations, she assumes, without knowing it, superior dignity and new graces; so that the beauties of holiness seem to radiate about her, and the bystanders are almost induced to fancy her already worshipping amongst her kindred angels! (Dr James Fordyce, *Sermons to Young Women*, 1766, Vol. 2, p. 163)

12

Though religion is indispensably necessary to *both* sexes, and in every possible character and station, yet a woman seems, more peculiarly, to need its enlivening supports, while her frame must be confessed to be admirably calculated for the exercise of all the tender and devout affections.

The timidity, arising from the natural weakness and delicacy of your frame; the numerous diseases, to which you are liable; that exquisite sensibility, which, in many of you, vibrates to the slightest touch of joy or sorrow; the tremulous anxiety you have for friends, children, a family, which nothing can relieve, but a sense of their being under the protection of God; the sedentariness of your life, naturally followed with low spirits or *ennui*, whilst we are seeking health and pleasure in the field; and the many, lonely hours, which in almost every situation, are likely to be your lot, will expose you to a number of *peculiar* sorrows, which you cannot, like the men, either drown in wine, or divert by dissipation.

From the era that you become marriageable, the sphere of your anxieties and afflictions will be enlarged. The generality of men are far from acting on such strict principles of honour and integrity, in their connections with you, as they would rigidly observe, in matters of a much more trivial importance . . . Under these, or indeed any *other* distresses, religion is the only true and unfailing resource, and its hopes and prospects, the only solid basis of consolation. In your many, *solitary*, moments what can afford the mind so sovereign a relief, as the exercise of devotion to an all-present God? (Rev John Bennett, *Letters to a Young Lady on a Variety of Useful and Interesting Subjects*, 1789, Vol. 1, pp. 6–10)

(d) Femininity

13

. . . one thing the duty of a tender Uncle obliges me to blame in you; and that is, a certain affectation that of late obtains in your behaviour, of imitating the manners of the other sex, and appearing more masculine than either the amiable softness of your person or sex can justify.

I have been particularly offended, let me tell you, my dear, at your new Riding-habit; which is made so extravagantly in the mode that one cannot easily distinguish your sex by it. For you neither look like a modest girl in it nor an agreeable boy . . .

. . . I would have you remember, my dear, that as sure as anything intrepid, free, and in a prudent degree bold, becomes a man, so whatever is soft, tender, and modest, renders your sex amiable. In this one instance we do not prefer our own likeness; and the less you resemble us the more you are sure to charm: For a masculine woman is a character as little creditable as becoming. (Samuel Richardson, *Letters from Particular Friends, on the Most Important Occasions*, 1741, Letter xc, p. 125)

14

A masculine woman must be naturally an unamiable creature. I confess myself shocked, whenever I see the sexes confounded. An effeminate fellow, that, destitute of every manly sentiment, copies with inverted ambition from your sex, is an object of contempt and aversion at once. On the other hand, any young woman of better rank, that throws off all the lovely softness of her nature, and emulates the daring intrepid temper of a man – how terrible! The transformation on either side must ever be monstrous . . . But what though the dress be kept ever so distinct, if the behaviour be not; in those points, I mean, where the character peculiar to each sex seems to require a difference? . . . By dint of assiduity and flattery fortune and show, a female man shall sometimes succeed strangely with the women: but to the men an amazon never fails to be forbidding. (Dr James Fordyce, *Sermons to Young Women*, 1766, pp. 104–5)

15

The personal charms of young females . . . have occasioned them in all countries to be compared to flowers. Hence a young woman whose lungs are fatally affected, is a blossom nipped by untimely frost. The imagination proceeds with the metaphor; and in virtue of such poetical logic, it seems to be concluded that the drooping human being feels, no more than the drooping vegetable expresses.

. . . in a certain seminary, an elegant delicacy of appetite had been so successfully inculcated, not by actually professed limitation, but by the fear of ridicule, that forty girls were fed for two days on a single leg of mutton. (J. E. Stock, *Memoirs of the Life of Thomas Beddoes*, 1811, pp. 164, 202)

Part 2   And the Greatest of These Was Chastity

Tis a pretty way we have got, to seek the temptation, and then blame the tempter . . . (Daniel
Defoe, *A Weekly Review of the Affairs of France*,
(1704–13), from 1938 edn, ed. Arthur Wellesley
Secord, Vol. 3, p. 527)

> Great whores in coaches gang,
> Smaller misses
> For their Kisses
> Are in Bridewell banged.
> (*The Grub-Street Opera*, July
> 1731, air xxxv)

Introduction

Of all the desirable feminine attributes by far the most
important was chastity. Its importance lay in the accepted
unchastity of men, and the belief that men's passions were
uncontrollable and natural, if regrettable. It was on women,
therefore, that there rested the full responsibility for preserving their innocence and upholding the moral values laid
down for their instruction. It was they who must always be on
their guard, maintaining, as de Mandeville puts it, 'the ever-
watchful look of a forbidding eye' (2). 'Men are to ask –
Women are to deny', said Richardson's Lovelace (9).

The venom behind the language in which the sin of chastity
lost was expressed barely conceals the real motives behind
the emphasis on female chastity and the double moral
standard for men and women. Johnson puts it bluntly. On
women's chastity 'all the property in the world depends' (11).
Francis Place suggests that among tradesmen's families,
where property considerations were minimal, a very different
view of loss of chastity was taken. It is a view which is echoed
in different attitudes to courtship (see Part 4*b*).

Especially for the middle- and upper-class families, marriage contracts remained essentially commercial transactions
in which the price of a husband was the dowry a girl's father
could afford, plus her virginity. Where the law of primogeni-

ture had as its object the preservation intact of estates, and where men had the responsibility of providing for the offspring of a marriage, how essential was it for them to ensure that children born to their wives were their own. As William Alexander argued in his *History of Women*, 'it would be hard that a man should be obliged to provide for, and leave his estate to children which he could never with certainty call his own' **(12)**. 'Confusion of progeny', said Johnson, 'constitutes the essence of the crime' **(11)**.

Loss of chastity meant a sharp drop in a woman's marketable value. It might seem ironic that, in an age when women's property rights were so few, her one apparent asset, her chastity, was not really hers to dispose of as she pleased. As Mary Wollstonecraft put it, 'the honour of a woman is not made even to depend on her will' **(5)**. To her parents the preservation of that asset was often vital – if not to the improvement, certainly to the maintenance of their standard of living. To her husband, a woman's chastity was an essential part of the property transaction of marriage.

If there was a double standard as between the morals of men and women, there was also a double standard as between the punishment thought fitting for the crime of chastity lost as between rich and poor. As de Mandeville puts it, it was far easier for 'people of substance' to conceal 'their stolen pleasure' than it was for the poor, particularly if they became pregnant **(13)**. The penalty for poor women was severe. Elizabeth Inchbald suggested in her *Nature and Art* that 'it was not .. the crime, but the rank which the criminal held in society' that called forth the most severe punishment **(20)**.

All estimates of the number of prostitutes at any point during the eighteenth century must be viewed with caution. Of course, prostitution was not confined to London. Most provincial towns shared the problem – if on a far smaller scale.

By 1820 the population of London was double what it had been in 1700. Since prostitution is mainly an urban phenomenon, the growth of London would suggest that prostitution also increased. Other reasons for thinking it a worsening problem in the eighteenth century lie in the main sources from which prostitutes were recruited.

There is little evidence of parents selling children into prostitution **(27)**. There is rather more of seduction of country girls, whether maid servants or not, by the rural gentry, their abandonment by their families and, in consequence, their move to London, where they became particularly vulnerable to the arts of the procuress (**26**). But, above all, it was poverty, whether chronic or temporary, that forced many into the ranks of London prostitutes. As Sir John Fielding makes clear, one source was the increasing number of poverty-stricken and large families where prostitution offered one of the few trades open to untrained, and often illiterate, daughters (**25**). Both orphan girls and daughters abandoned by their parents and seeking a means of escape from the hardships of pauper apprenticeship, were easy prey for those anxious for recruits.

Among female domestic servants, particularly in the higher ranks where supply in London tended to outstrip demand, loss of a place could mean girls falling into debt and taking to the streets to avoid starvation. Often such servant girls came from the countryside, and Hogarth in plate 1 of his *The Harlot's Progress* showed the dangers awaiting such girls when they stepped down from their coach bringing them from their villages. One writer suggested that this was the 'sacrifice to the metropolis, offered by the thirty-nine counties' (**29**).

Daniel Defoe, early in the century, saw the increase in prostitution as, in part, the result of an increase in bachelordom particularly among the younger sons of the gentry and the delay in marriage of young apprentices and tradesmen through the conditions of indenture and economic circumstances. When marriage involved moving from the parental home its financial implications were considerable. The existence of such an army of bachelors necessitated, or so it is argued, an increase in prostitutes. Such a view is supported by the ambivalence in attitudes to attempts at both repressive and reforming policies. The double standard ensured that, on the one hand, the prostitute was seen as irretrievably fallen – certainly by the majority of the middle classes. So while the efforts of Fielding and Hanway in the middle of the century at voluntary rescue work were sincere and, compared with later institutions for penitent prostitutes, even humane, many remained totally sceptical of their object. At best, such experiments touched only an insignificant minority. On the other hand, prostitution was seen as a safety-valve for the irrepressible sexual appetites of men – both bachelors and married men, and therefore must not be repressed. Bernard de Mandeville attacked such efforts at repression by the Suppression of Vice Society (**22, 23**). His proposal for a controlled system of municipal brothels was dismissed as outrageous at the beginning of the century, but by the end there were many who shared his view that the purity and virtue of respectable women was dependent on the continuing existence of prostitution. The rigid distinction made between love and sexual passion that led to what Edward Bristow (*Vice and Vigilance*, 1977, p. 53) has called the 'idealisation and sexual anaesthetisation of middle class women' and the belief that prostitutes existed for the satisfaction of men's uncontrollable sexual urges goes some way to explain the ambivalence of attitudes towards eighteenth-century prostitution.

(a) Chastity Preserved and Chastity Lost

1

[Of Whoredom. In a dialogue between Erotion and Sophronistes]
SOPHRONISTES: '. . . I must own, that when a woman can prevail with her self, to set her conscience and her honour aside, to rush through her native modesty, and the reservedness of her education, she is strangely degenerated, and mightily alter'd from what God has made her. She that's untrue to her husband, and has broken the covenant of her God, is all bane and blemish. She stains the blood of the family, brings in a foreign issue, and quarters the enemy upon that estate . . .

. . . Lewdness, like treason, degrades a woman's quality, and makes her despicable and cheap; . . .' (Jeremy Collier, *Essays upon Several Moral Subjects*, 1705, pt 3, pp. 118–19)

2

A young woman moreover, that would be thought well-bred, ought to be circumspect before men in all her behaviour, and never known to receive from, much less to bestow favours upon them, unless the great age of the man, near consanguinity, or a vast superiority on either side plead her excuse. A young lady of refin'd education keeps a strict guard over her looks, as well as actions, and in her eyes we may read a consciousness that she has a treasure about her, not out of danger of being lost, and which yet she is resolved not to part with at any terms. Thousand satires have been made against prudes, and as many encomiums to extol the careless graces, and negligent air of virtuous beauty. But the wise sort of mankind are well assured, that the free and open countenance of the smiling fair, is more inviting and yields greater hopes to the seducer, than the ever-watchful look of a forbidding eye.

(Bernard de Mandeville, *The Fable of the Bees* (1714), 1724, Vol. 1, pp. 60–1)

3

[Squire Allworthy admonishes Jenny Jones for her confessed loss of chastity]

. . . It is the other part of your offence, therefore upon which I intend to admonish you, I mean the violation of your chastity; a crime, however lightly it may be treated by debauched persons, very heinous in itself, and very dreadful in its consequences.

The heinous nature of this offence must be sufficiently apparent to every Christian, inasmuch as it is committed in defiance of the laws of our religion, and of the express command of Him who founded that religion.

. . . For by it you are rendered infamous, and driven, like lepers of old, out of society; at least, from the society of all but the wicked and reprobate persons; for no others will associate with you. If you have fortunes, you are hereby rendered incapable of enjoying them; if you have none, you are disabled from accquiring any, nay almost of procuring your sustenance; for no person of character will receive you into their houses. Thus you are often driven by necessity itself into a state of shame and misery, which unavoidably ends in the destruction of both body and soul.

Can any pleasure compensate these evils? Can any temptation have sophistry and delusion strong enough to persuade you to so simple a bargain? Or can any carnal appetite so over-power your reason, or so totally lay it asleep, as to prevent your flying with affright, and terror from a crime which carries such punishment always with it?

How base and mean must that women be, how void of that dignity of mind, and decent pride, without which we are not worth the name of human creatures, who can bear to level herself with the lowest animal, and to sacrifice all that is great and noble in her, all her heavenly part, to an appetite which she hath in common with the vilest branch of the creation! Love, however barbarously we may corrupt and pervert its meaning, as it is laudable, is a rational passion, and can never be violent but when reciprocal . . .
(Henry Fielding, *Tom Jones*, 1749, bk 1, ch. 7, Everyman's Library, 1908–9, Vol. 1, pp. 16–17)

4

[Of Bell Yard, Temple Bar – 'as perfect a sample of second rate tradesmen's families as any place could be', in the 1780s]

From the heedless mode of education and the want of correct notions of propriety in their relatives, want of chastity in girls of the class of which I am speaking was common, but it was not by any means considered so disreputable in master tradesmens families as it is now in Journeymen mechanics families . . . being unchaste did not necessarily imply that the girl was an abandoned person as she would be now and it was not therefore then as now an insurmountable obstacle to her being comfortably settled in the world. (*The Autobiography of Francis Place (1771–1854)*, ed. Mary Thale, 1972, pp. 81–2)

5

Highly as I respect marriage, as the foundation of almost every social virtue, I cannot avoid feeling the most lively compassion for those unfortunate females who are broken off from society, and by one error torn from all those affections and relationships that improve the heart and mind. It does not frequently even deserve the name of error; for many innocent girls become the dupes of a sincere, affectionate heart, and still more are, as it may emphatically be termed *ruined* before they know the difference between virtue and vice, and thus prepared by their education for infamy, they become infamous. Asylums and Magdalens are not the proper remedies for these abuses. It is justice, not charity, that is wanting in the world!

A woman who has lost her honour imagines that she cannot fall lower, and as for recovering her former station, it is impossible; no exertion can wash the stain away. Losing thus every spur, and having no other means of support, prostitution becomes her only refuge, and the character is quickly depraved by circumstances over which the poor wretch has little power, unless she possesses an uncommon portion of sense and loftiness of spirit. Necessity never makes prostitution the business of men's lives; though numberless are the women who are thus rendered systematically vicious. This, however, arises in a great degree from the state of idleness in which women are educated, who are always taught to look up to man for maintenance, and to consider their persons as the proper return for his exertions to support them. Meretricious airs, and the whole science of wantonness, have then a more powerful stimulus than either appetite or vanity; and this remark gives force to the prevailing opinion, that with chastity all is lost that is respectable in woman. Her character depends on the observance of one virtue, though the only passion fostered in her heart is love. Nay, the honour of a woman is not made even to depend on her will. (Mary Wollstonecraft, *Vindication of the*

Rights of Woman (1792) ed. Miriam Kramnick, 1978, pp. 165–6)

(b) The Double Standard

6

EROT: Under favour, the Crime is not the same. When a woman proves perfidious, the Misfortune is incorporated with the Family, the Adulterous Brood are fed upon the Husband, and it may be run away with the Premisses. But when the Man goes astray, the Wife can't pretend to such great Damages.

EROT: Nothwithstanding what you say, a licentious Life is not so scandalous in a man as in a woman.

SOPHRON: That is, the men say so; but what does this prove more than confidence and partiality? Were they not bolder in their crimes they would not think so. Now, is face and forehead such a commendation? Or a libertine the better for the loss of his modesty? I confess, this vice is so very bad in both sexes, and so great a disturber of society that I think that it can hardly be put under too much shame and discipline.

SOPHRON: What think you of sending a wench to bridewell, and doing nothing to the fellow that debauch'd her, tho' sometimes the first is single and the other married? Is not this a sign that the sex is crep't into the administration, and that we live under a masculine government? (Jeremy Collier, *Essays upon Several Moral Subjects*, 1705, pt 3, pp. 121, 122–3, 129)

7

. . . is there no reprieve for honour lost? the gracious Gods more merciful to the sins of mortals, accept repentance, tho' the nobler part, the Soul, be there concern'd, and suffer our sins to be washed away by tears of penitence. But the world, truly inexorable, is never reconcil'd! unequal distribution! Why are your sex so partially distinguish'd? Why is it in your powers, after accumulated crimes, to regain opinion? when ours, tho' oftentimes guilty, but in appearance, are irretrievably lost? Can your regularity of behaviour reconcile us? Is it not this inhospitality that brings so many unhappy wretches to destruction? despairing of redemption, from one vile degree to another, they plunge themselves down to the lowest ebb of infamy! (Mary de la Riviere Manley, *The New Atlantis*, 1709, Vol. 2, pp. 190–1)

8

To gentlemen:
If a woman falls into your snares, so cruel and unjust are you, that
it is impossible she should ever retrieve her character, you can find
an hundred excuses to extenuate the crimes of your own sex, you
call them slips, tricks of youth, heat of young blood, or the like,
and such an one has no more to do, than to take a trip into the
country, or a voyage at most, and upon his return, put on a
demure countenance, carry an air of gravity, and all's forgiven and
forgotten; O he's become a mighty sober man! his wild oats are
sown, and he'll make the better husband, now he has had his
swing, and has seen his folly. But if a woman, decoy'd by the
flattery and subtile arguments of treacherous men, steps the least
awry, the whole world must ring with it, it's an indelible blot in her
'scutcheon, not to be wiped out by time, for it even pursues her
after death, and contrary to all justice, the very children are
upbraided with their mother's misfortune; no excuses are sought
for her, no pity can be afforded to a ruin'd woman, but the fault is
exaggerated with bitter expressions and railings against the whole
sex, they are all immediately condemn'd of lewdness and
wantonness . . . (Anon., *Woman Triumphant*, 1721, pp. xii–xiii)

9

[Mr Lovelace in a letter to John Belford]
. . . Never offer to invalidate the force which a virtuous education
ought to have in the sex, by endeavouring to find excuses for *their*
frailty from the frailty of ours. For, are we not devils to each
other? – They tempt us – we tempt them. Because we *men* cannot
resist temptation, is that a reason that *women* ought not, when the
whole of their education is caution and warning against our
attempts? Do not their grandmothers give them one easy rule –
Men are to ask – Women are to deny? (Samuel Richardson,
Clarissa (1748), 1811, Vol. 3, p. 313)

10

A man may live by gaming, be known for a prostitute of our sex,
may fail in trade, and defraud his creditors: nay, he may be guilty
of murder, under certain modifications, and yet the generality of
the world will neither despise him, nor discountenance him. On
the contrary, if he should happen to be successful in the course of
his villainy, he will be cherished and esteemed by those who class
themselves among the honest and worthy. But alas! if we do but

once deviate from the track delineated by custom on the chart of chastity (which, if any, is but a subordinate virtue), if we attempt to pass but one barrier without paying toll, or only mistake the intended barrier, we are arraigned at the bar of *honour*, and our *reputation* is pronounced irreparable by a jury of *prudes* and *old maids*! (Anon., *Genuine Memoirs of the Celebrated Miss Maria Brown*, 1766, Vol. 1, pp. 146–7)

11

[1768]
Confusion of progeny constitutes the essence of the crime; and therefore a woman who breaks her marriage vows is much more criminal than a man who does it. A man, to be sure, is criminal in the sight of God but he does not do his wife a very material injury, if he does not insult her; if, for instance, from a mere wantonness of appetite, he steals privately to her chambermaid. Sir, a wife ought not greatly to resent this. I would not receive home a daughter who had run away from her husband on that account. A wife should study to reclaim her husband by more attention to please him. Sir, a man will not, once in a hundred instances, leave his wife and go to a harlot, if his wife has not been negligent of pleasing . . .

I asked him if it was not hard that one deviation from chastity should so absolutely ruin a young woman. JOHNSON: Why no, Sir; it is the great principle which she is taught. When she has given up that principle, she has given up every notion of female honour and virtue, which are all included in chastity.

1773 . . . being once divulged, it ought to be infamous. Consider, of what importance to society, the chastity of women is. Upon that all the property in the world depends. We hang a thief for stealing a sheep; but the unchastity of a woman transfers sheep, and farm and all, from the right owner. I have much more reverence for a common prostitute than for a woman who conceals her guilt. The prostitute is known. She cannot deceive: she cannot bring a strumpet into the arms of an honest man, without his knowledge. (*Boswell's Life of Johnson* (1776), ed. G. B. Hill and L. F. Powell, 1934–50, Vol. 2, pp. 55–6; Vol. 5, pp. 208–9)

12

Matrimony, in all nations, being a compact between a male and female, for the purpose of continuing the species, the first and most necessary obligation of it has been thought fidelity; but, by various people, this fidelity has been variously understood: almost all nations . . . have agreed in requiring the most absolute unconditional fidelity on the part of the woman; while, on that of the man, greater latitude has been given . . . the hand of severity is held so closely over the incontinence of married women, and so much latitude given to the men, because the men generally have the care of providing for the offspring; and it would be hard that a man should be obliged to provide for, and leave his estate to children which he could never with certainty call his own, were the same indulgence given to the women as to the men. A shorter way of explaining the matter would have been, to have said, that men are generally the framers and explainers of the law. Where women have shared in the legislation, they have put their own sex on a more equal footing with ours. (William Alexander, *The History of Women*, 1779, Vol. 2, pp. 220–1)

(c) One Law for the Rich

13

People of substance may sin without being exposed for their stolen pleasure; but servants and the poorer sort of women have seldom an opportunity of concealing a big belly, or at least the consequences of it. It is possible that an unfortunate girl of good parentage may be left destitute, and know no other shift for a livelihood than to become a nursery, or a chambermaid: she may be diligent, faithful and obliging, have abundance of modesty and, if you will, be religious: she may resist temptation, and preserve her chastity for years together, and yet at last meet with an unhappy moment in which she gives up her honour to a powerful deceiver, who afterwards neglects her.

If she proves with child, her sorrows are unspeakable, and she can't be reconciled with the wretchedness of her condition, the fear of shame attacks her so lively, that every thought distracts her. All the family she lives in have a great opinion of her virtue, and her last mistress took her for a saint. How will her enemies, that envied her character, rejoice! How will her relations detest her! The more modest she is now, and the more violently the dread of coming to shame hurries her away, the more wicked and more cruel her resolutions will be, against her self or what she bears. (Bernard de Mandeville, *The Fable of the Bees* (1714), 1724, Vol. 1, pp. 66–7)

14

On Saturday last a young woman at Clerkenwell having been debauched by a young fellow, under pretence of marriage, and being with child, poison'd herself rather than be expos'd to the censures of the world: the Coroner's inquest sate on her, and brought it in Non Compos Mentis; it appearing she was in the utmost despair at the thoughts of being abandoned by the man, to whom she had deliver'd up her all. (*Northampton Mercury*, 28 July 1735)

15

Bath, March 21. The man-midwife of Bristol is dead, who about three weeks ago, was called up at midnight to deliver a lady about six miles off; and when he came on the outside of the Temple-Gate, was blinded by the messenger with a handkerchief 'till he arrived at the place, where he was shewn into a magnificent room, richly furnished in which was the lady lying on a couch with her face covered, whom he soon delivered, was well rewarded, and afterwards carried back blindfolded, 'till he came again to Temple-Gate. 'Tis supposed he never recovered the fright he was in upon this occasion. (*Jackson's Oxford Journal*, 29 March 1755)

16

The distinctions of fortune, do not alter the rights of mankind. But when a man forgets the great law of doing as he would be done by, it is not surprising he should debauch his neighbour's daughter, at the very time that an offer of marriage with his own, would be deemed the highest insolence. Such are the inconsistencies men fall into! And what shall be said of those who pretend to honour and justice, and yet, after gratifying their inclinations, expose her to every kind of misery, to whom they professed the sincerest love. How many men are engaged by promises, or by words that were understood as promises which they do not regard? The offers which are too commonly made to transport the deluded fair from want, confinement and restraint of passions, to liberty, gaiety and joy, are temptations which really deserve compassion. When women of education, who are supposed to be the guardians of their own honour, trespass, it is the greater shame; but the poor and ignorant are less guarded against such formidable seducers. (Jonas Hanway, *A Plan for Establishing a Charity-House, etc.*, 1758, pp. xiii–xiv)

17

Leeds, Jan. 22. One night last week, a young woman hanged herself in a barn at Wetherby. The cause of her committing this rash action is said to be this; she had unfortunately suffered a young fellow, who courted and had promised to marry her, to get her with child; but he afterwards villainously deserting her, and her parents inconsiderately turning her out of doors, she determined to release herself from present misery, by putting a period to her life. (*British Chronicle. Or Pugh's Hereford Journal*, 31 January 1771)

18

There is nothing more common than to hear youth of *modern honour* and *fashion* use this argument for female seduction:
'Why, such a plan, no doubt, would have been disgraceful and infamous to have attempted upon a woman of *rank* and *fashion*! – but to an ordinary girl, and below one's rank, Lord! where's the harm? . . .'
. . . I consider those below me as born to be subservient to me; and I think there is no harm in seducing a girl that is not entitled to expect me for a husband. If she allows liberties in such expectations, she is a fool.' (*Gentleman's Magazine*, 1788, p. 491, from 'Letters on Education', 17 April 1786)

19

PREGNANT LADIES
Whose situation requires a temporary retirement, may be accommodated with genteel separate Apartments, to lie-in, either in town or country, agreeable to their circumstances, and depend on being treated with the utmost care, attention and secrecy; their infant put out to nurse, and humanely taken care of, by applying to Mr. White, Surgeon and Man-Midwife, or Mrs. White, Midwife, at the Square Lamp, in London House Yard, the North side of St. Paul's Church yard.
Where may be had, Mr. White's address to Pregnant Women prise 1s. Also his Restorative Salo Pills, at £1 2s. per box; an effectual remedy to remove all obstructions or irregularities. Letters, post paid, attended to. (*Bath Chronicle*, 13 March 1790)

20

[Of the wife of Lord Bendham]

Whether in town or country, it is but justice to acknowledge, that in her own person she was strictly chaste; but in the country she extended that chastity even to the persons of others: and the young woman who lost her virtue in the village of Anfield had better have lost her life. Some few were now and then found hanging or drowned, while no other cause could be assigned for their despair, than in imputation on the discretion of their characters, and dread of the harsh purity of Lady Bendham. She would remind the parish priest of the punishment allotted for female dishonour and by her influence had caused many an unhappy girl to do public penance, in their own or neighbouring churches.

But this country rigour, in town, she could dispense withal; and, like other ladies of virtue, she there visited and received into her house the acknowledged mistresses of any man in elevated life: it was not therefore the crime, but the rank which the criminal held in society that drew down Lady Bendham's vengeance: she even carried her distinction of classes in female error to such a very nice point, that the adulterous concubine of an elder brother was her most intimate acquaintance, whilst the less guilty unmarried mistress of the younger, she would not sully her lips to exchange a word with. (Elizabeth Inchbald, *Nature and Art* (1796), from *The British Novelists*, ed. Mrs Barbauld, 1820, Vol. 27, p. 263)

21

[From the regulations for a House of Industry, the Isle of Wight] No. 20   That every single woman, becoming chargeable to this corporation the second time, on account of bastardy, shall be carried before two justices of the peace, to be dealt with according to law, and that all such women in the house, (except those who are employed in the hard work of the house, and those who have been punished, as aforesaid,) . . . shall be placed in separate apartments from the other poor, provided for that purpose; shall have their names entered in the black book; shall be allowed no solid meat on meat-days; and wear coarse yellow coats or gowns, or other disgraceful distinctions, at the discretion of the weekly committee.

[Published rules and regulations of provision for the poor from Preston, Lancs.] No. 10   That they use their utmost endeavours to obtain the earliest information of all single women in a state of pregnancy resident within the township, and give notice thereof to the next weekly court.

. . .

No. 22   That a caution be given twice every year, the first week in January and first week in July, by advertisement, that no person take in and harbour single women pregnant or not, who do not belong to the township, and offering a reward to any person giving information where such women are harboured and concealed. (F. M. Eden, *The State of the Poor*, 1797, Vol. 2, pp. 236, 356–7)

(d) Prostitutes and Prostitution

22

. . . publick whoring is neither so criminal in itself, nor so detrimental to the society, as private whoring.

Publick whoring consists in lying with a certain set of women, who have shook off all pretence to modesty; and for such a sum of money, more or less, profess themselves always in a readiness to be enjoy'd. The mischief a man does in this case is entirely to himself; for with respect to the woman, he does a laudable action, in furnishing her with the means of subsistence, in the only, or at least, most innocent way that she is capable of procuring of it. The damage he does to himself, is either with regard to his health, or the expence of money, . . . was there a probability of a women's amendment, and of her gaining a livelihood by some honest method, there might be some crime in encouraging her to follow such a profession: But the minds of women are observ'd to be so much corrupted by the loss of chastity, or rather by the reproach they suffer upon that loss, that they seldom or never change that course of life for the better; and if they should, they can never recover that good name, which is so absolutely necessary to their getting a maintenance in any honest way whatsoever; and that nothing but meer necessity obliges them to continue in that course, it is plain from this, that they themselves in reality utterly abhor it . . . (Bernard de Mandeville, *A Modest Defence of Public Stews*, 1724, p. 8)

23

If courtesans and strumpets were to be prosecuted with as much vigour as some silly people would have it, what locks or bars would be sufficient to preserve the honour of our wives and daughters? For 'tis not only that women in general would meet with far greater temptations, and the attempts to ensnare the innocence of virgins would seem more excusable even to the sober part of mankind than they do now: But some men would grow outrageous, and ravishing would become a common crime . . . how is it to be suppos'd that honest women should walk the streets unmolested, if there were no harlots to be had at reasonable prices? For which reason the wise rulers of that well-order'd city always tolerate an uncertain number of houses, in which women are hir'd as publicly as horses at a livery stable . . .

. . . it is manifest, that there is a necessity of sacrificing one part of womankind to preserve the other. (Bernard de Mandeville, *The Fable of the Bees* (1714), 1724, Vol. 1, pp. 95, 99)

24

[When her accusers lament her 'abuse of such uncommon perfections of mind and body', Sarah Millwood, the London prostitute, turns on them]
If such I had, well may I curse your barbarous sex, who robb'd me of 'em, e'er I knew their worth; then left me, too late, to count their value by their loss. Another and another Spoiler came, and all my gain was poverty and reproach. My soul disdain'd, and yet disdains dependance & contempt. Riches, no matter by what means obtain'd, I saw secur'd the worst of Men from both; I found it therefore necessary to be rich; and, to that end, I summon'd all my Arts. You call 'em wicked, be it so, they were such as my conversation with your sex had furnish'd me withal. (George Lillo, *The London Merchant*, 1731, Act iv, sc. viii)

25

Infinite are the number of chairmen, porters, labourers, and drunken mechanics in this town, whose families are generally too large to receive even maintenance, much less education, from the labour of their parents; and the lives of their fathers being often shortened by their intemperance, a mother is left with many helpless children, to be supplied by her industry; whose resource for maintenance is either the wash-tub, green-stall or barrow. What must then become of the daughters of such women, where poverty and illiterateness conspire to expose them to every temptation? And they often become prostitutes from necessity, even before their passions can have any share in their guilt.
. . . on a search night, when the constables have taken up near forty prostitutes, it has appeared on their examination, that the major part of them have been of this kind, under the age of eighteen, many not more than twelve, and those, though so young, half eat up with the foul distemper.

Who can say that one of these poor children had been prostitutes through viciousness? No. They are young, unprotected, and of the female sex; therefore become the prey of the bawd and debauchee. (Sir John Fielding, *A Plan for a Preservatory and Reformatory, etc.*, 1758, pp. 5–6)

26

You must be sensible, that the ruin of many of the girls now about the town, is owing to the infernal arts of the keepers of bawdy-houses, who by some means or other contrive to have young women run into their debt for lodging, diet, clothes, etc. and then, by the terror of that debt, and the consequences of it, imprisonment, etc., hanging over them, force them to submit to their hellish designs, to the ruin of their souls and bodies . . . I am assured by some persons . . . that there are near forty brothels kept by such persons, in and near the parishes of St. Paul's Covent-Garden, St. Martin's, and St. James's . . .

These miscreants are constantly enquiring of the pretty girls that are a little in debt, and if they can contrive to buy up their notes, perhaps at a crown in the pound, they arrest them, detain them at their house in quality of a spunging-house, and make their property of them. The debt, perhaps of two or three pounds, still remains if they were to earn them a hundred pounds; so that they are never often, out of their clutches, till they are rotten and unfit for service, when they are cast into the streets, and become real objects for a reformatory.

Of all the stations in life, the most deplorable is that of persons who are brought up in affluence, and reduced to poverty, without any means of support from their own skill and industry. This I take to be the case of many of our prostitutes, who are the daughters of poor tradesmen, or of clergymen of poor livings in the country, who during their fathers' life time are company for the Squire and frequently debauched by him. If by this institution proposed they are kept at work, though they begin late in life, it will be a means of a comfortable support, and many of them may become the joyful mothers of children.

As domestic servitude is the fruitful supply of prostitutes, and female servants in the metropolis, generally much more numerous than can be accommodated . . . it shall be the constant maxim of this charity, that every other method of procuring a comfortable support for those who have approved themselves worthy, under the institution shall be preferred to that of sending them to service.

(Jonas Hanway, *A Plan for Establishing a Charity-House, etc.,* 1758, pp. xxix, pp 29–30, fn. 39)

27

A mother wrote a letter to a gentleman to offer up her daughter as a prostitute, being about fourteen years of age. The gentleman neglecting to take notice of the first letter, received a second; he then from curiosity appointed an interview. The child was brought by another woman, and the gentleman chusing rather to protect than ruin innocence, caused them both to be committed to Bridewell. Dreadful as this crime is, it is to be feared, that it is oftener practised than detected. (*Annual Register*, 21 April 1759)

28

22nd of June, 1763, a writ of Habeas Corpus was directed to Sir Francis Blake Delaval, commanding him to produce the body of Ann Catley, in the court of King' Bench. And a charge was likewise brought against him, together with William Bates and John Faine, for joining in an unlawful combination and conspiracy to remove the girl, an infant, about eighteen years of age, out of the hands of the defendant Bates, a musician, to whom she was bound apprentice by her father, a gentleman's coachman without the knowledge or consent of the said Catley, her father, and to place her in the hands of Sir Francis for the purposes of prostitution. (Anon., *The Laws respecting Women*, 1777, pp. 362–3)

29

[Of London Prostitutes]
. . . the principal cause is idleness. To the generality of the world, ease is preferable to labour. Perhaps it is difficult to produce an instance of a girl, of an industrious turn, going upon the town. It is seldom an act of choice, but of necessity. Inclination seems no part of the excitement for this is much the same as in the rest of women. It is not the man they want, but the money.

They suffer what they do not relish, to procure the bread they do. In the connections between the sexes, the heart is not of the party. Their language, like that of the leech, is give; and like it, they squander their profits and become lean. – Their price is various, but always a little more than they get.

Most of the ladies I conversed with were not natives of London, but were a sacrifice to the metropolis, offered by the thirty-nine counties. (William Hutton, *A Journey to London*, 1785, pp. 44–5, 47–8)

30

[Of London apprentices in Fleet Street and neighbourhood, 1785–9]

. . . most of them were 'fine men' to some of the prostitutes who walked Fleet Street, spending their money with them in debauchery and occasionally receiving money from them. It may seem strange but it is true, that on no occasion did I ever hear one of these women urge any one of these youths to bring her more money than he seemed willing to part from, and what they gave was generally spent, the women were generally as willing as the lads to spend money when they were flush.

When I was an apprentice I went frequently among these girls that is I went with other lads and spent many evenings at the dirty public houses frequented by them. At that time, they wore long quartered shoes and large buckles, most of them had clean stockings and shoes, because it was to them the fashion to be flashy about the heels, many of that time wore no stays, their gowns were low round the neck and open in the front, those who wore handkerchiefs had them always open in front to expose their breasts this was a fashion which the best dressed among them followed, but numbers wore no handkerchiefs at all in warm weather, and the breasts of many hung down in a most disgusting manner, their hair among the generality was straight and 'hung in rats tails' over their eyes, and was filled with lice, at least was inhabited by considerable colonies of these insects. Drunkenness was common to them all and at all times when the means of drunkenness could be found. Fighting among themselves as well as with the men was common and black eyes might be seen on a great many. (*The Autobiography of Francis Place (1771–1854)*, ed. Mary Thale, 1972, pp. 75–6, 77–8, quote in fn. from Add. MS 27829, f.119)

31

. . . Many married women who live in the distant parts of the town, prostitute themselves in Westminster, where they are unknown. I have beheld with a surprise, mingled with terror, girls from eight to nine years old, make a proffer of their charms; and such is the corruption of the human heart, that even they have their loves. Towards midnight when the young women have disappeared, and the streets become deserted, then the old wretches, of fifty or sixty years of age, descend from their garrets, and attack the intoxicated passengers, who are often prevailed upon to satisfy their passions in the open street, with these female monsters. (J. W. von Archenholz, *A Picture of England*, 1791, p. 193)

Part 3   Female Education

A set of phrases learn'd by rote;
A passion for a scarlet coat;
When at a play, to laugh, or cry,
Yet cannot tell the reason why;
Never to hold her tongue a minute,
While all she prates has nothing in it . . .
(Jonathan Swift, *The Furniture of a Woman's Mind*, 1727)

I am persuaded, if there was a commonwealth of rational horses (as Dr. Swift has supposed), it would be an established maxim among them, that a mare could not be taught to pace! (*Letters and Works of Lady Mary Wortley Montagu*, ed. Lord Wharncliffe, 1837, Vol. 3, p. 5)

Introduction

Underlying the views of all but a minority of eighteenth-century writers on the education of girls of the middle and upper classes is the conviction that women were of different and inferior intellectual abilities. Nor was it a view confined to men. Many women writers, however critical of the nature of the education provided for girls, shared the belief that an education different in kind from that of men was appropriate to them. So Hannah More at the very end of the century (**5, 7**) while highly critical of the education most women received, shared the view of the majority that women were incapable of serious intellectual study. They lacked the 'sound and penetrating judgement' (**1**) of men, they were far more superficial in their responses, more concerned with outward appearances and less with the heart of the matter. Many writers went even further in their analysis of women's fundamental inferiority of intellect. Women, it was said, had shallow minds incapable of 'intense and continued application' or of a 'close and comprehensive reasoning'. To James Fordyce the 'imbecility of those who were formed to delight us' should make men more tolerant of their weaknesses (**3**). It was the recognition of such weaknesses that made William Alexander (**4**) warn young men against spending too much time with women. It was these intellectual disabilities of women that made them unsuitable for 'employments of any real importance' (Part 13, extract 3). Maria Edgeworth while satirising the views of such men and wholeheartedly rejecting them, nevertheless, was far from subscribing to any idea of real intellectual equality between the sexes.

At the beginning of the century a suitable education for the daughters of the middle and upper classes consisted of essentially useful accomplishments – cooking, sewing, embroidery, spinning, housewifery – all of which would later enable her as a wife and mother to run the household economically and efficiently, and to entertain elegantly.

If the trend was towards an education in the more ornamental accomplishments, there was still the belief, at least in the early years of the century, that while useful knowledge was more suited to the labouring poor, even the rich would benefit from instruction in the domestic virtues. How important was it to avoid, through ignorance of domestic matters, a situation where domestic servants might 'usurp too much power' (**9**).

There were some writers (**8**) who, recognising that the education of sons as well as daughters was often left to the mother in the family, felt that women must improve themselves in order that their children would have a better chance of a good education.

The effort needed to break through the conventional limits placed on women's intellectual capacity was considerable. Learning, if a woman possessed it, was best concealed. The 'learned lady' was an object for ridicule, and learning was seen as unwomanly and masculine (**15, 17**). There was an assumption not only that such women neglected husbands, children and homes (**16**), but that learning de-sexed women. They lost all sexual attraction for men and became 'no better than old maids'.

French, dancing, music, drawing – these were the ornamental accomplishments which provided the core of the education of most girls in the middle classes and these, along with reading, writing and elementary arithmetic, formed the curriculum of most girls' schools. A few women like Maria Edgeworth had no illusions as to the motive behind the cultivation of such accomplishments (**23**). They saw the importance that they were given in the matrimonial market. To those newly arrived in the middle class, who sought an education to fit their daughters for entry to fashionable society, accomplishments were seen as the key to admission. There were those like Hester Chapone (**20**) who, while accepting the ornamental accomplishments as the necessary basis for a girl's education, wanted much more emphasis on occupations of the mind and particularly on reading. Yet even such women shared the views of those who stressed the role accomplishments played in filling the otherwise empty and idle hours from which so many women of the upper classes suffered. Lady Pennington (**18**) thought that to effectively occupy such time diversions must be carefully organised and time allotted for each. The way in which many men really viewed such accomplishments is revealed by John Gregory (**21**) who suggested that, far from being of any value in themselves, accomplishments merely enabled women to judge more effectively the standards of workmanship of others – presumably menials – and to fill up those 'many solitary hours' all women had to endure. It was important for 'women of quality' to have some interest other than their husbands, *The Guardian* added, for these 'are generally strangers to them' (**8**).

Catherine Macaulay (*Letters on Education*, 1790, p. 46) was one of the very few who criticised the total separation between the education of girls and boys, and the idea that, as she put it, 'the education of females should be of an opposite kind to that of the male'. She rejected the restricted nature of fashionable education imposed by false ideas of decorum and called for coeducation.

If the whole purpose of their education was display, argued Thomas Gisborne (**24**), then little wonder if such education produced women who saw their entire role as one of attracting the admiration of the opposite sex. If women were seen as 'senseless creatures' and educated accordingly, then senseless creatures they would become.

In the course of the eighteenth century, women readers increased – particularly after the spread of circulating libraries brought books within reach, financially and geographically, of many middle-class women. The outcry against novel-reading seems to have been an over-reaction to the true situation. Most women readers continued to read as much serious literature – particularly pious works – as before. But, among young girls, novel-reading may well have become all-engrossing. Maria Edgeworth (**25**), among many others, warned of the dangers of cultivating 'what is called the heart prematurely'. Girls were misled about the realities of life and marriage, grew discontented and became bad wives.

Parents sought a schooling that would equip girls for entry to the social class to which they aspired. Many writers emphasise how tradesmen and artisans strained their finances to send their daughters to such schools only to find them return with a total contempt for their parents, their social class and the trade which they practised (**28**).

To meet the demand for schooling for girls a new type of private venture school emerged in the form of girls' boarding schools, the number of which multiplied rapidly from the mid-century. Unfortunately, the standard of teaching at these establishments showed no parallel improvement in quality. Standards were almost invariably low. The curriculum varied little. It was devoted almost exclusively to the acquisition of the ornamental accomplishments. While parents saw such accomplishments as playing a vital part in their daughters' success in the marriage market, it was impossible for much improvement in the quality of the education offered to take place (**32**).

If the education that boarding schools provided for the daughters of the middle class showed little improvement in the course of the century there was certainly plenty of it. For the daughters of the poor, educational provision remained totally inadequate – both in number of schools and the nature the curriculum followed. It is no longer certain that, as some historians of education have claimed, an improvement in primary education for girls came about as a result of the work done by the charity school movement.

Charity schools were by no means the only sort of school catering for the poor in the eighteenth century. Some few authorities had established free schools supported by the rates. There were innumerable dame schools for young children charging a minimal fee of a penny or so a week. There were free places in parish schools and, towards the end of the century, there were spinning schools and Sunday schools. It is often extremely difficult to categorise neatly schools for the poor since any poor widow or impecunious spinster could set up a school in her own home. For the same reason where exactly such school provision existed was often entirely fortuitous. It varied greatly between one area and another, one village and the next.

Bedevilling all efforts at improving such provision for the daughters of the poor was the constantly expressed fear that the result of such education was to make the female poor less willing to offer themselves for servile work. Nothing perhaps demonstrates better the widening gulf between rich and poor and the growing awareness of social class than this debate on just how much education was necessary for the poor. Was it not possible, it was asked, to educate them to work, but not to think? What was the minimum that was needed? Poor girls had less need of education than poor boys given the nature of the employments they were likely to follow. So it was argued that as they would make little use of writing in their working lives it could well be excluded from the curriculum (**35**). Girls in charity schools were constantly reminded of their humble origins and that they were the objects of charity. To allow them to forget this was to go against the whole aim of charity schools – to provide industrious and servile female domestic servants.

For many daughters of poor parents the pressure of economic circumstances militated against any but the minimum of education. At best, schooling was irregular and soon ended. Many girls, like the wife of Francis Place, had finished their schooling at the age of 12 or even earlier (**39**). If by the end of the century there was some recognition of the shortcomings of education for the poor, there was no real improvement in the education most girls of the working class enjoyed until well into the nineteenth century.

Mention must be made of the blue-stockings, a group of women who not only insisted on their ability to converse on equal terms with men but, in their salons, demonstrated such ability and received public recognition for their intellectual attainments and their conversational wit. Many of the women included in this anthology were blue-stockings – Lady Mary Wortley Montagu, Mrs Elizabeth Montagu, Mrs Chapone, Catherine Macaulay and Hannah More. All were exceptional women, some were outstanding scholars. They were not so much daughters of the aristocracy as of the successful middle class – lawyers, doctors, merchants and the clergy. In the main, they were privately or self-educated. If they despised the sort of education girls received at fashionable boarding schools, they failed to have any real influence on raising those standards. Few of them questioned the role of women, *all* women, in society. Even those who were writers and authors seemed content to accept the inferior position allotted to them because they were women. It was enough for the great majority of them to enjoy the recognition that they received in a limited sphere.

(a) The Intellectual Differences between the Sexes

1

LUCINDA: . . . In reasoning, women can never cope with men, they have a thousand advantages beyond us; our wit may be equal with theirs, but in everything else they exceed us, as well as in strength of body; it is thought sufficient, if a woman can but read and write, we receive no other education, as to learning. But where we leave off, they set out; they are not trusted to manage their own affairs, before they are sent to schools, and universities, to have their intellectuals mended and sharpen'd; not by one master, or by ordinary men, but by several, that are picked and culled out of thousands, for excelling everyone in his own profession; here they have the quintessence of arts and science, politics, and worldly cunning infused into them; and for seven or eight years, all manner of knowledge, as it were, beat into their brain, with all the application imaginable, whilst we are pricking a clout. Why should we venture then (their headpieces being so much better furnished than ours) to hold arguments, or to parley with them? What is short and plain we understand perhaps as well as they; but when business is too intricate or of too long a coherence, 'tis beyond our reach: Women are shallow creatures, we may boast of prattling, and be quick at jest, or repartee, but a sound and penetrating judgement only belongs to man, as the masters of reason and solid sense. (Bernard de Mandeville, *The Virgin Unmask'd* (1709), 1724, pp. 27–8)

2

It is not from want of capacity that so many women are such trifling insipid companions – so ill qualified for the friendship and conversation of a sensible man – or for the task of governing and instructing a family; it is much oftener from the neglect of exercising the talents which they really have, and from omitting to cultivate a taste for intellectual improvement. (Hester Chapone, *Posthumous Works* (1773), 1807, Vol. 3, pp. 223–4)

3

To whatever cause the difference is owing, good nature will forgive a female, who appears to be fond of her person or dress, much more readily than a man who betrays the same weakness. Perhaps, indeed, this indulgence to the other sex is at bottom a compliment to our own: perhaps, Gentleman, we are willing on such occasions, to make more allowance for the imbecility of those who were formed to delight us, not so much by an emulation of intellects, as by external graces and decorations, united with the softer virtues of the heart, and the sprightlier charms of the fancy. (Dr James Fordyce, *The Character and Conduct of the Female Sex*, 1776, p. 54)

4

By the learned and studious, it has often been objected to female company, that it so enervates and relaxes the mind, and gives it such a turn for trifling, levity, and dissipation, as renders it altogether unfit for that application which is necessary in order to become eminent in any of the sciences . . . Nothing . . . seems more certain, than that the youth who devotes his whole time and attention to female conversation and the little offices of gallantry, never distinguishes himself in the literary world; . . . we sincerely wish to caution the young and unexperienced part of our sex, and we advise them to be careful how they associate with any of the other, who are not endowed with sense as well as virtue . . . (William Alexander, *The History of Women*, 1779, Vol. 1, pp. 329–30)

5

Women have generally quicker perceptions; men have juster sentiments. — Women consider how things may be prettily said; men how they may be properly said. — In women (young ones at least), speaking accompanies, and sometimes precedes reflection; in men, reflection is the antecedent. — Women often speak to shine or to please; men, to convince or confute. — Women admire what is brilliant; men what is solid. — Women prefer an extemporaneous sally of wit, or a sparkling effusion of fancy, before the most accurate reasoning, or the most laborious investigation of facts. In literary compositions, women are pleased with point, turn, and antithesis; men with observation, and a just deduction of effects from their causes. — Women are fond of incident, men of argument. — Women admire passionately, men approve cautiously. — One sex will think it betrays a want of feeling to be moderate in their applause, the other will be afraid of exposing a want of judgement by being in raptures with any thing. — Men refuse to give way to the emotions they actually feel, while women sometimes affect to be transported beyond what the occasion will justify. (Hannah More, *Essays on Various Subjects*, 1791, p. 9)

6

The science of legislation, or jurisprudence, of political economy; the conduct of government in all its executive function; the abstruse researches of erudition; the inexhaustible depths of philosophy; the acquirements subordinate to navigation; the knowledge indispensable in the wide field of commercial enterprise; the arts of defence, and of attack by land and by sea, which the violence or the fraud of unprincipled assailants render needful; these, and other studies, pursuits and occupations, assigned chiefly or entirely to men, demand the efforts of a mind endued with the powers of close and comprehensive reasoning, and of intense and continued application, in a degree to which they are not requisite for the discharge of the customary offices of female duty. It would therefore seem natural to expect, and experience, I think, confirms the justice of the expectations, that the Giver of all good, after bestowing those powers on men with a liberality proportionate to the subsisting necessity, would impart them to the female mind with a more sparing hand . . .

Were we called upon to produce examples of the most amiable tendencies and affections implanted in human nature, of modesty, of delicacy, of sympathising sensibility, of prompt and active benevolence, of warmth and tenderness of attachment; whither should we at once turn our eyes? To the sister, to the daughter, to the wife. These endowments form the glory of the female sex. (Thomas Gisborne, *An Enquiry into the Duties of the Female Sex* (1797), 1798, pp. 20–3)

7

In almost all that comes under the description of polite letters, in all that captivates by imagery, or warms by just and affecting sentiment, women are excellent. They possess in a high degree that delicacy and quickness of perception, and that nice discernment between the beautiful and defective which comes under the denomination of taste. Both in composition and action they excel in details; but they do not so much generalise their ideas as men, nor do their minds seize a great subject with so large a grasp. They are acute observers, and accurate judges of life and manners, as far as their own sphere of observation extends; but they describe a smaller circle. A woman sees the world, as it were, from a little elevation in her own garden, where she makes an exact survey of home scenes, but takes not in that wider range of distant prospects which he who stands on a loftier eminence commands. Women have a certain tact which often enables them to feel what is just more instantaneously than they can define it. They have an intuitive penetration into character, bestowed on them by providence, like the sensitive and tender organs of some timid animals, as a kind of natural guard to warn of the approach of danger, beings who are often called to act defensively. (Hannah More, *Strictures on the Modern System of Female Education* (1799), 1800, pp. 225–6)

(b) The Objectives of Female Education

8

. . . I would the more recommend the improvements of the mind to my female readers, that a family may have a double chance for it; and if it meets with weakness in one of the heads, may have it made up in the other. It is indeed an unhappy circumstance in a family, where the wife has more knowledge than the husband; but it is better it should be so, than that there should be no knowledge in the whole house. It is highly expedient that at least one half of the persons, who sits at the helm of affairs, should give an example of good sense to those who are under them.

I have often wondered that learning is not thought a proper ingredient in the education of a woman of quality or fortune. Since they have the same improveable minds as the male part of the species, why should they not be cultivated by the same method? Why should reason be left to itself in one of the sexes, and be disciplined with so much care in the other?

There are some reasons why learning seems more adapted to the female world, than to the male. As in the first place, because they have more spare time upon their hands, and lead a more sedentary life. Their employments are of a domestic nature, and not like those of the other sex, which are often inconsistent with study and contemplation . . .

There is another reason why those especially who are women of quality, should apply themselves to letters, namely, because their husbands are generally strangers to them . . . (*The Guardian*, no. 155, 1713)

9

. . . it is the custom of the nation . . . to educate daughters in the knowledge of things that relate to the affairs of the household, to spin and to use the needle, both for making garments and for the ornaments of embroidery: they have been generally employed in the preparation of food, in the regular disposal of the affairs of the house, for the conveniences and accommodation of human life; in the furniture of the rooms, and the elegancies of entertainment . . .

Some of these things are the constant care and labour of women in our day, whereby they maintain themselves: the most laborious parts of them belong to the poor: And it is the opinion of the best judges, that, even in superior and wealthy circumstances, every daughter should be so far instructed in them as to know when they are performed aright, that the servants may not usurp too much power, and impose on the ignorance of the mistress. (Isaac Watts, *The Improvement of the Mind* (1725), 1819, p. 346)

10

To cultivate and adorn your understanding with the improvements of learning (I mean such as is suitable to your sex) is a matter vastly more worthy of your attention, than any external graces you can put on. The learning I recommend to you, is an inquiry into such truths, as will fix in you your duty; and the reading of so much, in moral and religious authors, as will enable you to form, in your own mind, true conceptions of the deity, especially of his goodness and mercy; of your own being, and the purposes for which you were made; that you may be able to conform this knowledge to the practice of virtue . . . (Rev Mr Wettenhall Wilkes, *A Letter of Genteel and Moral Advice to a Young Lady* (1740), 1766, pp. 157–8)

11

There are no public institutions for the education of women, and there is accordingly nothing useless, absurd, or fantastical, in the common course of their education. They are taught what their parents or guardians judge it necessary or useful for them to learn, and they are taught nothing else. Every part of their education tends evidently to some useful purpose; either to improve the natural attractions of their person, or to form their mind to reserve, to modesty, to chastity, and to economy; to render them both likely to become the mistresses of a family, and to behave properly when they have become such. In every part of her life, a woman feels some conveniency or advantage from every part of her education. (Adam Smith, *The Wealth of Nations*, 1776, World's Classics, Vol. 2, p. 416)

12

. . . Confine not the education of your daughters to what is regarded as the ornamental parts of it, nor deny the graces to your sons. Suffer no prejudices to prevail on you to weaken Nature, in order to render her more beautiful; take measures for the virtue and the harmony of your family, by uniting their young minds early in the soft bonds of friendship. Let your children be brought up together; let their sports and studies be the same; let them enjoy, in the constant presence of those who are set over them, all that freedom which innocence renders harmless, and in which Nature rejoices.

. . . I have given similar rules for male and female education, on the following grounds of reasoning.

First, that there is but one rule of right for the conduct of all rational beings; consequently that true virtue in one sex must be equally so in the other, whenever a proper opportunity calls for its exertion; and, vice versa, what is vice in one sex, cannot have a different property when found in the other.

Secondly, that true wisdom, which is never found at variance with rectitude, is as useful to women as to men; because it is necessary to the highest degree of happiness, which can never exist with ignorance.

Lastly, that as on our first entrance into another world, our state of happiness may possibly depend on the degree of perfection we have attained in this, we cannot justly lessen, in one sex or the other, the means by which perfection, that is another word for wisdom, is acquired. (Catherine Macaulay, *Letters on Education*, 1790, pp. 50, 201–2)

13

. . . an advantageous settlement in marriage is the universal prize, for which parents of all classes enter their daughters upon the lists; . . . To this one point tends the principal part of female instruction; for the promotion of this design, their best years for improvement are sacrificed to the attainment of attractive qualities; showy, superficial accomplishments; polished manners; and, in one word, the whole science of pleasing, which is cultivated with unceasing assiduity, as an object of the most essential importance.

. . . as a more rational education prevails, women will be better acquainted with their relative situation; and as their ideas are more defined, they will perceive that there can be but one head or chief in every family. Nature and reason, as well as custom, have established this power in the hands of the men; therefore, so far from puffing them up, and making them self-willed or presumptuous, an increase of real knowledge will conduce to give them a just estimate of what they owe to themselves, and what is due to their husbands: it will not teach them a servile, unqualified obedience, such as can only be observed by slaves, (for that is an absurdity in a connection which involves the mutual happiness of two persons,) but it will promote a diffidence of their own judgement in concerns of moment, and an habitual reference on such occasions, to the more enlarged experience of mankind in their husbands.

[On the objects of education of the female poor]
In addition to reading, they ought to be well instructed in plain work, knitting, marking, cutting-out, and mending linen, a branch of domestic economy with which too many are unacquainted, who know how to finish a fine shirt completely. Washing, ironing, and cleaning house, should likewise be taught them, with every other qualification that will prepare them to become useful as servants, or as the wives of labourers. They may be allowed to acquire as much skill in writing as will enable them to set down the articles of their expenditure, or to write a receipt, which will be small advantage, unless they also learn addition of money. The multiplication table is so applicable, on various occasions, that a knowledge of that, and the pence table, will profitably repay the time spent in learning them. (Priscilla Wakefield, *Reflections on the Present Condition of the Female Sex* (1798), 1817, pp. 30, 86, 138–9)

14

The profession of ladies, to which the bent of their instruction should be turned, is that of daughters, wives, mothers and mistresses of families. They should be therefore trained with a view to these several conditions and be furnished with a stock of ideas, and principles, and qualifications, and habits ready to be applied and appropriated, as occasion may demand, to each of these respective situations: for though the arts which merely embellish life must claim admiration; yet when a man of sense comes to marry, it is a companion whom he wants, and not an artist. It is not merely a creature who can paint, and play, and dress, and dance; it is a being who can comfort and counsel him; one who can reason, and reflect, and feel, and judge, and act, and discourse, and discriminate; one who can assist him in his affairs, lighten his cares, soothe his sorrows, purify his joys, strengthen his principles, and educate his children.

The chief end to be proposed in cultivating the understanding of women, is to qualify them for the practical purposes of life. Their knowledge is not often, like the learning of men, to be reproduced in some literary composition, nor even in any learned profession; but it is to come out in conduct. A lady studies, not that she may qualify herself to become an orator or a pleader; not that she may learn to debate, but to act. She is to read the best books, not, so much to enable her to talk of them, as to bring the improvements which they furnish, to the rectification of her principles, and the formation of her habits. The great uses of study are to enable her to regulate her own mind, and to be useful to others. (Hannah More, *Strictures on the Modern System of Female Education* (1799), 1800, pp. 72–3, 208–9)

(c) 'Learned Ladies'

15

I own I do not approve of great learning in women. I believe it rarely turns out to their advantage. No farther would I have them to advance, than to what would enable them to write and converse with propriety, and, make themselves useful in every stage of life. I hate to hear Latin out of a woman's mouth. There is something in it, to me masculine. I would fancy such a one weary of the petticoat, and talking over a bottle. (Letter from Lady Bradshaigh to Samuel Richardson, from *Correspondence of Samuel Richardson*, ed. A. L. Barbauld, 1804, Vol. 6, p. 52)

16

It has been objected against all female learning, beyond that of household economy, that it tends only to fill the minds of the sex with a conceited vanity, which sets them above their proper business – occasions an indifference to, if not total neglect of, their family affairs – and serves only to render them useless wives, and impertinent companions . . . a sensible woman will soon be convinc'd, that all the learning her utmost application can make her mistress of, will be, from the difference of education, in many points, inferior to that of a schoolboy: – this reflection will keep her always humble . . . (Lady Sarah Pennington, *An Unfortunate*

Mother's Advice to her Absent Daughters (1761), 1770, pp. 44–6)

17

You apprehend that knowledge must be hurtful to the sex, because it will be the means of their acquiring power. It seems to me impossible that women can acquire the species of direct power which you dread: the manners of society must totally change before women can mingle with men in the busy and public scenes of life. They must become amazons before they can affect this change; they must cease to be women before they can desire it. The happiness of neither sex could be increased by this metamorphosis. (Maria Edgeworth, *Letters from Literary Ladies*, 1795, p. 52)

(d) Accomplishments – Ornamental or Useful

18

It is an excellent method to appropriate the mornings wholly to improvement; – the afternoon may then be allow'd to diversions: – under the last head, I place company, books of the amusing kind, and entertaining productions of the needle, as well as plays, balls, cards, etc., which more commonly go by the name of diversions: . . . One half hour or more, either before or immediately after breakfast, I would have you constantly give to the attentive perusal of some rationally pious author, or to some part of the New Testament . . .

It is necessary for you to be perfect in the four first rules of Arithmetic – more you can never have occasion for, and the mind should not be burthen'd with needless application.

The management of all domestic affairs is certainly the proper business of woman – and, unfashionably rustic as such an assertion may be thought, it is not beneath the dignity of any lady, however high her rank, to know how to educate her children, to govern her servants . . . Make yourself, therefore, so thoroughly acquainted with the most proper method of conducting a family, and with the necessary expense which every article, in proportion to their number, will occasion, that you may come to a reasonable certainty of not being materially deceived without the ridiculous drudgery of following your servants continually, and meanly peeping into every obscure corner of your house; – nor, is this at all difficult to attain, as it requires nothing more than an attentive observation. (Lady Sarah Pennington, *An Unfortunate Mother's Advice to her Absent Daughters* (1761), 1770, pp. 40–1, 43, 46–50)

19

Always be employed in somewhat innocent, or useful; for various, and beyond description, are the inconveniences which besiege the mind in vacancy of employment. . . .

Various are the innocent diversions of life, by which you may lengthen time in general, and prevent any part of it from being useless or tedious.

Needlework, pastry, cookery, limning, drawing, music, singing, gardening; learning of French, Italian, or Latin (as you may have a particular taste and genius for these arts) are all accomplishments, worthy of your care, but not of all your time. (Rev Mr Wettenhall Wilkes, *A Letter of Genteel and Moral Advice to a Young Lady* (1740), 1766, pp. 200–5)

20

With regard to accomplishments, the chief of these is a competent share of reading, well chosen and properly regulated; . . . Dancing and the knowledge of the French tongue are now so universal that they cannot be dispensed with in the education of a gentlewoman; and indeed they both are useful as well as ornamental; the first, by forming and strengthening the body, and improving the carriage: the second, by opening a large field of entertainment and improvement for the mind . . .

To write a free and legible hand, and to understand common arithmetic, are indispensable requisites.

As to music and drawing, I would only wish you to follow as genius leads: you have some turn for the first, and I should be sorry to see you neglect a talent, which will at least afford you an innocent amusement, though it should not enable you to give much pleasure to your friends: I think the use of both these arts is more for yourself than for others . . . but, with regard to yourself, it is of great consequence to have the power of filling up agreeably those intervals of time, which too often hang heavily on the hands of a woman . . . as to the learned languages, though I respect the abilities and application of those ladies, who have attained them, and who make a modest and proper use of them, yet I would by no means advise you – or any woman who is not strongly impelled by a particular genius – to engage in such studies. The labour and time which they require are generally incompatible with our natures and proper employments. (Hester Chapone, *Posthumous Works* (1773), 1807, Vol. 3, pp. 166–9)

21

The intention of your being taught needle-work, knitting and such like, is not on account of the intrinsic value of all you can do with your hands, which is trifling, but to enable you to judge more perfectly of that kind of work, and to direct the execution of it in others. Another principal end is to enable you to fill up, in a tolerably agreeable way, some of the many solitary hours you must necessarily pass at home. (John Gregory, *A Father's Legacy to his Daughters*, 1774, p. 30)

22

Girls learn something of music, drawing and geography; but they do not know enough to engage their attention, and render it an employment of the mind. If they can play over a few tunes to their acquaintance, and have a drawing or two (half done by the master) to hang up in their rooms, they imagine themselves artists for the rest of their lives. It is not the being able to execute a trifling landscape, or anything of the kind, that is of consequence – these are at best but trifles, and the foolish, indiscriminate praises which are bestowed on them only produce vanity. But what is really of no importance, when considered in this light, becomes of the utmost, when a girl has a fondness for the art, and a desire of excellence. Whatever tends to make a person in some measure independent of the senses, is a prop to virtue. Amusing employments must first occupy the mind . . . (Mary Wollstonecraft, *Thoughts on the Education of Daughters*, 1787, pp. 25–7)

23

Accomplishments, it seems, are valuable, as being the objects of universal admiration. Some accomplishments have another species of value, as they are tickets of admission to fashionable company. Accomplishments have another, and a higher species of value, as they are supposed to increase a young lady's chance of a prize in the matrimonial lottery. Accomplishments have also a value as resources against ennui, as they afford continual amusement and innocent occupation. This is ostensibly their chief praise; it deserves to be considered with respect. False and odious must be that philosophy which would destroy any one of the innocent pleasures of our existence . . . Women are peculiarly restrained in their situation, and in their employments, by the customs of society: to diminish the number of those employments, therefore, would be cruel; they should rather be encouraged, by all means, to cultivate those tastes which can attach them to their home, and which can preserve them from the miseries of dissipation. Every sedentary occupation must be valuable to those who are to lead sedentary lives, and every art, however trifling in itself, which tends to enliven and embellish domestic life, must be advantageous, not only to the female sex but to society in general. As far as accomplishments can contribute to all or any of these excellent purposes, they must be just objects of attention in early education. (Maria Edgeworth, *Practical Education*, 1798, Vol. 1, pp. 522–3)

24

In schools almost universally, and very commonly, I fear in domestic tuition, ornamental accomplishments occupy the rank and estimation which ought to have been assigned to the objects of infinitely greater importance . . . If a girl is treated by her instructress, if she is taught to labour and act, in the way that would be reasonable, if to improve in personal grace, to study fashionable decorations of the body and of the mind, were the appointed purposes of her existence; . . . is it surprising that she, when grown up, should starve herself into shapeliness, and overspread her face with paint, who was trained at a boarding-school to swing daily by the chin, in order to lengthen her neck, and perhaps even accustomed, as is sometimes the case, to peculiar modes of discipline contrived to heighten the complexion? If she was taught throughout the whole course of her education, though not by express precept, yet by daily and hourly admonitions which could convey no other meaning, that dancing is for display, that music is for display, that drawing and French and Italian are for display; can it be a matter for astonishment, that during the rest of her life she should be incessantly on the watch to shine and to be admired? (Thomas Gisborne, *An Enquiry into the Duties of the Female Sex* (1797), 1798, pp. 80–3)

(e) Novel-Reading

25

. . . sentimental stories, and books of mere entertainment . . . should be sparingly used, especially in the education of girls. This species of reading cultivates what is called the heart prematurely, lowers the tone of mind, and induces indifferences for those common pleasures and occupations which, however trivial in themselves, constitute by far the greatest portion of our daily happiness . . . To those who acquire this taste every object becomes disgusting which is not an attitude for poetic painting; a species of moral picturesque is sought for in every scene of life, and this is not always compatible with sound sense, or with simple reality.

Women, from their situation and duties in society, are called upon rather for the daily exercise of quiet domestic virtues, than for those splendid acts of generosity, or those exaggerated expressions of tenderness, which are the characteristics of heroines in romances. Sentimental authors who paint with enchanting colours all the graces and all the virtues in happy union, teach us to expect this union should be indissoluble. Afterwards, from the natural influence of association, we expect in real life to meet with virtue when we see grace, and we are disappointed, almost disgusted, when we find virtue unadorned. This false association has a double effect upon the conduct of women; it prepares them to be pleased, and it excites them to endeavour to please by adventitious charms, rather than by those qualities which merit esteem. Women, who have been much addicted to common novel-reading are always acting in imitation of some Jemima or Almeria, who never existed, and they perpetually mistake plain William and Thomas for 'My Beverly!' They have another peculiar misfortune; they require continual great emotions to keep them in tolerable humour with themselves; they must have tears in their eyes, or they are apprehensive that their hearts are growing hard. (Maria Edgeworth, *Practical Education*, 1798, pp. 332–3, 296–7)

(f) Schooling for Daughters of the Rich

26

[Of around 1720]
In order to perfect young ladies in what was then thought a necessary part of their education, a pastry-school was set up in Manchester, which was frequented, not only by the daughters of the town's-people, but those of the neighbouring gentlemen. (J. Aikin, *A Description of the Country from Thirty to Forty Miles round M'Chester*, 1795, p. 188)

27

[Of a boarding school education]

. . . there they may be taught to sing and dance, to work and dress, and if you will, receive good instructions for a genteel carriage, and how to be mannerly; but these things chiefly concern the body, the mind remains uninstructed. They lead easy and lazy lives, and have abundance of time upon their hands, especially those whose relations are rich, and foolish enough to furnish them with as much money as may enable them to bribe their teachers to neglect their duty, and wink at their faults, and cramming themselves with custards and cheesecakes all day long, oblige their mistresses with having no stomach to their dinner . . . All the week long they are commonly barr'd from the sight of man, Sundays excepted; some are arch, most of em wanton, and when they grow up, all fill one another's heads with so much rubbish of courtship, and love, that it is a wonder they don't run away with the first man they see . . . (Bernard de Mandeville, *The Virgin Unmask'd* (1709), 1724, pp. 48–9)

28

I beg your assistance to convey some hints on . . . the improper education given to a great number of the daughters of low tradesmen and mechanics. Every village in the neighbourhood of this great city has one or two little boarding schools, with an inscription over the door, 'Young ladies boarded and educated'. The expense is small, and hither the blacksmith, the ale-house keeper, the shoemaker etc., sends his daughter, who, from the moment she enters these walls, becomes a young lady. The parent's intention is an honest one: his time is too much taken up, as well as his wife's, by the necessary duties of their profession, to have any to bestow on the education of their children; they are therefore obliged to send them from home. As this is the case, there ought certainly to be proper schools for their reception: but surely, the plan of these schools ought to differ as much from that of the great schools, intended for the daughters of the nobility and gentry, as the station in life of the scholars at the one, differs from those of the other . . . the daughter of the lowest shopkeeper at one of these schools, is as much Miss, and a young lady, as the daughter of the first Viscount in England, at one of the other . . . and Miss, whose mamma sells oysters, tells Miss, whose papa deals in small coal, that her governess shall know it, if she spits in her face, or does anything else unbecoming a young lady . . . French and dancing is also to be taught at these schools, neither of which can be of any use to young ladies of this sort. The parents may imagine the first may procure them a place, but in this they may be greatly mistaken as, I believe, there is hardly a single instance of a girl's having learnt that language to any degree of perfection at one of these schools. As to the last, . . . it would be of much more consequence they should be well instructed how to wash the floor than how to dance upon it . . . The needlework taught at these schools is of a kind much more likely to strengthen the natural propensity in all young minds to show and dress, than to answer any housewifely purpose . . .

How disappointed will the honest shopkeeper be, if, at any age when he thinks proper to take his daughter from school, he should expect any assistance from her! Can he suppose a young lady will weigh his soap for him? . . . Though ignorant of everything else, she will be so perfect in the lessons of pride and vanity, that she will despise him and his nasty shop, and quit both, to go off with the first man who promises her a silk gown and a blonde cap . . . young people should be taught submission and humility to their superiors, decency and modesty in their own dress and behaviour . . . they should all be well instructed in all kinds of plain-work, reading, writing, accompts, pastry, pickling, preserving, and other branches of cookery; be taught to weave, and wash lace and other linen. Thus instructed, they may be of great comfort and assistance to their parents and husbands; . . . whereas young ladies are the most useless of all God's creatures. (*Annual Register*, 1759 [from the *London Chronicle*], pp. 424–6)

29

What girls learn at these schools is trifling, but they unlearn what would be of great disservice – a provincial dialect, which is extremely ungenteel, and other tricks that they learn in the nursery. The carriage of the person, which is of great importance, is well attended to, and dancing is well taught. As for the French language, I do not think it necessary, unless for persons in very high life. It is rarely much cultivated at schools. I believe all the boarding-schools are much on the same plan. (Dr Doran, *A Lady of the Last Century (Mrs. Elizabeth Montagu)*, 1873, pp. 181–2)

30

There is a school in this metropolis, at which females are educated of the first fashion, and I believe, such only . . . When a young lady, daughter of a duke or earl, or whatever her quality may be, has, by some great offence, exposed herself to particular severity

of animadversion, she is stript of her own apparel, and attired in that of a charity-girl.
. . . How then? is a charity-girl, as such an object of contempt and ridicule? . . . is it thus that the good lady inculcates on the hearts of her fair pupils the great duties of humility and consideration of the poor! (*Gentleman's Magazine*, 1789, p. 489)

31

[Of the 1780s]
. . . my two sisters were sent to school at what was called a very respectable day school . . . here almost every thing was professed to be taught. It was the best of the sort in the neighbourhood. My sisters were taught various kinds of needle work and the rudiments of the French language. (*The Autobiography of Francis Place (1771–1854)*, ed. Mary Thale, 1972, p. 40)

32

[Of exercise]
He pleads for its more extensive adoption among the inhabitants of female boarding schools; whose walks are too generally of so constrained a case, that they probably tend rather to injure than to do any service. The end of salutary exercise is not answered by those solemn processions, from the line of which no individual dares to depart, and which are often protracted to a dangerous extent, beneath an atmosphere, the chilling influence of which, the exertion made use of is by no means adequate to repel.

Another remark may be offered in excuse for the plans generally pursued at such seminaries. To use a familiar illustration, the article must be manufactured in a style to meet the demand. If, in consequence of an ill-judging taste, superficial accomplishments attract the attention due only to virtue, to real good sense and solid information; and if parents cannot rise superior to the desire that their children should be educated conformably to such a standard, what remains for the conductors of such institutions, but to 'sign and submit'? (J. E. Stock, *Memoirs of the Life of Thomas Beddoes*, 1811, pp. 204, 277)

33

. . . my . . . child . . . went to school in January, in good health but never in good spirits for she abhorred school. Oh! what infatuation to send her to one. In the country she had health, spirits, and strength, as if there were not enough with what she might have learned at home, instead of going to that region of constraint and death, Camden House.

The rules for health are detestable, no air but in a measured, formal walk, and all running and quick motion prohibited. Preposterous! She slept with a girl who could hear only with one ear, and so ever laid on one side; and my dear child could do no otherwise afterwards without pain; because the vile beds are so small that they must both lie the same way. The school discipline of all sorts, the food, etc. etc., all contributed. She never had a bellyful at breakfast. Detestable this at the expence of £80 a year. Oh! how I regret ever putting her there . . . they are all theatres of knavery, illiberality and infamy. (Arthur Young, *The Autobiography of Arthur Young*, ed. M. Betham-Edwards, 1898, p. 263)

(g) Schooling for Daughters of the Poor

34

Some rules for the well ordering of the Charity School.

In ye summer all the children shall rise at 6 and go to bed at 9 at night. In the winter they shall rise at 7 and go to bed at 8. Prayers shall be read every morn by one of the biggest girls before the children are set to work and the like in the evening when they give over working in the presence of the 2 mistresses, housekeeper and servant belonging to the school.

The children shall all breakfast at 9 dine at 12 and have supper at 7 all the year round.

Fourteen of the biggest girls shall attend the work of the housekeeper (viz) 2 each day by turns who are to obey ye housekeeper's orders in the work that is to be done but on the days of washing ironing or the like the housekeeper shall have authority to employ as many of the said 14 girls as is necessary. Fourteen of ye children shall be employed every day in the knitting with one mistress present or the like work.

Seven of each fourteen shall read a chapter every day alternately whilst the rest are kept to their work.

The children shall be taught to write and cast accounts one afternoon in a week.

If at any time linen shall be brought in to be made, and the mistress shall order from the above 28 girls so many as may be necessary to do the same and so in the like manner for making and mending the children's apparel . . . ('Rules for the School', *Minute Book of Burlington School*, 1723, quoted from Marion Ardern Burgess, *A History of Burlington School*, 1937, p. 29)

35

I will by no means contend for writing as a matter of equal necessity or advantage with that of reading. And there may also be some of the poor who dwell in very obscure villages, and are confined to rural labours, and others in towns and cities, and especially girls, whose business is most within doors at home, who may have but very little occasion, and as little inclination to use a pen. I would not therefore by any means have it made a necessary part of a Charity-School, that the children should be taught to write. (Isaac Watts, *An Essay towards the Encouragement of Charity Schools*, 1728, p. 729)

36

[Of the advantages of the education provided at a Foundling hospital]
Husbandry and manufacturing will thrive by means of these children, who might otherwise have had no existence – The girls being accustomed to regularity, the use of their needle, and the drudgery of domestic life, will fill up some of the most useful offices in families. If everything that is bad is kept from them, and everything that is good and proper to their condition, is set before their eyes, . . . we may hope to see these children, some of the more useful, and therefore the most valuable subjects. (Jonas Hanway, *A Journal of Eight Days' Journey*, 1757, Vol. 2, pp. 131–2)

37

With respect to girls, whose condition obliges them to work for their living, their genius is still more useless to them. They are taught some trade or calling suitable to their sex as soon as they come to the age of discretion, and the necessity they are in of constantly attaching themselves to it, prevent their properly thinking of anything else. (Anon., *Female Rights Vindicated*, 1758, pp. 100–1)

38

1772 – In my second year I was sent to a dame school, kept by Mrs. Loseby, who lived in the house now converted into Payne's fish shop, in High Street, Leicester. There was only one other male youngster . . . We were made to sit on a small form by ourselves, distinct from the little girls, who filled the school . . .

Mrs. Loseby was a little sharp old woman, so crooked and lame that she could not move from her chair. She was the horror of my working and sleeping thoughts . . . when the old lady was ill we were turned over to the maiden government of her niece, Jane Glover, a good-tempered, and pleasing young person, . . . (William Gardiner, *Music and Friends*, 1838–53, Vol. 3, pp. 2–3)

39

[Francis Place married in 1791. His wife was 17 years of age] The education of my intended wife, I mean the school education was very narrow reading and writing and common sewing constituted the whole. Other useful education she obtained by seeing what others did and from such instructions as they could give her. At twelve years of age she was taken by a very good woman who was housekeeper to Mr. Styles a pastry cook near Temple Bar, he was a batchelor at nearly seventy years of age and almost continually afflicted with the gout, and needed someone to wait upon him, in this capacity she remained until Mr. Styles died . . . She now occasionally served in the shop the care of which had devolved upon the housekeeper. Her wages were not more than sufficient to provide her with a good stock of clothes and . . . she had no money by her. (*The Autobiography of Francis Place (1771–1854)*, ed. Mary Thale, 1972, p. 100)

40

Since the day-labourer can scarcely with his utmost exertions supply his family with the daily bread which is to sustain their bodies, no wonder that he should so seldom strive to procure for them that other bread, which is to nourish their souls, and prepare them for a future state of being. For though the schooling of a child costs but two-pence or three-pence a week, yet this pittance is wanted for so many other purposes, that it would be missed in the family. (David Davies, *The Case of Labourers in Husbandry*, 1795, pp. 28–9)

41

[From the Manchester Workhouse rules]:
Rule 24. The matron shall take care that such girls as are of proper age be, by rotation, employed and instructed, as much as may be, in cookery, housewifery, washing, scouring, and such other work as may best qualify them for service. (F. M. Eden, *The State of the Poor*, 1797, Vol. 2, p. 347)

42

. . . as there are not any little trades which the lower classes of women can be taught, the best thing that can be done for girls in that rank of life, is to make them fit for servants: But as it may happen without any fault of theirs that they may not always be able to find places, they should likewise be taught some probable means of gaining a livelihood in such an emergency; also they should be instructed in such employments as will be most useful to them if they marry and have children of their own.

In order to be fitted for servants, they should be taught to sew, knit, and spin line [flax], to wash, to milk, to clean a house, and should have such other general instructions in housewifery as their situation can admit of; and in order to enable them to maintain themselves if they should be out of place, and also to enable them in after life to assist in bringing up a family: They should in this country be well instructed in spinning worsted. (Catharine Cappe, *An Account of Two Charity Schools*, 1800, pp. 103–4, app. no. 6)

Part 4   Approaching Marriage

> Obey your parents' wishes, and you will offend
> neither delicacy or propriety. (*Ladies' Magazine*,
> 1792)

> SIR HARRY: . . . Our daughters lie upon our hands,
> brother Tipkin; girls are drugs, sir, mere drugs.
> (Richard Steele, *The Tender Husband*, 1705)

> Daughters are chickens brought up for the tables of
> other men. (Samuel Richardson, *Clarissa* (1748),
> 1811, Vol. 1, pp. 80–1)

> O these men! fathers or husbands much alike! the
> one tyrannical, the other insolent; so that, between
> one and t'other, a poor girl has nothing for it, but a
> few weeks courtship, and perhaps a first month's
> bridalry, if that; and then she is as much a slave to a
> husband, as she was a vassal to her father. (Samuel
> Richardson, *Pamela*, 1740, Vol. 3, pp. 78–9)

Introduction

Relations between parents and daughters in the eighteenth
century were closely associated with attitudes to marriage.
Parents persistently express concern about relations with
their daughters. This suggests that their relationship was
being questioned. Just as after the Restoration attitudes to
sex and to the institution of marriage had reflected a growing
cynicism, so now children were increasingly challenging their
traditional role of submission to parental authority. The
decline of such authority was of uneven development, but in
the course of the eighteenth century with the growing emerg-
ence of the middle class it seems to have accelerated. It
coincides with a new liberalism in notions of child-rearing
which made for a far more permissive relationship between
parents and children. In so far as attempts to enforce obedience in daughters persisted, they predominated among parents of the rural upper classes.

So long as parents' main criterion of a successful marriage

was expressed in terms of money, property and rank, daughters continued to be treated as valuable commodities. However much parents might subscribe to the idea of a daughter's consent to a marriage, mercenary considerations often outweighed such principles. While the trend in all classes during the century was towards marrying for love, greater resistance to acceptance of such a principle was offered by the very rich. Yet in the course of the century pressure on parents not to enforce a marriage against their children's inclinations grew (3, 5). Many recognised that daughters, while ultimately having the right, even the duty, to resist a marriage they disliked, nevertheless should consult their parents and win their agreement to any marriage they might contemplate (4). Thomas Gisborne (7) suggests that in matters of the heart, the judgement of daughters is likely to be affected, so all the more need for them to seek the advice of parents or relatives – and to heed it.

Most writers make clear that they are writing of the upper classes. We know all too little of relations between daughters and parents further down the social scale.

Attitudes to courtship also range over a wide spectrum. Among the upper classes courtship meant a satisfactory marriage settlement arrived at by negotiations between parents and their lawyers rather than between the husband and wife to be. Among the labouring class there is evidence that courtship sometimes meant a kind of trial marriage in which both partners to the arrangement were free to contract out even if it ended in the pregnancy of the woman (18, 19). Daniel Defoe (10) and Thomas Turner (13) express the attitude of the middle class to pre-marital sex. If such examples suggest a greater equality in courtship among the labouring class, more evidence is needed before any conclusive judgement can be made. For the middle and upper classes courtship remained a very one-sided process. As an anonymous writer (8) put it 'men court the women' and not vice versa. For a woman to acknowledge, by the slightest gesture, her feelings for a man before she was sure they were fully reciprocated showed want of 'prudence and delicacy' (14, 16). As Jonas Hanway suggests (15) such accepted etiquette led to the thwarting of what could have been many happy marriages.

Behind most attitudes to marriage among the respectable classes there lies one major assumption: that only by marriage could a woman really fulfil her destiny in the role of mother as well as wife. Defoe thought propagation the sole reason for marriage in women, and that a childless marriage was a mockery of the institution (**26**). From these assumptions arose the often almost pathological pursuit of a husband by daughters and parents. The object was the best husband that money could buy. Parents, particularly those desperately anxious to win acceptance in the social class to which they aspired, were prepared almost to cripple themselves financially in these efforts.

Mercenary marriages were not new, but in the eighteenth century such marriages became more blatantly commercial. The newspapers of the period are full of reports of marriages couched in the same terms as those from the *London Chronicle* and *Daily Post-Boy* (**27, 28**). Parents were anxious to publicise not only the happy event but the wealth of the bride to be and the social ranking of the bridegroom (**25, 34**).

The dowry that was offered with daughters naturally became of crucial importance. Contemporaries thought that more women were competing for fewer potential husbands than earlier, and that this accounted for the rise in the price that must be paid for a husband. As Moll Flanders found, marriage seemed far more favourable to husbands than to wives (**23**).

The middle-class Defoe was not alone in thinking love an essential ingredient of a happy marriage. But Defoe went some way to seeing marriage as a partnership based on equality or, at least, one in which neither of the participants were regarded as subject to the other (**26**). It was not just that love was the only basis on which a happy working partnership could be based, but that the absence of love was to prostitute marriage, to make of it a mere 'matrimonial whoredom'.

The nature of this 'love' was more akin to friendship or an affectionate companionship, than anything related to sexual passion (**29, 36**). Few writers in the eighteenth century saw sexual attraction as having anything to do with marriage. Indeed, to discuss the existence of such 'carnal appetites' was taboo. It was, as Defoe put it, 'to gratify their vicious part' (**26**).

John Gregory saw women as incapable of love for they lacked 'that sensibility which disposed to such attachments' (**31**). Overendowed as they were with 'sensibility', it is difficult to believe that they could still be inadequately supplied! Most writers took it for granted that women were incapable of strong feelings and sexual urges. Hester Chapone (**29**), while recognising the existence of desire on both sides, saw it as ending with marriage. Little wonder, then, that so many men of her social class went outside marriage for sexual satisfaction.

Mary Wollstonecraft (**37**) was almost alone in criticising the assumption about wives that lay behind such attitudes, that women lacked all passion and only yielded to their lovers out of compassion.

The role that women were to play as wives was made clear by Mary Astell (Part 6, extract 7). The best that women could hope for was that they would be given the opportunity to refuse what was offered, to reject a fool for a husband, to 'choose' a man at least agreeable and understanding, and one, Hester Chapone was at pains to add, she could 'willingly acknowledge as her superior'. For many wives of the upper and middle classes, matrimony was little more than 'a fund in which prudent women deposit their fortunes to the best advantage in order to receive a larger interest for them than they could elsewhere' (Henry Fielding's *Tom Jones*).

As has been said, we do not know how marriage was regarded by the labouring class, what importance the institution of marriage had for them, and what were the motives behind the formation of a stable partnership whether inside or outside of matrimony. From middle-class writers like Hanway (**30**) a sneaking suspicion is sometimes expressed that maybe it was all so much easier for the poor to experience happy relationships without the complications of fortune and rank that pervaded all marriage arrangements among their betters. That economic considerations cannot have been entirely absent from decisions to enter into such relationships is clear (**35**). To escape from their parents' home on marriage and set up house on their own involved having the wherewithal to rent a cottage, if such could be found, and providing sufficient livestock to keep the wife employed and so able to supplement the labourer's wage. It would seem clear that whatever motives the labouring class might have for a 'married' relationship they must have been different from those of the 'respectable' classes. Both sides were expected to contribute something to setting up house together, it was vital that both were at least capable of labour if they were to have any chance of avoiding dependence on the poor rate, but after these considerations, was there perhaps a greater possibility that real affection could be the basis on which they came and stayed together?

(a) Parent–Daughter Relations and the Choice of a Husband

1

[A sister addresses her brother]

. . . if your daughter desires to marry any person you do not like, I grant that you have power, by the law of God, to forbid her positively; the scripture is plain, you have power to dissolve even a vow or promise of hers to marry or not to marry at all. But if your daughter is not willing to marry one you may like, I do not think you have the same right of command, for you might then command her to marry a person she may have an abhorrence of, and an aversion to, which could not be; the very laws of matrimony forbid it . . . (Daniel Defoe, *Religious Courtship* (1722), 1840–1, dialogue III)

2

. . . the old man, having no other notion of making his daughter happy, than by making her rich, had pitch'd upon a son-in-law, that had a vast estate, but was very deformed, and slighting the aversion which he perceived his daughter had against him, granted access to nobody but him . . . She defending herself . . . made a vigorous opposition, and was so constant in her refusal, that her father, who was of an obstinate, wilful temper, seeing her so resolute, began to be rough with her, told her he would be obey'd, and being very covetous, resolved to make use of all his authority, to force her inclinations, and rather marry her by violence, than miss of so rich a prize. (Bernard de Mandeville, *The Virgin Unmask'd* (1709), 1724, pp. 39–40)

3

. . . filial gratitude obliges children to the same submission to the will of their parents, when grown up, as in their infant years; in all cases, except where a higher duty interferes, or where the sacrifice they are expected to make is greater than any degree of gratitude can require. And as one case, and that the most general and common case wherein parents and children differ where a higher duty *does* interfere, and where the sacrifice expected is greater than any degree of gratitude can require, I instanced that of marriage with a hated object: (if I had said an indifferent one, I think I should not have gone toò far;) which is contrary to our duty to God, to a husband, and to ourselves; and which would disturb, if not destroy, the happiness of the child's whole life. You agree with me in thinking that parents have no right to force a child to marry against inclination; that where this is attempted, children have a right to resist, and to use every method their own prudence can suggest to get out of their parent's power; in short to disclaim an authority which is made use of, not according to its true end, etc.

... those marriages which are made up by the parents are *generally* (amongst people of quality or great fortune,) mere Smithfield bargains, so much ready money for so much land, and my daughter flung in into the bargain! ... I took it into my head ... that fathers and mothers, now-a-days, frequently dressed out their daughters, and sent them into public places, with an appearance of five times the fortune they could give them, in hopes that they might catch – what? – Not a man of sense and worth, who should make them happier and better, but a fool, a rich fool . . . I thought that parents in *general*, (at least amongst the rich and great) consulted not their children's inclinations, or their *real* happiness in marriage, but sought to procure them the goods of fortune only. (Hester Chapone, *Posthumous Works* (1773), 1807, Vol. 2, pp. 100–1, 121–3)

4

Fortune and family it is the sole province of your father to direct – he certainly has always an undoubted right to a negative voice; though not to a compulsive one – as, a child is very justifiable in the refusal of her hand, even to the absolute command of a father, where her heart cannot go with it – so is she extremely culpable, in giving it contrary to his approbation. (Lady Pennington, *An Unfortunate Mother's Advice to her Absent Daughters*, 1770, pp. 84–5)

5

MARY: Do you not reckon that the greatest abuse of all, is that of – of forcing a woman, to marry a man she does not like?
THOMAS: This is a crime, which ought to be carried to the account of ambitious or covetous parents. (Jonas Hanway, *Virtue in Humble Life*, 1774, Vol. 2, p. 451)

6

Females, it is true, in all countries are too much under the dominion of their parents; and few parents think of addressing

their children in the following manner, though it is in this reasonable way that Heaven seems to command the whole human race:–
It is in your interest to obey me till you can judge for yourself; and
the almighty Father of all has implanted an affection in me to serve
as a guard to you whilst your reason is unfolding; but when your
mind arrives at maturity, you must only obey me, or rather respect
my opinions, so far as they coincide with the light that is breaking
in on your own mind . . .
   A slavish bondage to parents cramps every faculty of the mind;
and Mr. Locke very judiciously observes. that 'if the mind be
curbed and humbled too much in children; if their spirits be abased
and broken much by too strict an hand over them, they lose all
their vigour and industry.' This strict hand may in some degree
account for the weakness of women; for girls, from various causes,
are more kept down by their parents, in every sense of the word,
than boys. The duty expected from them is, like all the duties
arbitrarily imposed on women, more from a sense of propriety,
more out of respect for decorum, than reason; and thus taught
slavishly to submit to their parents, they are prepared for the
slavery of marriage. (Mary Wollstonecraft, *Vindication of the
Rights of Woman* (1792), ed. Miriam Kramnick, 1978, pp. 269–70)

7

The truths which have been inculcated as furnishing the only
foundation for rational hopes of happiness in marriage are such as
ought to be established in the mind, while the affections are yet
unengaged. When the heart has received an impression, reason
acts feebly or treacherously. But let not the recent impression be
permitted to sink deeper, ere the habitual principles and conduct
of him who has made it shall have been ascertained. On these
points, in particular, points which a young woman cannot herself
possess adequate means of investigating, let the advice and
inquiries of virtuous relatives be solicited. Let not their opinions,
though the purport of them should prove unacceptable, be under-
valued; nor their remonstrances, if they should remonstrate, be
construed as unkindness. Let it be remembered that, although
parental authority can never be justified in constraining a daughter
to marry against her will; there are many cases in which it may be
justified in requiring her to pause. (Thomas Gisborne, *An Enquiry
into the Duties of the Female Sex*, (1797), 1798, p. 254)

(b) Wooing and Courtship

8

. . . men court the women, and not women the men; which is a shrew'd token of the bashfulness of the one, and the boldness of the other: For maids, if they are so unfortunate as to fall in love, will rather choose to die, than to declare it to the person, so great is their modesty . . . (Anon., *Woman Triumphant*, 1721, pp. 11–12)

9

LUCINDA: What your opinion of wooing may be, I cann't tell, but I always thought it very ridiculous; tell me, pray Antonia, which is more unacccountable, the pride of the woman, or the humility of the man? She is resolved to be very cross, and with abundance of coyness sits in state, insults over the man, and treats him with as much scorn, as if he was not worthy to wipe her shoes; and why does she do all this? For no other reason but because she designs to make him her master, and give him all she has in the world. The man, on his side, seems to be fond of being ill-treated, and with the most profound veneration to his idol, begs on his knees, that a certain modest petition may be granted him; the upshot of which is, that the person, to whom he pays his devotion, would be so kind, as to oblige herself solemnly before witnesses, upon the penalty of being damn'd, to be his slave as long as she lives, unless he should happen to die before her. (Bernard de Mandeville, *The Virgin Unmask'd* (1709), 1724, p. 30)

10

. . . for a man to make a whore of the very woman who he intends and designs to make his wife . . . defiles his own bed, pollutes his own seed, spreads bastardy in his own race, and shows a most wicked vitiated appetite, that could not withhold himself from her merely as a woman, till the performance of a lawful marriage might make it seasonable, as well as lawful; . . . he apparently exposes and dishonours his wife as well as himself; nor is it sufficient to say, that the woman dishonours her self too, or that there is much more of the blame lies on him than on her, for as she sufficiently bears her share of the reproach, so she bears more of the scandal, than the man . . . (Daniel Defoe, *Conjugal Lewdness*, 1727, pp. 65–6)

11

SIR POSITIVE TRAP: . . . I never saw my lady then till an hour before our marriage. I made my addresses to her father, her father to his lawyer, the lawyer to my estate . . . the bargain was struck . . . What need have young people of addressing, or anything, till they come to undressing?

LADY TRAP: Ay, this courtship is an abominable, diabolical practice, and the parent of nothing but lies and flattery . . .

SIR POSITIVE TRAP: . . . I hope to see the time, when a man may carry his daughter to market with the same lawful authority as any other of his cattle . . . (Henry Fielding, *Love in Several Masques*, 1728, Act II, Sc. vi)

12

. . . are there some situations, in which a woman must conceal her true sentiments? in which it would be thought immodesty to speak out? . . . why . . . should women be blamed, for owning modestly a passion for a worthy and suitable object? Is it, that they will not speak out, lest, if their wishes should not be crowned with success by *one* man, they should deprive themselves of the chance to succeed with *another*? Do they not propose to make the man they love happy? And is it a crime to acknowledge, that they are so well disposed to a *worthy* object . . . What a littleness is there in the custom that compels us to be insincere? And suppose we do not succeed with a first object, shall we cheat a future lover with the notion that he was the first? (Samuel Richardson, *Sir Charles Grandison*, 1753–4, Vol. 3, letter I)

13

[27 January 1762]
The wife of Tho. Davy was this day delivered of a girl, after being married only six months; two people whom I should least have suspected of being guilty of so indiscreet an act. But what can be said of this passion? – how careful should we be of ourselves in this particular, when we daily see people of the strictest virtue apparently guilty of it. (Thomas Turner, *The Diary of a Georgian Shopkeeper 1754–64*, ed. G. H. Jennings, 1979, p. 52–3)

14

A woman, in this country, may, easily prevent the first impressions of love, and every motive of prudence and delicacy should make her guard her heart against them, till such time as she has received the most convincing proofs of the attachment of a man of such merit, as will justify a reciprocal regard. Your hearts indeed may be shut inflexibly and permanently against all the merit a man can possess. That may be your misfortune, but cannot be your fault. In such a situation, you would be equally unjust to yourself and your lover, if you gave him your hand when your heart revolted against him. But miserable will be your fate, if you allow an attachment to steal on you before you are sure of a return; or, what is infinitely worse, where there are wanting those qualities which alone can ensure happiness in a married state. (John Gregory, *A Father's Legacy to his Daughters*, 1774, pp. 115–16)

15

MARY: Most people think it unbecoming in a young woman to talk as if she ever intended to marry; at the very moment they suppose she would be exceeding glad to find a good and proper husband.

THOMAS: There is a kind of ridiculous farce carried on upon this subject: It is prudent and modest in young women, to decline the discovery of their thoughts, when it is of no use to make them known: but reserve hath prevented the union of thousands, who would have gladly met; and after a little knowledge of each other's humour, been happy together. (Jonas Hanway, *Virtue in Humble Life*, 1774, Vol. 2, pp. 457–8)

16

If a wish to possess the heart of some worthy man, co-operating with the partiality which most persons have for themselves, shall induce a woman to conclude too hastily, that such a man is attached to her; it will be decent at least to conceal a persuasion, which women of prudence and delicacy will ever be slow to entertain. To entertain it rashly, we have seen, is always wrong, and frequently pernicious. We now subjoin, that to declare it bluntly is both unwise and contemptible . . . Surely, Gentlemen, one of the last things a man of sense and modesty will suspect is, that a woman is enamoured of him. (Dr James Fordyce, *The Character and Conduct of the Female Sex*, 1776, p. 63)

17

The poor are the only class who still retain the liberty of acting from inclination and from choice, while the rich, in proportion as they rise in opulence and rank, sink in the exertion of the natural rights of mankind, and must sacrifice their love at the shrine of interest or ambition.

. . . courtship, at least that kind of it which proceeds from mutual inclination and affection is, among the great, nearly annihilated, and the matrimonial bargain . . . is made between the relations of the two families, with all the care and cunning that each is master of to advance its own interest by over-reaching the other. (William Alexander, *The History of Women*, 1779, Vol. 2, p. 179)

18

The mode of courtship here is, that a young woman never admits of the serious addresses of a young man, but on supposition of a thorough probation. When she becomes with child, she tells her mother; the mother tells her father; her father tells his father, and he tells his son, that it is then a proper time to be married . . . If the woman does not prove with child, after a competent time of courtship, they conclude they are not destined by Providence for each other; and as it is an established maxim, which the Portland women observe with great strictness, never to admit a plurality of lovers at one time, their honour is no ways tarnished: she just as soon (after the affair is declared to be broke off) gets another suitor, as if she had been left a widow, or that nothing had ever happened, but that she remained an immaculate virgin. (John Smeaton, *A Narrative of the Building and a Description of the Construction of the Eddystone Lighthouse with Stone*, 1791, p. 65 n., quoted from R. W. Malcolmson, *Life and Labour in England 1700–1780*, 1981, pp. 104–5)

19

. . . on Portland Island . . . where the inhabitants seldom or never intermarry with any on the main-land, where the young women, selecting lovers of the same place (but with what previous rites, ceremonies, or engagements, I could never learn), account it no disgrace to allow them every favour, and that too from the fullest confidence of being made wives, the moment such consequences of their stolen embraces begin to be too visible to be any longer concealed. (John Brand, *Observations on Popular Antiquities* (1777), 1813, Vol. 2, p. 21)

(c) Motives for Marriage

20

. . . alas! what poor woman is ever taught that she should have a higher design than to get her a husband? Heaven will fall in of course; and if she makes but an obedient and dutiful wife, she cannot miss of it. A husband indeed is thought by both sexes so very valuable, that scarce a man who keeps himself clean and makes a bow, but thinks he is good enough to pretend to any woman, no matter for the difference of birth or fortune, a husband is such a wonder-working name as to make an equality, or something more, whenever it is pronounc'd. (Mary Astell, *Some Reflections upon Marriage* (1700), 1706, pp. 62–3)

21

[To Wortley Montagu, 26 February 1711]
Farewell, then, since you will have it so; I renounce all the ideas I have so long flattered myself with, and will entertain my fancy no longer with the imaginary pleasure of pleasing you. How much wiser are all those women I have despised than myself! In placing their happiness in trifles, they have placed it in what is attainable. I fondly thought fine clothes and gilt coaches, balls, operas, and public adoration rather the fatigues of life; and that true happiness was justly defined by Mr. Dryden (pardon the romantic air of repeating verses), when he says,

'When Heav'n would bless it does from pomp remove
And makes their wealth in privacy and love.'

These notions have corrupted my judgement . . .

[idem, 12 August, 1712]
If we marry, our happiness must consist in loving one another. (*Letters and Works of Lady Mary Wortley Montagu*, ed. Lord Wharncliffe, 1837, Vol. 1, pp. 162–3, 180)

22

. . . I thought my circumstances were not proper at all for matrimony at present. If she has but a small fortune it would ruin me to marry her, keep me low in the world and prevent my rise. And if she has a considerable fortune her father would never consent I should have her without a proportionable fortune. I cannot suppose my father can or will give me enough to answer £2,000 fortune without the addition of a business or employment, but then here comes in the balance of my love and inclination to her and I did not find that so strong as to be equivalent for all the rest.

My father . . . said her fortune could not be anything consider-able, a £1,000 or £1,500 would be the most could be expected, besides her family was nothing, could bring me no acquaintance no friends that could serve me in my business. That her father was nothing but a common ordinary tailor at first, but by great industry arrived at something considerable. He might perhaps be worth 5 or £6,000 but hardly more. (*The Diary of Dudley Ryder, 1715– 1716*, ed. William Matthews, 1939, pp. 251, 326)

23

. . . the market is against our sex just now; and if a young woman have beauty, birth, breeding, wit, sense, manners, modesty, and all these to an extreme, yet if she have not money, she's nobody, she had as good want them all, for nothing but money now recommends a woman; the men play the game all into their own hands.

This knowledge I soon learned by experience, viz. that the state of things was altered as to matrimony, and that I was not to expect at London what I had found in the country; that marriages were here the consequences of political schemes for forming interests, and carrying on business, and that Love had no share, or but very little, in the matter.

That . . . beauty, wit, manners, sense, good humour, good behaviour, education, virtue, piety, or any other qualification, whether of body or mind, had no power to recommend; that money only made a woman agreeable; that men chose mistresses indeed by the gust of their affection, and it was requisite to a whore to be handsome, well-shaped, have a good mien and a graceful behaviour; but that for a wife, no deformity would shock the fancy, no ill qualities the judgement; the money was the thing; the portion was neither crooked nor monstrous, but the money was always agreeable, whatever the wife was. (Daniel Defoe, *Moll Flanders* (1721), 1924, pp. 12, 54)

24

3RD DAUGHTER: For all you are both my eldest sisters I question whether you understand what a good offer means; and, it may be, have considered it no more than I: there's a great deal in that word.

1ST DAUGHTER: O! I'll explain it in a few words: a good estate, and a man you like.

2ND DAUGHTER: Nay, you might have stopped at the first: 'tis no matter what the man is, if the estate be but good.

3RD DAUGHTER: Is that the example my eldest sisters intend to set me?

FATHER: Aye, and a good example too, child. (Daniel Defoe, *Religious Courtship* (1772), 1840–1, Dialogue I)

25

ANTONIA: Don't you think it is almost an unconceivable pleasure for a woman, to have so charming a creature for an only daughter, as she has and to see her so well disposed of?

LUCINDA: How well, child?

ANTONIA: How well! To a baronet, a gentleman of three thousand a year: that has settled a thousand pound a year upon her; is that not well disposed of? At least it is more than answerable to her fortune; for she gave but five thousand pound with her. (Bernard de Mandeville, *The Virgin Unmask'd* (1709), 1724, pp. 34–5)

26

The great duty between the man and his wife, I take to consist in that of love, in the government of affection, and the obedience of a complaisant, kind, obliging temper: the obligation is reciprocal, 'tis drawing in an equal yoke. Love knows no superior or inferior, no imperious command on one hand, no reluctant subjection on the other; the end of both should be the well-ordering their family, the good-guiding their household and children, educating, instructing and managing them with mutual endeavour.

Ask the ladies why they marry, they tell you 'tis for a good settlement; tho' they had their own fortunes to settle on themselves before. Ask the men why they marry, it is for money. How few matches have any other motive except as I mention here-after, and indeed will hardly bear any mention at all, for many known reasons. How little is regarded of that one essential and absolutely necessary part of the composition, called love, without which the matrimonial state is, I think, hardly lawful, I am sure is not rational, and, I think, can never be happy.

In their permission and licence, they must be sure to observe the order of Nature, and the ends of God. He is an ill husband, that uses his wife as a man treats a harlot, having no other end but pleasure. Concerning which our best rule is, that although in this, as in eating and drinking, there is an appetite to be satisfied, which cannot be done without pleasing that desire; yet since that desire and satisfaction was intended by nature for other ends, they should never be separate from those ends, with a desire of children, or to avoid fornication, or to lighten and ease the cares and sadnesses of household affairs, or to endear each other; but never with a purpose, either in act or desire to separate the sensuality from these ends which hallow it.

But as the persons of a lower station are, generally speaking, much more happy in their marriages, than princes and persons of distinction; so I take much of it, if not all of it, to consist in the advantages they have to choose and refuse.

Will you live with a man, and lie with a man you don't love? . . . 'tis but a kind of legal prostitution, in the plain English of it, too gross and wicked to express. We must not say she is a whore, because the law makes it a literal contract and marriage. But God forbid I should ever say 'twill pass for matrimony in heaven; the young lady in short, is willing . . . to lie with a man; and she takes a fellow that is just in the same condition, under the influence of some lewd appetite, as he desires to lie with a woman. They are both willing to gratify their vicious part in the formality of a legal appointment, and so they agree to marry in form, and they are called man and wife; as such she throws off the mask of modesty, goes into the naked bed to him, or suffers him to come to bed to her; and as they came together upon the mere principles of desire, as above, so they act the several excesses and all the conjugal madnesses, chamberings and wantonnesses . . . and all the while not one ounce of affection, not a grain of original, chaste, and rivetted love . . . is to be found between them.
Is this matrimony! . . . Forbid it, O heaven! that I should call it by that honourable and religious title: On the contrary, it merits . . . nothing less or more than the title of matrimonial whoredom, or, at least, of a matrimonial prostitution. (Daniel Defoe, *Conjugal Lewdness*, 1727, pp. 26, 27–8, 54–5 where Defoe quotes with approval Dr Taylor's 'Discourse on Chastity', 97, 105–6)

27

Yesterday morning Thomas Probin of the County of Surrey, Esq.;

was married at Newington Church to Miss Lacy, the only daughter of the late Mr. Joshua Lacy of Middlesex, an eminent linen draper, a beautiful young lady possessed of an estate of £400 per annum, besides large sums of money she has in the bank and funds. (*Daily Post-Boy*, 4 October 1735)

28

Yesterday, George Craster, Esq.; only son of John Craster, of Craster in the County of Northumberland, Esq.; was married at St. Clement-Danes to Miss Sharpe, daughter of the late John Sharpe, of Lincoln's Inn Fields, Esq.; a young lady with a fortune of 30,000 1.

On Friday last Edmund Probyn, of Newland Gloucestershire, Esq., eldest son of John Probyn, Esq. Member of Parliament for Wotton-Bassett, was married at Newland, to Miss Dalton, an heiress of the said county, with a fortune of 20,000 1. (*London Chronicle*, Vol. 1, 1757, pp. 121, 521)

29

It is not intended that we should pass our lives in the delirium of passion: but whilst this subsides, the habit of affection grows strong. The tumult and anxiety of desire must of course be at an end when the object is secure; but a milder and more serene happiness succeeds, which in good hearts creates a tenderness that is often wanting amidst the fervours of violent passion. Before this palls, your business is to build the solid foundations of a durable friendship. (Hester Chapone, *Posthumous Works* (1773), 1807, Vol. 4, p. 131)

30

[Thomas Trueman and his Daughter, Mary, converse]

THOMAS: At present they are not the less friends for being poor and wedded. Poverty may come in at their door; but there is less danger that love will fly out of their window, than with people who once lived in affluence. They are not the less obliged to hold their marriage vow as sacred as the greatest of mankind.

THOMAS: Marriage is a serious affair; you are engaged in a business which requires much caution. As to love, it is common to mortals; and having nothing to do with pomp, our humble condition seems less subject to wretchedness, on this account, than that of the rich.

MARY: I believe people naturally follow affection when they are poor.

THOMAS: Those who have no wealth, nor ever had any prospect of living in affluence, hope they may support love without any such aid; and it seems to be more in favour of love, to have no want but of money, than to want everything except money. Where true love subsists, in the marriage state, adversity cannot divide it from the heart. (Jonas Hanway, *Virtue in Humble Life*, 1774, Vol. 2, pp. 14, 447–8)

31

. . . I do not think that your sex, at least in this part of the world, have much of that sensibility which disposes to such attachments. What is commonly called love among you is rather gratitude, and a partiality to the man who prefers you to the rest of your sex; and such a man you often marry, with little of either personal esteem or affection. Indeed, without an unusual share of natural sensibility, and a very peculiar good fortune, a woman in this country has very little probability of marrying for love. (John Gregory, *A Father's Legacy to his Daughters*, 1774, p. 46)

32

. . . there are persons in the world who are young without passions, and in health without appetite: these hunt out a wife as they go to Smithfield for a horse; and inter-marry fortunes not minds, or even bodies: In this case the Bridegroom has no joy but in taking possession of the portion, and the bride dreams of little besides new clothes, visits and congratulations. Thus, as their expectations of pleasure are not very great, neither is the disappointment very grievous; they just keep each other in countenance, live decently, and are exactly as fond the twentieth year of matrimony, as the first. But I would not advise any one to call this state of insipidity happiness, because it would argue him both ignorant of its nature and incapable of enjoying it . . . Matches of this kind are downright prostitution, however softened by the letter of the law; and he or she who receives the golden equivalent of youth and beauty, so wretchedly bestowed, can never enjoy what they so dearly purchased. (*The Writings of Thomas Paine 1774–1779*, ed. M. D. Conway, 1894, Vol. 1, pp. 51–3)

33

Nor is it to be disguised, that too many women of elegance and sense have submitted to a piece of deceit, on which the very best friends of the sex must ever reflect with grief and amazement; I mean, Sirs, that of vowing at the altar of God unceasing love and honour to men, for whom it is not possible that sense or elegance should entertain either sincere affection or esteem; to men so flagrantly profligate, so palpably insignificant, or so exceedingly disagreeable, that all the world must be convinced such sacrifice of understanding, taste, ingenuity, and the pleasures connected with the heart, could only be made to the demon of Covetousness, the idol of Rank, or the passion for Splendour. (Dr James Fordyce, *The Character and Conduct of the Female Sex*, 1776, p. 65)

34

[Mrs Montagu in a letter to Mrs Robinson, 15 March 1785]
. . . I know my brother and you and your daughters will be glad to hear Montagu is going to be married, in a manner which is agreeable to himself and to me. The young lady is so form'd and qualified to please both the fancy and the judgement, and her fortune such as to content any reasonable wishes. She has 45,000 l. in present; 3,000 l. more is to remain in the funds to secure an annuity to a very old person during his life, and who has been sometime bedridden; so it will soon come into Miss Charlton. She has also an annuity of 300 l. a year on the life of a young prodigal; but the regular payment of this is not to be depended upon. She has also some other little contingencies; so that her fortune is not estimated at less than fifty thousand pounds, by her guardians. (Dr Doran, *A Lady of the Last Century (Mrs. Elizabeth Montagu)*, 1873, pp. 327–8)

35

The children of these cottagers brought up under an industrious father and mother, are sent to yearly service amongst farmers, etc. and if in the course of a few years service, the young man can scrape up 20 l. or 30 l. and finds a young woman that he likes, possessed with nearly an equal sum, they strike a bargain and agree to marry as soon as they can find a cottage near the common; they then stock their cottage with cows, calves, sheep, hogs, poultry, etc. as much as their little fortunes will admit of. He then hires himself as a day labourer to a neighbouring farmer, and the wife stays at home to look after the live stock. (Anon., *A Political*

Enquiry into the Consequences of Enclosing Waste Lands, 1785, p. 44)

36

[Louise Clifton writes to Anna St Ives]
My opinion is that parties should themselves reciprocally discover those qualities which ought mutually to fit them for the friendship of marriage. Is not that the very phrase, Anna, *the friendship of marriage?* Surely, if it be not friendship, according to the best and highest sense in which the word is used, marriage cannot but be something faulty and vicious.

[Anna's ideas on a woman's motives for marriage undergo a change]
We have duties to fulfil. Few opportunities present themselves to a woman, educated and restrained as women unfortunately are, of performing any thing eminently good. One of our most frequent and obvious tasks seems to be that of restoring a great mind, misled by error, to its proper rank. . . .

The reformation of man or woman by projects of marriage is a mistaken, a pernicious attempt. Instead of being an act of morality, I am persuaded it is an act of vice. Let us never cease our endeavours to reform the licentious and the depraved, but let us not marry them. . . .

I am more and more convinced of the error of marrying a bad man in order to make him good. I was not entirely ignorant of this before, and therefore flattered myself the good might be affected previous to marriage. I forgot, when passion has a purpose to obtain, how artful it is in concealment. (Thomas Holcroft, *Anna St. Ives*, 1792, Vol. 1, pp. 75–6, 89; Vol. 4, pp. 150, 181)

37

Those who support a system of what I term false refinement, and will not allow a great part of love in the female, as well as the male breast, to spring in some respects involuntarily, may not admit that charms are as necessary to feed the passions, as virtues to convert the mellowing spirit into friendship. To such observers I have nothing to say, anymore than to the moralists, who insist that women ought to, and can love their husbands, because it is their duty. To you, my child, I may add, with a heart tremblingly alive to your future conduct, some observations, dictated by my present feelings, in calmly reviewing this period of my life. When novelists or moralists praise as a virtue, a woman's coldness of constitution, and want of passion; and make her yield to the ardour of her lover out of sheer compassion, or to promote a frigid plan of future comfort, I am disgusted. They may be good women, in the ordinary acceptation of the phrase, and do no harm; but they appear to me not to have those 'finely fashioned nerves', which render the senses exquisite. They may possess tenderness, but they want that fire of the imagination, which produces *active* sensibility, and *positive* virtue. How does the woman deserve to be characterised, who marries one man, with a heart and imagination devoted to another? Is she not an object of pity or contempt, when thus sacrilegiously violating the purity of her own feelings? Nay, it is as indelicate, when she is indifferent, unless she be constitutionally insensible; then indeed it is a mere affair of barter; and I have nothing to do with the secrets of trade. (Mary Wollstonecraft, *The Wrongs of Woman*, 1798, quoted from *Mary and the Wrongs of Woman*, ed. Gary Kelly, 1980, Vol. 2, pp. 152–3)

Part 5 Marriage and After

In a word, the married state, with and without the affection suitable to it, is the completest image of heaven and hell we are capable of receiving in this life. (*The Spectator*, 9 September 1712)

. . . the good treatment of wives in England, is not such as may be boasted of at present (Daniel Defoe, *The Great Law of Subordination Consider'd*, 1724)

Introduction

The results of arranged marriages, as some writers had predicted, were all too often disastrous. The woman found herself tied to a man who, at best, was her undisputed master demanding complete obedience and submission. In most cases, the role was performed out of a sense of duty not of love. No wonder Mary Astell (**1**) thought that the role she was called on to play demanded heroic qualities. At worst, the husband could be a fool, a sot, a bully or a tyrant, or a combination of all four. (For violence in marriage see Part 8, Section (c).) Among the upper classes such marriages invited the cynicism with which both parties to the marriage soon regarded it and the ease with which the husbands, at least, embarked on a succession of affairs. There were those who like Fielding's 'Blister' never possessed any illusions as to the nature of the matrimonial bond – good for a fortnight of 'lying together' after which one turned one's sights elsewhere (**4**).

The consequence of mercenary marriages, often contracted at a very young age between children of very different social backgrounds with different expectations of life, was a rapid deterioration in their relations. To avoid the inevitable quarrels and bickerings and bitterness, they tended to live increasingly separated lives (**6**). In their ability to do so they differed from the labouring class where home conditions imposed an enforced intimacy from which there was no escaping. For the husband of such upper-class marriages, if he was not already living in town, a prolonged visit to London or Bath or some other county town was always possible. For the woman, particularly if she lived in the countryside, it must have been far more difficult. To the misery of the marriage was added loneliness, a desperate need for companionship – and, at the same time, a knowledge of the dangers to her reputation that might lie in any attempt to find such companionship. The only solution in Mary Astell's view was more education so that future wives would avoid unwise choices.

Hogarth's *Marriage à la Mode* of 1745 followed the course of a marriage of convenience contracted between the parents of the couple, where there was all the force of social convention operating against their parting and living separate lives. Hogarth saw the couple as victims of a choice not their own, and of a set of values taken over from their parents that were merely an extension of those in which the marriage had been contracted. The subjects of Hogarth's work were a young lord of title but no money and a rich merchant's daughter with social aspirations. It was a work aimed at high society but its message of the hypocrisy of all those marriages based on money and property considerations had meaning for a far wider audience.

While in the eighteenth century there must have been many couples living together more than temporarily, who had never gone through any form of marriage, there were few writers who were prepared to go beyond criticising the basis of a 'prudent' marriage and the misery which ensued. Even Charlotte Palmer (7) who dared to suggest that attachments outside marriage could be as virtuous as, and even more virtuous than, those sanctioned by 'holy matrimony', thought it best for the good of society that a couple should conform, if possible by going through a legal marriage ceremony. Frank Henley in Thomas Holcroft's *Anna St. Ives* (8) while welcoming greater freedom in the contracting and dissolving of the marriage bond, nevertheless believed that some form of marriage would be concluded between willing partners.

Before 1753 and Hardwicke's Marriage Act, the law pertaining to marriage was sufficiently loose in its definition to allow for a variety of forms, both regular and irregular, constituting legal marriage. On the one hand, were regular marriages, celebrated in church, after the publication of banns three times before the ceremony took place (or the obtaining of a licence which cost money but avoided the delay). On the other, there were verbal declarations of a couple's intentions of marrying in the future, the spousals, made before witnesses or even a declaration by a couple that they were already married – both, once consummated, constituting a legal form of marriage and, as such, indissoluble. The disadvantages of the old law from the point of view of the authorities was that it was often impossible to know whether or not a marriage had taken place. No records were required of the irregular marriages so there were no means of proving bigamy or of those 'polygamies, easily conceal'd, and too much practised', let alone adultery, or illegitimacy. It was all too easy to achieve the advantages of a divorce merely by claiming that the marriage was invalid and all too difficult to disprove.

The old law limited parental control by permitting children over 7 years of age to marry without the consent of their parents. Young heiresses could be carried off and married in a trice with no sort of legal redress for the parents **(9, 13)**. Unsuitable matches – unsuitable socially – could be concluded with no hope of dissolving such marriages. Such a situation was an open invitation to fortune-hunters anxious to contract a marriage without undue delay and free from parental interference. Usually no licence was required. There were many impecunious parsons ready to celebrate marriages without asking any questions and without making any record of the event, in exchange for a fee **(11, 12)**. In London the Fleet prison and its immediate environs was notorious for such 'Fleet' marriages, but it was a practice by no means confined to the Metropolis **(15)**.

There were those **(14)** who married secretly to avoid the expense and trouble of 'regular' marriages. Most of the poor, if they went through any form of marriage, probably chose the cheaper form, thus avoiding the necessity of purchasing a licence.

Hardwicke's Act in its object of ending Fleet marriages was probably successful. Daughters of wealthy parents were no longer in danger of being carried away, for parental consent was now obligatory for all girls under 21. It is possible it may even have had the good result of relaxing somewhat parental control over daughters.

The second object of the Act, to do away with secret marriages and to make bigamy more difficult, may not have been achieved – at least immediately. The Act made invalid any marriage not celebrated by an ordained minister of the Church of England after the calling of the banns on three successive Sundays and the careful recording of that marriage before witnesses. For many of the poor the effect of the Act was to lead them to dispense with any form of marriage, as is suggested by writers here.

For Defoe (**17**) the only possible reason for women submitting to the fetters of matrimony was that they desired children. As most women spent a large part of their child-bearing lives actually having children, the conditions of pregnancy and birth were not unimportant to them.

A very small minority of women can have had their children in hospital under expert supervision. But even hospitals could be a mixed blessing. The British Lying-In Hospital in London was quite unique in its high standards of cleanliness and nursing (**19**), but it catered for only thirty-six women. Dr Young of Edinburgh (**18**) bears witness to a far more common occurrence in hospitals, the incidence of mortality from puerperal fever. Little was known even by the experts of the medical profession of pre- and post-natal care.

Most women had their children at home or wherever they happened to be when labour commenced. Whether or not they had the assistance of a midwife depended on their means. The lying-in expenses of the wife of a labourer were not inconsiderable and had to be carefully budgeted for. Even for Francis Place, a skilled artisan (**21**), only careful saving enabled him to purchase the assistance of a midwife.

Adam Smith claimed that barrenness was far rarer among women of the poor than of the rich. He accounted for this by the effects of soft and luxury-living on fertility. If this was true of fertility, it was not true of the survival rate of those children once born. The survival rate of children while generally abysmally low, was, if anything, lower among the poor than the rich.

The standards of nursing of young children were poor. Babies were all too frequently fed on alcohol and totally unsuitable food (**23**). They were nearly suffocated by the layers of tight-fitting clothes in which they were swaddled and, among the better off, they were grossly overheated (**24**). But the object of Cadogan and Hanway's greatest criticism was the practice, near-universal among the well-to-do, of sending their babies out to wet nurses to suckle. The practice was followed by those institutions catering for the very poor – the foundling hospital and workhouses, as well as by parishes who farmed out their children to parish nurses. Many must have been the Mrs Pooleses (**26**). The only difference between one wet-nurse and another was the fee paid and the number of children they nursed at any one time.

There is little evidence to support the view that the high mortality rate among children lessened the affection parents felt for them. The trend was towards greater expression of affection – even overindulgence of children. This area of parent/children relations is one in which recently considerable interest has been shown. For this reason, and that of space, it is omitted here.

The miracle is that, despite everything, some married women managed to lead relatively happy lives. Many, however, lacking the outstanding Christian principles Mary Astell listed as necessary in a wife, must have led miserably unhappy ones.

(a) The 'Forlorn State of Matrimony'

1

To be yok'd for life to a disagreeable person and temper; to have folly and ignorance tyrannise over wit and sense; to be contradicted in every thing one does or says, and bore down not by reason but the will and pleasure of an absolute Lord and Master, whose commands she cannot but despise at the same time she obeys them; is a misery none can have a just idea of, but those who have felt it.

Again, it may be said, if a wife's case be as it is here represented, it is not good for a woman to marry, and so there's an end of [the] human race. But this is no fair consequence, for all that can justly be inferr'd from hence, is that a woman has no mighty obligation to the man who makes love to her, she has no reason to be fond of being a wife, or to reckon it a piece of preferment when she is taken to be a man's upper servant; . . . For she who marries purely to do good, to educate souls for heaven, who can be so truly mortified as to lay aside her own will and desires, to pay such an entire submission for life, to one whom she cannot be sure will always deserve it, does certainly perform a more heroic action than all the famous masculine heroes can boast of, she suffers a continual martyrdom to bring glory to God and benefit to mankind, . . . She has need of a strong reason, of a truly Christian and well-temper'd spirit, of all the assistance the best education can give her, and ought to have some good assurance of her own firmness and virtue, who ventures on such a trial; and for this reason 'tis less to be wonder'd at that women marry off in haste, for perhaps if they took time to consider and reflect upon it, they seldom wou'd marry. (Mary Astell, *Some Reflections upon Marriage* (1700), 1706, pp. 4, 88–90)

2

[1723]

To speak plainly, I am very sorry for the forlorn state of matrimony, which is as much ridiculed by our young ladies as it used to be by young fellows: in short, both sexes have found the inconvenience of it, and appellation of rake is as genteel in a woman as a man of quality; it is no scandal to say Miss – the maid of honour, looks very well now she is up again, and poor Biddy Noel has never been quite well since her last confinement. You may imagine we married women look very silly; we have nothing to excuse ourselves but that it was done a while ago and we were very young when we did it. This is the general state of affairs. (*Letters and Works of Lady Mary Wortley Montagu*, ed. Lord Wharncliffe, 1837, Vol. 2, p. 160)

3

I told him, I had, perhaps, differing notions of matrimony from what the received custom had given us of it; that I thought a woman was a free agent, as well as a man, and was born free, and could she manage herself suitably, might enjoy that liberty to as much purpose as the men do; that the laws of matrimony were indeed otherwise, and mankind at this time acted quite upon other principles; and those such that a woman gave herself entirely away from herself, in marriage, and capitulated only to be, at best, but an upper servant, and from the time she took the man, she was no better or worse than the servant among the Israelites, who had his ears bored, that is, nailed to the door-post, who by that act gave himself up to be a servant during life.

That the very nature of the marriage contract was, in short, nothing but giving up liberty, estate, authority, and everything to the man, and the woman was indeed a mere woman ever after, that is to say, a slave. (Daniel Defoe, *Roxana* (1724), 1840–1, p. 157)

4

BLISTER: . . . as for liking me, do not give yourself any trouble about that, it is the very best reason for marrying me . . . hating one another is the chief end of matrimony . . . I fancy you have not a right notion of married life. I suppose you imagine we are to be fond and kiss and hug one another as long as we live.

LUCY: Why, an't we?

BLISTER: . . . Marrying is nothing but living in the same house together, and going by the same name; while I am following my business, you will be following your pleasure; so that we shall rarely meet but at meals, and then we sit at opposite ends of the table, and make faces at each other.

LUCY: Ah, but there is one thing though – an't we to lie together?

BLISTER: A fortnight, no longer.

LUCY: A fortnight! that's a long time; but it will be over.

BLISTER: Ay, and then you can have anyone else.

LUCY: May I? Then . . . by Golis! Why this is pure. (Henry Fielding, *An Old Man Taught Wisdom*, 1734, Act I, sc. iv)

5

What a happy state must a young woman imagine herself entering into, where she is to be lov'd, honour'd, cherish'd, nay, even worshipped; she has a protector till the hour of death, who is to forsake all, even his parents, for her, if it be required, who endows her with his fortune, and promises all that at the altar . . .

No sooner is the honeymoon expir'd but the fawning servant turns a haughty lord: Instead of honouring his wife, 'tis odds if he treats her with common civility; he shall tell her, to her face, he wishes her death, in order to marry another. The custom authorises this free way of speaking; yet I never knew it agreeable to any wife, nor did I ever doubt but the husband spoke in the sincerity of his heart.

As for our being endow'd with the worldly goods of our husbands 'tis known they are so little apt to share with us, that it has always been found necessary, in a marriage-settlement, to stipulate for pin-money, a very useful clause even to the husband, and it is much better his wife should have a share of his fortune, than be obliged to a gallant for a trifle, which gratitude may make her repay in too tender a manner.

. . . 'tis not lawful to separate on any cause save that of adultery. A woman of spirit, who is married to a sordid disagreeable wretch, has nothing to do but make him a cuckold; and then welcome thrice dear liberty: Yet methinks the husbands should, in justice, return to their wives, when they abandon them, the dowry they brought with them. (Laetitia Pilkington, *Memoirs of Mrs. Laetitia Pilkington* (1749–54), 1770, pp. 114–16)

6

. . . if such whose fortunes are affluent, whose desires were mutual, who equally languished for the happy moment before it came and seemed for a while to be equally transported when it had

taken place, if even these should in the end prove . . . unhappy
. . . As ecstasy abates, coolness succeeds which often makes way
for indifference: and that for neglect: sure of each other by the
nuptial bond, they no longer take any pains to be mutually
agreeable; careless if they displease; and yet angry if reproached;
with so little relish for each other's company, that anybody's else is
welcome and more entertaining. Their union thus broke, they
pursue separate pleasures; never meet but to wrangle, or part but
to find comfort in other society. After this the descent is easy to
utter aversion, which having itself out with heart-burnings, cla-
mours and affronts, subsides into a perfect insensibility; when
fresh objects of love step in to their relief on either side, and
mutual infidelity makes way for mutual complaisance, that each
may be the better able to deceive the other. (*The Writings of
Thomas Paine 1774–1779,* ed. M. D. Conway, 1894, Vol. 1,
1774–9, pp. 52–3)

(b) A Sacred Institution?

7

In consequence of what I have asserted, do not impute to me a
talent for universal censure on all whose attachments are not
sanctioned by matrimony. There are many exceptions; and a man
and woman of honour, who hold their word sacred, though given
in private, when perhaps secret reasons put it out of their power to
marry, are as virtuous, and perhaps *more* so, than some who boast
of their *lawful* marriages: Yet it is incumbent that every individual
should (if possible) obey the ordinances of the legislature, for the
general benefit of society. (Charlotte Palmer, *It Is and It Is Not a
Novel,* 1792, Vol. 1, p. 177)

8

[Frank Henley considers the nature of future relations between the
sexes]
I doubt whether in that better state of human society, to which I
look forward with such ardent aspiration, the intercourse of the
sexes will be altogether promiscuous and unrestrained; or whether
they will admit of something that may be denominated marriage.

  The former may perhaps be the truth but it is at least certain that
in the sense in which we understand marriage and the affirmation –
This is my wife – neither the institution nor the claim can in such a
state, or indeed in justice exist. Of all the regulations which were

ever suggested to the mistaken tyranny of selfishness, none perhaps to this day have surpassed the despotism of those which undertake to bind not only body to body but soul to soul, to all futurity, in despite of every possible change which our vices and our virtues might effect, or however numerous the secret corporal or mental imperfections might prove which a more intimate acquaintance should bring to light!

It [marriage] ought not to be a civil institution. It is the concern of the individuals who consent to this mutual association, and they ought not to be prevented from beginning, suspending or terminating it as they please. (Thomas Holcroft, *Anna St. Ives*, 1792, Vol. 4, pp. 16–17, 18)

(c) Regular, Clandestine and Irregular Marriage, and the Effects of Hardwicke's Marriage Act

9

[Written in 1719 before Hardwicke's Marriage Act:]
In England, a boy may marry at fourteen years old, and a girl at twelve, in spite of parents and guardians, without any possibility of dissolving their marriage, tho' one be the son of a hog-driver, and the other a duke's daughter. This often produces very whimsical matches. There is another thing in it odd enough; for those children by this means not only become their own masters, but obtain this advantage at a very easy rate. If to be marry'd it were necessary to be proclaim'd three times in a full congregation, their friends would be informed of the matter, and might find a way to dissuade a little girl that had taken it into her head to have a husband, by giving her fine clothes, pretty babies, and every thing else that might amuse her; but the wedding is clapp'd up so privately, that people are amaz'd to see women brought to bed of legitimate children, without having heard a word of the father. The law, indeed, requires that the banns should be publish'd; but the strange practice of a dispensing power makes the law of no manner of use. To proclaim banns is a thing no body now cares to have done; very few are willing to have their affairs declar'd to all the world in a public place, when for a guinea they may do it snug, and without noise; and my good friends the clergy, who find their accounts in it, are not very zealous to prevent it. Thus, then, they buy what they call a licence, and are marry'd in their closets, in presence of a couple of friends, that serve for witnesses; and this ties them for ever: Nay, the abuse is yet greater, for they may be

marry'd without a licence in some chapels, which have that
privilege . . .

Hence come the matches between footmen and young ladies of
quality, who you may be sure live no very easy life together
afterwards. Hence, too, happen polygamies, easily conceal'd, and
too much practised.

Persons of quality, and many others who imitate them, have lately
taken up the custom of being marry'd very late at night in their
chamber, and very often at some country house. They increase
their common bill of fare for some days, they dance, they play,
they give themselves up for some small time to pleasure; but all
this they generally do without noise, and among very near
relations.

One of the reasons that they have for marrying secretly, as they
generally do in England, is, that thereby they avoid a great deal of
expense and trouble . . . The ordinary ones . . . are generally
incognito. The bridegroom, that is to say, the husband that is to
be, and the bride, who is the wife that is to be, conducted by their
father and mother, or by those that serve them in their room, and
accompany'd among others by two bride-men and two bride-
maids, go early in the morning with a licence in their pocket and
call up Mr. Curate and his clerk, tell him their business; are
marry'd with a low voice, and the doors shut; tip the minister a
guinea, and the clerk a crown; steal softly out, one one way, and
t'other another, either on foot or in coaches; go different ways to
some tavern at a distance from their own lodgings, or to the house
of some trusty friend, there have a good dinner, and return home
at night as quietly as lambs . . . (M. Misson, *Memoirs and
Observations in his Travels over England*, 1719, trans. by Mr
Ozell, pp. 182–4, 349, 351–2)

10

20th May, 1737. John Smith, Gent. of St. James's Westminster
Batchelor & Eliz. Huthall of St. Giles's Spinster at Wilsons. By ye
opinion after matrimony, my clerk judg'd they were both women,
if ye person by name John Smith be a man, he's a little short fair
thin man, not above 5 foot. After marriage I almost could prove
you both women, the one dressed as a man, thin pale face, &
wrinkled chin. (*The Register Books of Fleet Marriages*, quoted
from John Ashton, *The Fleet: Its River, Prison and Marriages*,
1888, p. 382)

11

On Tuesday last, a woman indifferently well dress'd came to the sign of the Bull and Garter, next door to the Fleet Prison, and was there married to a soldier; in the afternoon she came again, and would have been married to a butcher, but that Parson who had married her in the morning refused to marry her again, which put her to the trouble of going a few doors further, to another parson who had no scruple. (*Whitehall Evening Post,* 24 July, 1739)

12

Jan. 5, 1742. On Tuesday last two persons, one of Skinner Street, and the other of Webb's Square, Spittle Fields, exchang'd wives, to whom they had been married upwards of twelve years; and the same day to the content of all parties, the marriages were consummated at the Fleet. Each husband gave his wife away to the other, and in the evening had an entertainment together. (Quoted from John Ashton, *The Fleet: Its River, Prison and Marriages,* 1888, p. 371)

13

[On the effects of Hardwicke's Marriage Act:]
The consent or concurrence of the parent to the marriage of his child under age, was also *directed* by our ancient law to be obtained: but now it is absolutely *necessary;* for without it the contract is void. And this also is another means which the law has put into the parent's hands, in order the better to discharge his duty; first, of protecting his children from the snares of artful and designing persons, and next, of settling them properly in life, by preventing the ill consequences of too early and precipitate marriages.

The offence of clandestine marriages: for by the statute 26 Geo. II, c. 33 1. To solemnise marriage in any other place besides a church, or public chapel wherein banns have been usually published, except by licence from the archbishop of Canterbury; – and, 2. To solemnise marriage in such church or chapel without due publication of banns, or licence obtained from a proper authority; – do both of them not only render the marriage void, but subject the person solemnising it to felony, punished by transportation for fourteen years: as, by three former statutes, he and his assistants were subject to a pecuniary forfeiture of 100 1. 3. To make false entry in a marriage register; to alter it when made; to forge or counterfeit such entry, or a marriage licence: to

cause or procure, or act or assist in such forgery; to utter the same
as true, knowing it to be counterfeit; or to destroy or procure the
destruction of any register; in order to vacate any marriage, or
subject any person to the penalties of this act, all these offences,
knowingly and wilfully committed subject the party to the guilt of
felony without benefit of clergy. (Sir William Blackstone, *Commentaries on the Laws of England* (1753), 1793 Vol. 1, p. 452; Vol.
4, p. 162)

14

'after mutual consent, said he, all the rest is mere ceremony'. –
'How, Sir, said I, do you look upon the holy institution of marriage
as mere ceremony, that may be dispensed with whenever our
inclination may prompt us to consider it in that light?' – 'My dear,
said he, . . . there are so many obstacles now to surmount, and so
many disagreeable steps to be taken, since the marriage-act has
passed, that all sensible people are entirely of the opinion that it is
only putting money in the priest's pocket, to publish three weeks
before hand to all the parish, that on such a night a girl is to lose
her virginity!' (Anon., *Genuine Memoirs of the Celebrated Miss
Maria Brown,* 1766, Vol. 1, pp. 97–8)

15

The circumstances of a clergyman's being sentenced to transportation at the last Leicester Assizes, for solemnising a marriage
contrary to the statute, has made so much noise as to demand an
accurate statement of particulars. His name is Wragge . . . 'The
Parties were servants to Mr. Hudson of Wanlip, of the same
county. Their master being averse to their marriage, they applied
to this compliant joiner of hands, who asked for five guineas for
his trouble, and, on a plea of poverty, agreed to three. The couple
were, in the country phrase *asked-out,* in the parish church of
Frisby, and regularly married. An entry was at the same time as
regularly made in the register, specifying, that the parties were
residents of that parish, and married by banns. (*Gentleman's
Magazine,* 1790, p. 304)

(d) Childbirth

16

LUCINDA: Are there not hundreds of women, that from the time they
have been three or four months with child, to the minute they

are deliver'd, in such continual torments, that, all that while, they enjoy not one half night's rest, or one hour's ease, in which they can say, they are wholly free from pain? When they begin to feel this misery, what an uncomfortable reflection must it not be, to think that without hope of cure, it is to last so many months; and that then they cannot get rid of it, but by undergoing an uncertain set of pains, each of which is a greater torture, than by dying any other way. Mind what I tell ye Antonia, 'tis not a trifle, a pain that racks, distorts, and wrings at one and the same instant, every nerve, nay every fibre, from the crown of the head, to the sole of the foot: A torture so exquisite, and so universal, that art nor cruelty, could ever imitate it; and nature knows not such another. When this is over, then begins the danger: an unconceivable weariness seizes the body all over: The strength of muscles and sinews is spent, the organs of hearing are become so tender, that the least noise disturbs their brain, and the lowest speech is offensive; the very eye-strings are strain'd, the sight impair'd, and nothing but darkness can ease them: And besides, that the stomach is weak, and for want of spirits unable to digest, the whole mass of blood is disorder'd: We may well imagine, that missing so many parts, through which of late it us'd to circulate, it cannot easily confine itself to its ancient limits: Being in this confusion, every small accident is able to inflame it, and be the cause of a fatal fever. What numbers have lost their lives in child-bed, your own mother for one, a whole fortnight she was like to do well and yet dy'd within the month.

ANTONIA: Dear Aunt, let me hear no more of it.

LUCINDA: Dear Niece, I am so full of it, methinks I have said but little yet. I have not spoke of the faintings, cramps, the intolerable headaches, and violent cholicks, that are so familiar to them: I have not told you what multitudes, tho' they survive, are made miserable, not mention'd the unskilfulness and neglect of mid-wives, or the many lingering distempers and lesser ailments, that attend some women as long as they live: But if this they escape, the skin will be wrinkled, the little capillary veins, that are so ornamental to it, must be broken in many places; the flesh be loosen'd, the ligaments relaxed, the joints be stiffen'd, and made unactive: This perhaps you may slight, but be assured, that the bearing, as well as bringing forth of children, wastes women, wears 'em, shakes, spoils, and destroys the very frame and constitution of them. (Bernard de Mandeville, *The Virgin Unmask'd* (1709), 1724, pp. 109–10)

17

. . . what woman in her senses would tie herself up in the fetters of matrimony, if it were not that she desires to be a mother of children, to multiply her kind, and, in short, have a family?

If she did not, she would be next to a lunatic to marry, to give up her liberty, take a man to call master, and promise when she takes him to honour and obey him. What! give herself away for nothing! Mortgage the mirth, the freedom, the liberty, and all the pleasures of her virgin-state, the honour and authority of being her own, and at her own dispose, and all this to be a barren doe, a wife without children; a dishonour to her husband, and a reproach to herself! Can any woman in her wits do thus? (Daniel Defoe, *Conjugal Lewdness*, 1727, p. 129)

18

[From a letter to Mr White from a Dr Young of Edinburgh, 21 November 1774]
We had a puerperal fever in the infirmary last winter. It began about the end of February, when almost every woman, as soon as she was delivered, or perhaps about twenty-four hours after, was seized with it; and all of them died, though every method was tried to cure the disorder. What was singular, the women were in good health before they were brought to bed, though some of them had been long in the hospital before delivery. One woman had been dismissed the ward before she was brought to bed; came into it some days after with her labour upon her; was easily delivered, and remained perfectly well for twenty-four hours, when she was seized with a shivering and the other symptoms of the fever. I caused her to be removed to another ward; yet notwithstanding all the care that was taken of her she died in the same manner as the others. (C. White, *Treatise on the Management of Pregnant and Lying-In Women*, 1777, app., pp. 45–6)

19

[Of the British Lying-In Hospital in Brownlow Street:]
Here are six wards, and in each six beds. The wards were clean and quiet: provision good: kitchen and pantry clean. This is a good institution, and proper attention is paid to the patients; who continue here three weeks after they are delivered . . .

Here female pupils are instructed in the art of midwifery, and after residing four or six months receive certificates of their ability to practise. Women are admitted here in the most generous manner, for no fee or gratification of any kind is allowed to the nurses or servants. (John Howard, *An Account of the Principal Lazarettos in Europe,* 1789, sect. 8, p. 137)

20

[Letter to Gilbert Imlay, 1 January 1794]
Considering the care and anxiety a woman must have about a child before it comes into the world, it seems to me, by a *natural right,* to belong to her. When men get immersed in the world, they seem to lose all sensations, excepting those necessary to continue or produce life! – Are these the privileges of reason? Amongst the feathered race, whilst the hen keeps the young warm, her mate stays by to cheer her; but it is sufficient for man to condescend to get a child, in order to claim it. – A man is a tyrant! (*Collected Letters of Mary Wollstonecraft,* ed. Ralph M. Wardle, 1979, p. 242)

21

On the 28 of April 1794 my wife had her second child a girl whom we named after her Elizabeth, we had been hard at work all day and I had been out at business in the evening, my wife had been putting the room in order when she was taken in labour, and when I came home I found her in that state. At her first lying-in she was attended by a woman, but as we were not quite satisfied with her treatment, we resolved to have a man of some reputation, and one had been engaged, two guineas were laid by for him, and as good clothes had been provided for the child as any working man could reasonably desire. She was delivered at two o'clock in the morning. Our room was on the second floor, the landlady of the house was with my wife, and I was invited to sit in the room on the first floor.

. . . on the 28 June 1798 my eldest son Francis was born. After the birth of our first child as has been related we employed a medical man in good practice, he had two guineas for his first attendance and a guinea for each of the succeeding two. This guinea was always carefully saved and immediately paid. As my wife was young strong and healthy, as none of the absurdities of nursing and feeding were indulged in, as there were no curtains to the bed, no candle, nor heating and stimulating messes we had no occasion for a regular nurse, some assistance was indispensable and this was easily procured. My wife remained in bed not more and seldom as much as two days, on the third day she got up to dinner and in a few days went about as usual, only refraining from any laborious employment. (*The Autobiography of Francis Place (1771–1854)*, ed. Mary Thale, 1972, pp. 126, 184)

22

Lying in: the child's linen 3 or 4s.; the midwife's fee 5s.; a bottle of gin or brandy always had upon this occasion, 2s.; attendance of a nurse for a few days, and her diet, at least 5s.; half a bushel of malt brewed, and hops, 3s.; to the minister for churching 1s.; call the sum £1 and suppose this to happen but once in two years. (David Davies, *The Case of Labourers in Husbandry*, 1795, p. 16)

(e) Nursing and Child Care

23

There are some wicked nurses, reckoned more skilful than the rest, who commonly attend lying-in women during the month, and are not afraid to give wine and brandy, sweetened perhaps with sugar, to new born infants, with great secrecy, as often as they can conveniently, to still their crying, and procure ease to themselves; whence dreadful symptoms arise from hidden causes . . . (Walter Harris, *Treatise of the Acute Diseases of Infants*, 1742, pp. 18–19)

24

In the lower class of mankind, especially in the country, disease and mortality are not so frequent, either among the adult, or their children . . . The mother who has only a few rags to cover her child loosely, and little more than her own breast to feed it, sees it healthy and strong, and very soon able to shift for itself; while the puny insect, the heir and hope of a rich family, lies languishing under a load of finery, that overpowers his limbs, abhorring and rejecting the dainties he is cramm'd with, 'till he dies a victim to the mistaken care and tenderness of his fond mother.

Children in general are over-cloath'd and over-fed, and fed and cloath'd improperly. To these causes I impute almost all their diseases . . . The first great mistake is, that they think a new-born infant cannot be kept too warm; from this prejudice they load and bind it with flannels, wrappers, swaths, stays, etc. commonly called cloaths; which all together are almost equal to its own weight; by which means a healthy child in a month's time is made so tender and chilly, it cannot bear the external air; and if, by any accident of a door or window left carelessly open too long a refreshing breeze be admitted into the suffocating atmosphere of the lying-in bed-chamber, the child and mother catch irrecoverable colds.

But besides the mischief arising from the weight and heat of these swaddling-cloaths, they are put on so tight, and the child is so cramp'd by them, that its bowels have not room, nor the limbs any liberty, to act and exert themselves in the free and easy manner they ought . . . The circulation restrained by the compression of any one part, must produce unnatural swellings in some other; especially as the fibres of infants are so easily distended. To which doubtless are owing the many distortions and deformities we meet with everywhere; chiefly among women, who suffer more in this particular than the men.

The general practice is, as soon as a child is born, to cram a dab of butter and sugar down its throat, a little oil, panada, caudle, or some such unwholesome mess. So that they set out wrong, and the child stands a fair chance of being made sick from the first hour. It is the custom of some to give a little roast pig to an infant; which it seems, is to cure it of all the mother's longings. I wish these mothers were a little more enquired into, for the honour of the sex; to which many imperfections of this kind are imputed, which I am sure it does not lie under. When a child sucks its own mother, which, with a very few exceptions would be best for every child, and every mother, nature has provided it with such wholesome and suitable nourishment; supposing her a temperate woman, that makes some use of her limbs; it can hardly do amiss . . . I could wish, that every women that is able . . . would give suck to her child. I am very sure, that forcing back the milk, which most young women must have in great abundance, may be of fatal consequence.

I am quite at a loss to account for the general practice of sending infants out of doors, to be suckled, or dry-nursed by another woman, who has not so much understanding, nor can have so much affection for it, as the parents; . . . No other woman's milk can be so good for her child; and dry-nursing I look upon to be the most unnatural and dangerous method of all; and, according to my observation, not one in three survives it.

Sending the children out to Country nurses, under the care of inspectors, is undoubtedly the best method they could take; but how far these nurses and their inspectors (who, I suppose, are to be some good gentlewomen in the neighbourhood) may be persuaded out of their old forms, to treat their nurselings a little more reasonably, is matter of much doubt . . . I make no doubt, but great care is taken, that the nurses, recommended to the hospital, be clean and healthy women. But this is not enough, the preference should be given to the middle-aged; because they will have more milk than the very young, and more and better than the old . . . Those between twenty and thirty are certainly of the best age. (W. Cadogan, *An Essay upon Nursing and the Management of Children*, 1748, pp. 7, 9, 10–11, 13–14, 24–5, 25–6)

25

[On the choice of a wet-nurse]
A nurse should be betwixt the age of twenty and thirty-five or forty years at most; should not have the Menses, or Fluor Albus; should be of an healthy complexion, not pale and wan; of a firm, not loose and flabby flesh; of a cheerful, easy temper, and lively; free from all distempers, and all sorts of pains, defluxions, sore eyes, or the like. She should be clean and neat, have a sweet breath and sound teeth. She should have a clear distinct voice, and free from all kinds of impediment of speech: Her breasts should be large enough for a sufficient quantity of milk, but not to excess, they should be equal, full, soft, and free from lumps, or any particular hardness, or scars, yet trim and plump; and she should be full-chested. The nipples should be rather long and slender, of a moderate size and firmness; . . . and the milk should easily flow out, by gentle pressure, and spout out in several streams. (John Burton, *An Essay towards a Complete New System of Midwifery*, 1751, p. 357)

26

. . . many children born of poor, idle or unfortunate parents, though they should have the best constitutions, yet die in great numbers under five years old. Many children instead of being nourished with care, by the fostering hand of a wholesome country nurse, are thrust into the impure air of a work-house, into the hands of some careless, worthless young female or decrepit old woman, and inevitably lost . . .

As far as I can trace out the evil, there has been such devastation within the bills of mortality, for half a century past, that at a moderate computation 1,000 or 1,200 children have annually perished under the direction of parish officers. I say under their direction, not that they ordered them to be *killed*, but that they *did not order* such means to be used as are necessary to keep them *alive* . . .

An acquaintance of mine once solicited a parish officer for 2s. a week for a servant while she was nursing her child; alleging that a common parish nurse had at least that sum, if not 2s. 6d. 'Yes', says the officer, 'it is very true; but the young woman in question will most probably preserve her child, whereas in the hands of our nurses, after 5 or 6 weeks we hear no more of them . . .'

There is no wonder in this, when it is considered, that these children were put into the hands of indigent, filthy or decrepit women, three or four to one woman, and sometimes sleeping with them. The allowance of these women being scanty, they are tempted to take part of the bread and milk intended for the poor infants. The child cries for food, and the nurse beats it because it cries. Thus with blows, starving and putrid air, with the additions of lice, itch, and filthiness, he soon receives his *quietus*.

Mrs. Poole [a nurse] had, in . . . 1765, the nursing of 23 children belonging to St. Clement Danes . . . The account of the 23 children stands thus:

Discharged at the age of 2 years	1
Discharged at the age of 5 months	1
Remaining alive	3
Departed out of this transitory life, in her hands after breathing the vital air about one month	18

For this piece of service to the parish, Mrs. Poole has been paid 2s. each per week, which, considering the importance of the enterprise, must be deemed a very moderate price. (Jonas Hanway, *An Earnest Appeal for Mercy to the Children of the Poor*, 1766, pp. 4, 8, 39–42, 138)

27

On Hampton Common are several nurse-children from the parish of St. Martins in the Fields, Westminster: a woman that had 5 of them told me, she was allowed 3s. a week, for each, by the parish; that she had brought them all up by hand; and that a parish-officer came from town twice a year, to see that they were well taken care of. They are sent back to London, when 8 or 9 years old. She teaches them to read: and the parish clothes them once a year. (F. M. Eden, *The State of the Poor*, 1797, Vol. 2, p. 439)

Part Women's Legal Position:
6   Marriage Law and Custom

> . . . even the disabilities, which the wife lies under,
> are for the most part intended for her protection and
> benefit. So great a favourite is the female sex of the
> laws of England. (Sir William Blackstone, *Commen-*
> *taries on the Laws of England* (1753), 1793, Vol. 1,
> p. 445)

> I fear there is little reason to pay a compliment to
> our laws for their respect and favour to the female
> sex. (ibid., Edward Christian's fn)

Introduction

The role allotted to eighteenth-century women was nowhere
more clearly seen than in their legal position. That women
had no part in the framing of that law is all too obvious, for it
was the law that excluded them from almost all the professions, that deprived them of all political rights and which,
whether in or outside of marriage, subjected them to men (3).

Under the law of primogeniture, at the death of the father,
the eldest son succeeded to the estate. The succession
passed through all the sons before descending to the daughters, and if this posed problems for the younger sons, it often
posed even greater problems for the daughters (4).

Blackstone makes clear the legal position of women in
marriage (5). Their legal existence, in so far as they had one
at all, was that of under-age children.

The inability of women to own property, as Eden suggests
(6), may well have acted as a deterrent to women working.
Certainly, it rendered useless any attempts to insure against
the costs of lying-in and sickness. According to canon law no
valid marriage could be dissolved. In consequence, divorce
was virtually impossible unless the marriage could be proved
invalid. Where a marriage had broken down, whether for
reasons of adultery or cruelty, all that was possible was the
equivalent of a legal separation which carried with it a
financial settlement. In this case, neither party could remarry.
Where no legal separation existed, as Charlotte Charke re-

veals, there was no protection of the wife's property (**10**).

By the end of the seventeenth century a marriage could be annulled provided proof could be established of a pre-contract with some other person, consanguinity, or impotence at the time of marriage. It could also be annulled if proof was available that the marriage had been made under duress, or on proof of insanity, or on the ground that the parties to the marriage were too young to consent to marriage. Until Hardwicke's Act, in 1753, the age of consent was fixed at 7 – but until the age of puberty either party could avoid the marriage. Puberty was fixed in a somewhat arbitrary manner at 12 for girls and 14 for boys (**8**). By this time, there had been plenty of evidence of the ability of Parliament to intervene in the process of the marriage law. Given that the church would permit no divorce, Parliament was prepared to sanction a divorce on the ground of adultery by the passage of a Private Act. Of course, it was still necessary to prove adultery in the ordinary courts but, once proved, a petition could be presented to the House of Lords and a divorce obtained. But this was a very lengthy and extremely expensive business only possible for the very wealthy. For the vast majority of the population divorce remained impossible.

It is significant that while divorce by Private Act as a matter of right was obtainable by a husband against a wife who had committed adultery, the reverse was not the case (**7**). Adultery alone was not sufficient ground on which an injured wife could claim a divorce. Proof of additional injury such as incest, bigamy, or extreme cruelty had to accompany it (**9, 11**). The fact that over 150 years there were only four cases of the passage of a Private Act at the suit of a wife makes the point that divorce, even for the wealthy, was almost exclusive to husbands.

In these circumstances, if a marriage broke down it is not all that surprising that many took the law into their own hands. There must have been a great deal of bigamy in the eighteenth century – most of it undetected and only a very few cases prosecuted (**22**). There were innumerable cases of desertion, in most cases by the husband. By custom there were certain accepted practices which many regarded as having the force of law. One of these was wife-sale. If the majority of the cases of wife-sale quoted here come from *Jackson's Oxford Journal*, (and these represent a fraction of the total), it is likely that other journals would yield similar and frequent examples.

It is probable that many such sales were the result of

mutual agreement and only occurred after the marriage had broken down irreparably. Indeed, very often the couple were already living apart and, in some cases, the purchaser was known to the woman if not already her lover (**24, 26, 28**). The sum paid was merely a token – money, a lottery ticket, or a leg of mutton. Often such sales were only an accepted ritual giving sanction to the dissolution of one marriage and the subsequent remarriage. Nevertheless, the ritual placing of a halter around the neck of the woman in order to lead her to the market-place is difficult to dissociate from the similar treatment of cattle. Behind the practice is a view of women that regarded them, as 'goods and chattels' (**18**). Yet it seems clear that the women were, in general, acquiescent partners to such proceedings (**20**). Its acceptance by women serves to remind us that men of whatever class still regarded women as property to be disposed of in the same way as cattle and, also, that the vast majority of women were prepared to play a role of submission.

(a) A Man-Made Law

1

. . . I shall state the matter clearly; as I understood it myself. I knew that while I was a mistress, it is customary for the person kept to receive from them that keep; but if I should be a wife, all I had then was given up to the husband, and I was thenceforth to be under his authority only; and as I had money enough, and needed not fear being what they call a cast-off mistress, so I had no need to give him twenty thousand pounds to marry me, which had been buying my lodging too dear a great deal. (Daniel Defoe, *Roxana* (1724), 1840–1, p. 153)

2

[The View of Millwood, the London prostitute, on man-made laws]
What are your Laws, of which you make boast, but the Fool's Wisdom & the Coward's Valour; the instrument and skreen of all your villanies, by which you punish in others what you act your selves, or wou'd have acted had you been in their circumstances. The judge who condemns the poor Man for being a Thief, had been a Thief himself had he been poor. Thus you go on

deceiving, & being deceiv'd, harrassing, plaguing, & destroying one another, But Women are your universal prey. (George Lillo, *The London Merchant*, 1731, Act IV, sc. viii)

3

[Women] for the most part, but improperly, or slightly educated; and at all times kept in a state of dependence, by the restrictions of a severe legislation, which, in the management and disposal of what property is allowed them, commonly cramps the freedom of their will. Dishonoured and disgraced beyond all possibility of redemption by the commission of faults, which in the men are hardly considered as anything but acts of gallantry; and even in the state of matrimony, a state to which they naturally aspire, more indissolubly bound than their husbands. The law affords them no relief, unless the cruel partner to whom they are tied, has attempted to take away their life; and while he may riot with impunity in adulterous amours, if the wife retaliates, by copying his example, he immediately procures a divorce, and may turn her out without subsistence, to the scorn and contempt of her own sex, who, in such cases, seldom look with pity even on a repenting sinner.

. . . in Britain, we allow a woman to sway our sceptre, but by law and custom we debar her from every other government but that of her own family, as if there were not a public employment between that of superintending the kingdom, and the affairs of her own kitchen, which could be managed by the genius and capacity of woman. We neither allow women to officiate at our altars, to debate in our councils, nor to fight for us in the field; we suffer them not to be members of our senate, to practise any of the learned professions, nor to concern themselves much with our trades and occupations; we exercise nearly a perpetual guardianship over them, both in their virgin and their married state; and she who, having laid a husband in the grave, enjoys an independent fortune, is almost the only woman among us who can be called free. Thus excluded from almost everything which can give them consequence, they derive the greater part of the power which they enjoy, from their charms; and these, when joined to sensibility, often fully compensate, in this respect, for all the disadvantages they are laid under by our law and custom. (William Alexander, *The History of Women*, 1779, Vol. 1, p. 210; Vol. 2, p. 336)

4

To females, towards whom the present customs of society are on other accounts peculiarly unfavourable, to whom therefore, parental regards ought at least to have shown impartiality; to females, I say, the law of primogeniture is peculiarly unfavourable. To this unnatural law are to be traced the prostitution of many young women of good birth, and the unsuitable connections which they form, merely to procure a maintenance. (George Dyer, *The Complaints of the Poor People of England*, 1793, p. 72)

(b) Married Women and the Law

5

By marriage, the husband and wife are one person in law: that is, the very being, or legal existence of the woman is suspended during the marriage, or at least is incorporated and consolidated into that of the husband: under whose wing, protection and cover, she performs every thing; . . .

. . . For this reason, a man cannot grant any thing to his wife, or enter into covenant with her: for the grant would be to suppose her separate existence; and to covenant with her, would be only to covenant with himself: and therefore it is also generally true, that all compacts made between husband and wife, when single, are voided by the inter-marriage . . .

. . . If the wife be injured in her person or her property, she can bring no action for redress without her husband's concurrence, and in his name, as well as her own: neither can she be sued, without making the husband a defendant . . .

A woman's personal property, by marriage, becomes absolutely her husband's which at his death he may leave entirely away from her; but if he dies without will, she is entitled to one third of his personal property, if he has children, if not to one half . . .

By the marriage, the husband is absolutely master of the profits of the wife's lands during the couverture; and if he has had a living child, and survives the wife, he retains the whole of these lands, if they are estates of inheritance, during his life: but the wife is entitled to dower, or one third, if she survives, out of her husband's estates of inheritance; but this she has, whether she has had a child or not . . .

. . . With regard to the property of women, there is taxation without representation; for they pay taxes without having the liberty of voting for representatives . . . (Sir William Blackstone,

Commentaries on the Laws of England (1753), 1793, Vol. 1, pp.
441–5)

6

. . . If the right which every labourer possesses, of disposing of the
produce of his labour, is the great incentive to industry; is it either
unfair or unreasonable to presume, that the incapacity which
married women labour under, of acquiring property, is one of the
principal causes why they contribute so little to the fund which is to
maintain a family? . . .
There are, however, various occupations, which the wife of a
peasant or artificer would, it is probable, be often inclined to
pursue, were she only allowed to have a voice as to the disposal of
her earnings. As the Law now stands, the moment she acquires
them, they become the absolute property of her husband; so that it
is not to be wondered at, that she conceives she has fulfilled her
duty in attending to the children; and that he, conscious that the
support of the family depends on his exertions, should so often
become imperious and tyrannical. The instances are not few,
where a stupid, drunken, and idle man, has an intelligent and
industrious wife, with perhaps both the opportunity and the ability
to earn enough to feed her children; but who is yet deterred from
working, from a thorough conviction that her mate would, too
probably, strip her of every farthing which she had not the
ingenuity to conceal. (F. M. Eden, *The State of the Poor*, 1797,
Vol. 1, pp. 625–8)

(c) Separation or Divorce

7

Let the business be carried as prudently as it can be on the
woman's side, a reasonable man can't deny that she has by much
the harder bargain. Because she puts herself entirely into her
husband's power, and if the matrimonial yoke be grievous, neither
law nor custom afford her that redress which a man obtains. He
who has sovereign power does not value the provocation of a
rebellious subject, but knows how to subdue him with ease, and
will make himself obey'd; but patience and submission are the only
comforts that are left to a poor people, who groan under tyranny,
unless they are strong enough to break the yoke, to depose and
abdicate, which I doubt wou'd not be allow'd of here. (Mary
Astell, *Some Reflections upon Marriage* (1700), 1706, p. 27)

8

The Case.

1   G. D. without the Knowledge and Consent of his Father (then alive, but accounted not of sound judgement) was at the Age of Fifteen, by the Procurement and Persuasion of those in whose Keeping he was, Marry'd, according to the Church form, to M. F. of the Age of Thirteen.

2   This young Couple was put to Bed, in the Day time, according to Custom, and continu'd there a little while, but in the Presence of the Company, who all testify they touched not one the other; and after that, they came together no more; – the young Gentleman going immediately Abroad, the young Woman continuing with her Parents.

3   G. D. after Three or Four Years Travel, return'd home to England, and being solicited to live with his lawful Wife, refus'd it, and frequently and publickly declar'd he never would compleat the Marriage.

4   Fourteen Years have pass'd since this Marriage Ceremony was perform'd, each Party having (as is natural to think) contracted an incurable Aversion to each the other, is very desirous to be set at liberty; and accordingly Application is made to the Legislative power to dissolve this Marriage, and to give each Party leave, if they think fit, to Marry elsewhere.

The reasons against such dissolution are:

First. That each party was consenting to the marriage, and was old enough to give such consent, according to the known laws of the kingdom; the male being fifteen years old, the female thirteen; whereas the years of consent are, by law, fourteen and twelve. Secondly. They were actually marry'd according to the form prescrib'd by the Church of England; the minister pronouncing those solemn words us'd by our Saviour, *Those whom God has joyn'd let no Man put asunder.* They are therefore man and wife both by the laws of God and of the land; and since nothing but adultery can dissolve a marriage, and no adultery is pretended here, the marriage continues indissoluble. (The Counsellor's Plea for the divorce of Sir G. D. and Mrs. F., 1715, quoted from John Ashton, *Social Life in the Reign of Queen Anne*, 1882, pp. 29–30)

9

Friday 10th. Was sued a divorce in Doctor's Commons by Elizabeth Keil from her husband Wm. Keil, for being guilty of adultery and incest with Joanna Rogers, sister of the said Elizabeth Keil; when, after a tryal of 5 hours, the facts being clearly proved, the court order'd a divorce. (*Gentleman's Magazine*, 1747, p. 341)

10

When I first went into my shop, I was horribly puzzled for the means of securing my effects from the power of my husband; who, though he did not live with me, I knew had a right to make bold with any thing that was mine, as there was no formal Article of Separation between us: And I could not easily brook his taking any thing from me to be profusely expended on his mistress. (Mrs Charlotte Charke, *A Narrative of the Life of Mrs. Charlotte Charke* 1755, pp. 75–6)

11

A cause came on to be tried in Doctors Commons, between an eminent tradesman in Piccadilly, and his wife, for repeated acts of cruelty, adultery, and giving her the foul disease, and other ill usage, when, after many learned arguments, (the innocence of his wife not being in the least impeached) the judge pronounced the man to have been guilty both of the cruelty and the adultery, and divorced the woman from her husband, and condemned him in full costs, to the satisfaction of the whole court. (*Annual Register,* 11 December 1767)

12

Adultery is the principal cause of divorce with us; but the spiritual court cannot pronounce a total divorce *a vinculo matrimonii* for this crime, in either party, although the legislative power indulges husbands thus aggrieved with annulling of their marriage contract; by which each party obtains free liberty to marry again; but with restriction on the part of the woman, that she shall not contract marriage with the man with whom she has held that illicit commerce, upon proof of which the divorce is obtained . . . Certain it is, the only atonement the transgressing parties can make, is by legally marrying with each other; by preventing which, a restoration of the woman to the notice of the virtuous part of her own sex, seems to be prevented. She must either live with her gallant meretriciously, or govern herself the rest of her life by the icy precepts of chastity. (Anon., *The Laws respecting Women*, 1777, p. 92)

13

Such are the partial laws enacted by men; for, only to lay a stress on the dependent state of a woman in the grand question of the comforts arising from the possession of property, she is (even in this article) much more injured by the loss of the husband's affection, than he by that of his wife; yet where is she, condemned to the solitude of a deserted home, to look for a compensation from the woman, who seduces him from her? She cannot drive an unfaithful husband from his house, nor separate, or tear, his children from him, however culpable he may be; and he, still the master of his own fate, enjoys the smiles of a world, that would brand her with infamy, did she, seeking consolation, venture to retaliate. (Mary Wollstonecraft, *The Wrongs of Woman*, (1798), quoted from *Mary and the Wrongs of Woman*, ed. Gary Kelly, 1980, Vol. 2, pp. 155–6)

(d) Customary Alternatives: Desertion and Bigamy

14

[Amy speaks: . . .] He calls you widow, and such indeed you are, for as my master has left you so many years, he is dead to be sure; at least he is dead to you; he is no husband; you are and ought to be free to marry who you will; and his wife being gone from him, and refusing to lie with him, then he is a single man again as much as ever; and though you cannot bring the laws of the land to join you together, yet one refusing to do the office of a wife, and the other of a husband, you may certainly take one another fairly.

. . . you own you love this gentleman, and he has given you sufficient testimony of his affection to you; your conditions are alike unhappy, and he is of the opinion that he may take another woman, his first wife having broke her honour, and living from him: and that though the laws of the land will not allow him to marry formally, yet he may take another woman into his arms, provided he keeps true to the other woman as a wife; nay, he says it is usual to do so, and allowed by the custom of the place, in several countries abroad; and, I must own, I am of the same mind; else it is in the power of a whore, after she has jilted and abandoned her husband, to confine him from the pleasure as well as convenience of woman all the days of his life, which would be very unreasonable, and, as times go, not tolerable to all people; and the like on your side, madam.

[Roxana considers: . . .] had I consulted conscience and virtue . . .

I ought to have remembered that neither he or I, either by the laws of God or man, could come together upon any other terms than that of notorious adultery. (Daniel Defoe, *Roxana* (1724), 1840–1, pp. 36–7)

15

[Mrs Waters speaks to Squire Allworthy of her predicament]
. . . in the eye of heaven I was married to him; for after much reading on the subject I am convinced that particular ceremonies are only requisite to give a legal sanction to marriage, and have only a worldly use in giving a woman the privileges of a wife, but that she who lives constant to one man after a solemn private affiance, whatever the world may call her, hath little to charge on her own conscience. (Henry Fielding, *Tom Jones*, 1749, Everyman's Library, Vol. 2, p. 380)

16

Catherine Jones was indicted at the Old Bailey on the 5th of September, 1719, for marrying Constantine Boone during the life of her former husband, John Rowland.

Proof was made that she was married to Rowland, in the year 1713, at a house in the Mint, Southwark, and that six years afterwards, while her husband was abroad, she was again married, in the same house to Constantine Boone; but Rowland, soon returning to England, caused his wife to be indicted for this crime.

The prisoner did not hesitate to acknowledge the double marriage, but insisted that the latter was illegal, as Boone was an hermaphrodite, and had been shewn as such at Southwark and Bartholomew fairs, and at other places.

To prove this a person swore he knew Boone when a child, that his (or *her*) mother dressed *it* in girls apparel, and caused it to be instructed in needlework, till it had attained the age of twelve years, when it *turned man, and went to sea.*

These last words were those of the deposition; and the fact was confirmed by Boone, who appeared in Court, acknowledged being an hermaphrodite, and having been shown publickly in that character.

Other witnesses deposed that the female sex prevailed on that of the male in the party in question; on which the jury acquitted the prisoner. (*Newgate Calendar, c.*1774)

17

A gentleman innkeeper in Hampshire the other day had the mortification to be visited by a wife whom he had reported in the country to have been dead; with the report, and assistance of a considerable estate, he about 10 years ago insinuated himself (though 70 years of age) into the good graces of a young damsel, whom he actually married, and by whom he has several fine children, whose, with the mother's situation is truly pitiable, she and her friends, who are people of repute, being entirely strangers to the business, though in fact he has always, 'till within these few weeks, allowed this unwelcome visitor a tolerable maintenance. (*Salisbury and Winchester Journal,* 27 July 1789, p. 3)

(e) Customary Alternatives: Wife Sale

18

Among the common people, a method is sometimes practised of dissolving a marriage no less singular than compendious. When a husband and wife find themselves heartily tired of each other, and agree to part; if the man has a mind to authenticate the intended separation by making it a matter of public notoriety, thinking with Petruchio, that his wife is his goods and chattels, he puts a halter about her neck, and thereby leads her to the next market place, and there puts her up to auction to be sold to the best bidder, as though she was a brood-mare, or a milch-cow. A purchaser is generally provided before hand on these occasions; for it can hardly be supposed, that the *delicate* female would submit to such public indignity, unless she was sure of being purchased when brought to market. To the highest bidder, the husband, by delivering up the end of the halter, makes a formal and absolute surrender of his wife, and, as he imagines, at once absolves her and himself from all obligations incident to marriage! – Although there are none so high as to be above the notice of the law; yet it should seem by the instance that there are some so low as to disregard its notice, thinking mutual consent law enough to set them free, little dreading remorse of conscience, and less the anathemas of the church.

   In a case in the court of Chancery it appeared, that a man had formally assigned his wife over to another man, and lord Hardwicke directed a prosecution for that transaction, as being notoriously and grossly against public decency and good manners. (Anon., *The Laws respecting Women,* 1777, pp. 55–6)

19

A few days since a woman near Oxford Road, was sold by her husband to another man for a leg of mutton, etc., with whom she cohabited three or four days, but by being too lavish in bestowing invigorating medicines on her new spouse, he expired without sufficiently satisfying her curiosity and inclination. (*Jackson's Oxford Journal*, 17 April 1756, p. 2)

20

A man and his wife falling into discourse with a grazier at Parham fair, in Norfolk, the husband offered him his wife in exchange for an ox, provided he would let him choose one out of his drove. The grazier accepted the proposal, and the wife readily agreed to it. Accordingly they met the next day, when she was delivered to the grazier with a new halter round her neck, and the husband received the bullock, which he afterwards sold for six guineas. (*Gentleman's Magazine*, 1764, p. 542)

21

One Higginson, a journeyman carpenter in the Borough, having last week sold his wife to a brother workman in a fit of conjugal indifference at the alehouse, took it in his head to hang himself a few days after, as the lady very peaceably cohabited with the purchaser, refused to return home at his most pressing solicitations. (*Annual Register*, 11 March 1766, p. 75)

22

On the 4th instant an extraordinary marriage was performed at Thorne, in Yorkshire: A man of that place sold his wife to a neighbour for five shillings, to whom he delivered her in a halter; but the purchaser being desirous of having her secured to him by marriage, a few days after went with the former husband to Doncaster to apply for licence to solemnise the same, which they obtained, and the ceremony was accordingly performed at the above time and place, when the first husband became father, and gave her away; the minister not knowing any thing of the circumstances of the affair.

London, June 4. About three weeks ago a bricklayer's labourer at Marylebone sold a woman, whom he had cohabited with for several years, to a fellow workman for a quarter-guinea and a gallon of beer. The workman went off with the purchase, and she has since had the good fortune to have a legacy of 200 l. and some plate left her by a deceased uncle in Devonshire. The parties were married last Friday. (*Jackson's Oxford Journal,* 22 November 1766; 6 June 1767)

23

Memorandum, Oct. 24, 1766.
It is this day agreed on between John Parsons, of the parish of Midsummer Norton, in the county of Somerset, clothworker, and John Tooker, of the same place, gentleman, that the said John Parsons, for and in consideration of the sum of six pounds and six shillings in hand paid to the said John Tooker, doth sell, assign, and set over unto the said Tooker, Ann Parsons, wife of the said John Parsons; with all right, property, claim, services, and demands whatsoever, that he, the said John Parsons, shall have in or to the said Ann Parsons, for and during the term of the natural life of her, the said Ann Parsons. In witness whereof, I the said John Parsons, have set my hand the day and year first above written.
John Parsons,
Witness: William Chivers. (British Museum, Add. MSS 32 084, 1768)

24

Friday last one Richard Unwin, a shepherd, at Iver, near Uxbridge, sold his wife to a farmer at Cowley for twenty pounds. The woman it seems had lived with the farmer a twelvemonth, and as her husband found he was unable to prevail with her to return home, he resolved to come to an eclaircissement with the farmer, and they soon settled matters in the above amicable manner. Unwin, after receiving the money gave the ringers a crown to ring a merry peal on the occasion. (*Jackson's Oxford Journal,* 4 August 1770)

25

Three men and three women went to the Bell-inn in Edgbaston-street, Birmingham, and made the following entry in the toll-book which is kept there:
'August 31, 1773. Samuel Whitehouse, of the parish of Willenhall, in the county of Stafford, this day sold his wife, Mary Whitehouse,

in open market, to Thomas Griffiths, of Birmingham, value one shilling,

> To take her with all her faults.
> Signed, Samuel Whitehouse, and Mary Whitehouse.
> Voucher, Thomas Buckley, of Birmingham.'

The parties were all exceedingly well pleased, and the money paid down as well for the toll as purchase. (*Annual Register,* 31 August 1773)

26

A man who had been some years abroad returned lately, and hearing that his wife cohabited with an acquaintance of his, a chimney sweeper, he went to their place of abode, and demanded her; but the sable knight of the brush, unwilling to part with what he considered a valuable acquisition proposed a legal transfer by purchase, to which the husband agreed, and writings being accordingly drawn up, and presented to a lawyer for inspection, who pronounced them invalid, and advised the parties, as a mutual security, to have the woman taken by her husband, with a halter round her neck, to a public market, and there exposed for sale. In consequence of this, the woman walked in form to the beast market on Saturday, and was there purchased by her paramour for a guinea. This done, the parties retired, each seemingly well satisfied. (*Sarah Farley's Bristol Journal,* 11 September 1784)

27

A very curious cause was tried last week at Lincoln: A man sold his wife to another man, for one guinea, and delivered her up with a halter about her neck. Some time after he demanded his wife, and the buyer refused the demand; whereupon the husband took out an action against the buyer for detaining his wife – The jury gave a verdict for the purchaser.

On Wednesday last, a Man who had sold his Wife for a *Guinea* and a *Crown Bowl of Punch,* delivered her to the purchaser, in the Beast Market at Worcester, with a Halter round her Waist, to the wonderful Amusement of the Populace.

After a Conversation about the Payment of 5s. as the Purchase-Money, the old Husband very deliberately pulled out a Penny Slip and tied it around the Waist of his Wife, the end of which he held fast till he pocketed 3s. in Part, the Purchaser not abounding in Cash. He then put the Cord into the Hands of the new Husband, and took French leave. The Woman then immediately called for her second Wedding-Ring which being put on, she eagerly kissed the Fellow with whom she walked off, leaving the Spectators in Amazement at such uncommon Assurance. (*Jackson's Oxford Journal*, 25 March 1786, 21 November 1789, 12 December 1789)

28

In England there are still a few of those singular laws which evince the barbarity of remote ages. For example, a husband is permitted to sell his wife, provided she gives her consent. I myself was witness to a transaction of this kind in the city of Worcester. A journeyman conducted his dear moiety to the market with a rope about her neck, as the law prescribes, and exactly in the same manner as an ox or an ass. A shoemaker, who was her lover, appeared according to appointment, and the bargain was soon made. The price of the woman was five pounds. (J. W. von Archenholz, *A Picture of England*, 1791, pp. 152–3)

29

Query – Do men sell their wives because there is no law which prohibits such a practice? or, because there is a specific statute which sanctions it? If the former, it is a shame that the magistrates do not take cognizance of a practice so repugnant to every idea of decency and of morality. If the latter, the legislature ought surely to take some steps against so gross a violation of the moral ties of the community.

A blacksmith, in the Cliffe, near Leeds, sold his wife, a smart young woman, with child, to one of his journeymen, for two guineas, agreeably to an engagement drawn up by an attorney. (*Jackson's Oxford Journal*, 22 July 1797)

Part 7 Women without Husbands

> In this happy life let me remain
> Fearless of twenty-five and all its train
> Of slights or scorns, or being call'd Old Maid,
> Those goblins which so many have betray'd.
> (Jane Barker, 'A Virgin Life', from *Poetical Recreations*, Pt 1, 1688)

> PEACHUM: And had not you the common views of a gentlewoman in your marriage, Polly?
> POLLY: I don't know what you mean, Sir.
> PEACHUM: Of a jointure, and of being a widow.
> POLLY: But I love him Sir: how then could I have thought of parting with him?
> PEACHUM: Parting with him! Why, that is the whole scheme and intention of all Marriage-articles. The comfortable estate of widowhood is the only hope that keeps up a wife's spirits. Where is the woman who would scruple to be a wife, if she had it in her power to be a widow whenever she pleas'd? (John Gay, *The Beggar's Opera*, 1728, Act I, sc. x)

Introduction

The 1801 Census of population revealed a large surplus of women over men. It seems probable that this situation had existed for some time. Many contemporary writers assume such a surplus. The reasons given for it are various: emigration, military service abroad, the toll of recent wars (**11**). Marriage, it was suggested, was out of fashion, or, with the marriage stakes rising rapidly, the families of many girls found themselves unable to compete for gentlemen but were unwilling to 'descend' to tradesmen (**10**). Bachelordom had increasing financial advantages and the ease of obtaining prostitutes diminished the attractions of marriage.

Regardless of whether or not the number of spinsters actually increased, there was certainly much greater awareness of them. At exactly what period the whole attitude to them changed it is difficult to say. Probably some time in the late seventh century for, by the beginning of the eighteenth, the opprobium attached to 'old maids' is very evident. If one cannot exactly date the alteration it is possible to suggest several reasons for it. The very change in the meaning of 'spinster' from a description of woman who spins to a term of abuse, suggests that the development occurred when women were deprived of opportunities for productive labour. As home spinning declined together with other domestic industry, the opportunities for single women to maintain themselves decreased. More and more rarely could they make any contribution towards the maintenance of their families. So, increasingly, they became an economic burden within the household of their parents, their brothers or their brothers' families, their friends, or, where no such help was available, a burden on the parish (**8, 12**). As the family unit became smaller and children tended to move away from their parents' home on marriage, the assimilation of unmarried daughters became less easy.

If the state of the marriage market was becoming less favourable to women, nevertheless the fear of becoming 'old maids' with all the passionate spite and scorn that term carried with it, ensured that however bad a marriage might be it was regarded as infinitely preferable to remaining single (**1, 6, 8, 15**).

The abuse levelled at spinsters might seem extreme. It was not unconnected with the vital importance attached to chastity in the commercial transaction so many marriages represented. The virginity of spinsters, to put it crudely, was seen as a frozen asset, unconvertible into any market value. So the spinster becomes a freak, an unnatural woman. Learning was unwomanly and masculine (see Part 3c). This goes some way to accounting for the assumption that 'learned ladies', whether married or single, must be sexually frigid. Equally unnatural was spinsterhood, so that the two were often linked in the public's imagination.

For the vast majority of women the prospect of widowhood was far from holding the promise that Willliam Alexander (20) suggested. As marriage became progressively less favourable to the woman than to the man, the size of the dowry increased while that of the jointure decreased proportionately. A well-provided-for widow might contemplate a life of greater economic independence and freedom than ever before. A widow was legally entitled to dower – a share (usually a third) of her husband's estate and often more. For the first time she gained a legal identity.

For the majority of widows, however, there was no such prospect. Jointures were often inadequate for their maintenance and the means of supplementing them no longer available. In 1696 Gregory King suggested that there were as many as 250,000 widows in England and Wales, constituting one-sixth of the adult female population. (*Observations on the State of England in 1696*, ed. George Chalmers (1804), 1810, p. 89). For the overwhelming majority of these widowhood meant poverty (see Part 9). Many widows of tradesmen were forced by ignorance of their husband's trade, on which maintenance of their standard of life depended, into hasty remarriages. Hence Defoe's urgent advice to husbands to teach their wives their trades (**18**). But the opportunity for remarriage for those without the advantages of youth or the attractions of a business was minimal.

Even where her family was well able to support her, there were problems. Such widows were 'dependants', with all that term involved. As the experience of William Stout's mother suggests (**16**) it was not always an easy role. There must have been few husbands with the foresight of Bonham Hayes (**17**) to ensure the rights of his widow after his death.

(a) Spinsters and Dependants

1

For the poor lady having past the prime of her years in gaiety and company, in running the circle of all the vanities of the town, having spread all her nets, and us'd all her arts for conquest, and finding that the bait fails where she wou'd have it take; and having all this while been so over-careful of her body, that she had no time to improve her mind, which therefore affords her no safe retreat, now she meets with disappointments abroad, and growing every day more and more sensible, that the respect which us'd to be paid her decays as fast as her beauty; quite terrified with the dreadful name of old maid, which yet none but fools will reproach her with, nor any wise woman be afraid of; to avoid . . . the scoffs that are thrown on superannuated virgins, she flies to some dishonourable match as her last, tho' mistaken refuge, to the disgrace of her family and her own irreparable ruin. (Mary Astell, *A Serious Proposal to the Ladies*, 1696, Pt 1, pp. 111–12)

2

[On a proposal for an 'office for marriages' in 1719]
. . . I cannot but approve of the gentleman's proposal in your last, of settling an Office for marriages . . . which I believe would be particularly useful to a set of despicable creatures, called old maids. I am of opinion the greatest part of those that would apply to an office upon that score, would be of that denomination; for I conceive that ladies of fortune, wit, beauty, etc. would have no occasion to offer themselves, seeing those qualifications must furnish them with frequent opportunities of doing it by more honourable methods. As for those wretches who have languished out their insipid lives, perhaps without ever having an offer of a husband; 'tis no wonder, if they (lost to all sense of modesty, and at their last cast) should (rather than sink with that heavy luggage of virginity into their graves) despising the calumnies of a censorious world (which would be sufficiently recompensed by the valuable prize,) flock in crowds to your office . . .

['Reply to a Satire on old Maids from an old maid' in 1723]
Sir, I have read your last journal wherein you have publish'd a letter scandalously reflecting upon the elder unmarried ladies, who your author universally reproaches, without exception . . .
    Now, I humbly conceive that there are two sorts of ladies who ought to be excepted out of his buffoonery, and are not the proper objects of the general satyr bestow'd upon the other, and these are:
I. Those who, either by religious vows, or by other private engagement; by choice, not necessity; remain single and unwed. These are neither touch'd with the scandal of having never been asked, or tainted with the sourness and moroseness of humour with which you reproach the old maids you mention.
II. Such as for defect of fortune . . . are sunk below the views they had, and the figure they were bred to; and, – scorning to dishonour their education, and the blood of their ancestors, will not, – for the mere satisfaction of being married, – be fettered to scoundrels, and degenerate into the rate of mechanicks; but choose to live single . . .
III. A third sort are such ladies who being perhaps a little over nice, and having good fortunes, (come of good families), good faces, and good breeding, have rejected many such as others have call'd good offers; being difficult and hard to be pleas'd, had rather live as they are, than marry where they cannot love; that is, in a word, had rather be completely happy in the dear enjoyment of themselves, than completely miserable in the bondage and chains

of unsuitable matrimony, which without doubt, is the worst condition in the world.

. . . There are more Ladies of fortunes, beauty, and breeding, who have had admirers, plenty, and never wanted opportunity to match equal to their rank, who yet remain unmarry'd, and venture the reproach of being old maids: . . . than ever were known in the memory of the oldest person alive. The reason is to be found in the degeneracy of the times; and, in a word, your sex is come to such a height in all the most disagreeable articles, that an honest virtuous woman must, and ought to have an aversion for marrying, it being a terrible venture . . . the just reproach of your sex's debauchery, will rather make the single Life of the ladies a mark of reserved virtue, than a brand of infamy. (William Lee, *Daniel Defoe*, 1869, Vol. 2, p. 115; Vol. 3, pp. 128–30)

3

I returned, that while a woman was single, she was a masculine in her politic capacity; that she had then the full command of what she had, and the full direction of what she did; that she was a man in her separated capacity, to all intents and purposes that a man could be so to himself; that she was controlled by none, because accountable to none, and was in subjection to none; . . .

I added, that whoever the woman was that had an estate, and would give it up to be the slave of a great man, that woman was a fool, and must be fit for nothing but a beggar; and that it was my opinion a woman was as fit to govern and enjoy her own estate, without a man, as a man was without a woman; and that if she had a mind to gratify herself as to sexes, she might entertain a man as a man does a mistress; that while she was thus single she was her own, and if she gave away that power, she merited to be as miserable as it was possible that any creature could be. (Daniel Defoe, *Roxana* (1724), 1840–1, p. 158)

4

[Harriet Byron on 'old maids']
I believe there are more bachelors now in England by many thousand than there were a few years ago: and probably, the number of them (and of single women, of course) will every year increase. The luxury of the age will account a good deal for this; and the turn our sex take in un-domesticating themselves, for a good deal more. But let not those worthy young women, who may think themselves destined to lead a single life, repine over-much at their lot; since, possibly, if they have had no lovers, or having had

one, two, or three, have not found a husband, they have had
rather a miss than a loss, as men go. And let me here add, that I
think, as matters stand in this age, or indeed ever did stand, that
those women who have joined with the men in their insolent
ridicule of old maids, ought never to be forgiven: . . . An old maid
may be an odious character, if they will tell us, that the bad
qualities of the persons, not the maiden state, are what they mean
to expose: but then they must allow, that there are widows and
wives of all ages and complexions, who in the abusive sense of the
words, are as much old maids, as the most particular of that class
of females. (Samuel Richardson, *Sir Charles Grandison* (1753),
1811, Vol. 2, letter II)

5

A discovery of a very extraordinary nature was made at Poplar,
where two women had lived together for six and thirty years, as
man and wife, and kept a public house, without ever being
suspected; but the wife happening to fall sick, and die, a few years
before she expired, revealed the secret to her relations, made her
will, and left legacies to the amount of half what she thought they
were worth. On application to the pretended, she at first endeavoured to support her assumed character, but being closely
pressed, she at length owned the fact, accommodated all matters
amicably, put off the male, and put on the female character, in
which she appeared to be a sensible well-bred woman, though in
her male character she had always affected the plain plodding
alehouse-keeper. It is said they had acquired in business money to
the amount of 3000 1. Both had been crossed in love when young,
and had chosen this method to avoid further importunities.
(*Gentleman's Magazine*, 1766, p. 339)

6

'As for old maids', continued I, 'they should not be treated with so
much severity, because I suppose none would be so if they could.
No lady in her senses would choose to make a subordinate figure at
christenings or lyings-in, when she might be the principal herself;
nor curry favour with a sister-in-law, when she might command a
husband; nor toil in preparing custards, when she might lie a-bed,
and give directions how they ought to be made; nor stifle all her
sensations in demure formality, when she might with matrimonial
freedom, shake her acquaintance by the hand, and wink at a
double entendre. No lady could be so very silly as to live single, if
she could help it' . . .

'Indeed, sir', replied my companion, 'you are very little acquainted with the English ladies, to think they are old maids against their will. I dare venture to affirm, that you can hardly select one of them all, but has had frequent offers of marriage, which either pride or avarice has not made her reject' . . . (*The Works of Oliver Goldsmith* (1772), 1845, Vol. 3, p. 80)

7

[Letter to Jane Arden, 1782 or 1783]
It is a happy thing to be a mere blank, and to be able to pursue one's own whims, where they lead, without having a husband and half a hundred children at hand to tease and control a poor woman who wishes to be free. (*Collected Letters of Mary Wollstonecraft*, ed. Ralph M. Wardle, 1979, p. 79)

8

If she has received a polite education . . . it is probable, that after having passed the sprightly years of youth in the comfortable mansion of an opulent father, she is reduced to the shelter of some contracted lodging in a country town, attended by a single female servant, and with difficulty living on the interest of two or three thousand pounds, reluctantly, and perhaps irregularly, paid to her by an avaricious or extravagant brother, who considers such payment as a heavy incumbrance on his paternal estate. Such is the condition in which the unmarried daughters of English gentlemen are too frequently found. To support such a change of situation, with that cheerfulness and content which several of these fair sufferers possess, requires a noble firmness, or rather dignity of mind; . . . we may justly suppose, that it is the natural wish and expectation of every amiable girl, to settle happily in marriage; and that the failure of this expectation, from whatever causes it may arise, must be inevitably attended by many unpleasant, and many depressive sensations.

The Old Maid who affirms, she never wished to marry, pronounces the severest of satires against her own heart. How utterly devoid of tenderness and of every amiable sensation, must that female be, who never felt at any period of life, a desire to engage in the duties or to share the delights of that state, to which all human beings are invited by the voice of nature and reason! . . . I would therefore wish her, whenever she has occasion to speak of the nuptial state, to . . . represent her own exclusion from it, not as the effect of choice, arising from a cold and irrational aversion to the state in general, but as the consequence of such perverse incidents as frequently perplex all the paths of human life, and lead even the worthiest of beings into situations very different from what they otherwise would have chosen.

How often does the amiable Old Maid smart under the flippant jocularity of the unfeeling rustic merchant, or the boorish squire, who never fail to comment on the variations of her countenance, repeatedly wonder why she does not get her a husband, and very kindly hint to her, with equal delicacy of sentiment and language, that if she does not take great care, she will slip out of the world without answering the end of her creation! (William Hayley, *A Philosophical, Historical, and Moral Essay on Old Maids*, 1786, Vol. 1, pp. 7–9, 13–14, 18)

9

. . . Many who have been well, or at least fashionably educated, are left without a fortune, and if they are not entirely devoid of delicacy, they must frequently remain single.

Few are the modes of earning a subsistence, and those very humiliating. Perhaps to be an humble companion to some rich old cousin, or what is still worse, to live with strangers, who are so intolerably tyrannical, that none of their own relations can bear to live with them, though they should even expect a fortune in reversion. It is impossible to enumerate the many hours of anguish such a person must spend. Above the servants, yet considered by them as a spy, and ever reminded of her inferiority when in conversation with the superiors. If she cannot condescend to mean flattery, she has not a chance of being a favourite; and should any of the visitors take notice of her, and she for a moment forget her subordinate state, she is sure to be reminded of it.

Painfully sensible of unkindness, she is alive to everything, and many sarcasms reach her, which were perhaps directed another way. She is alone, shut out from equality and confidence, and the concealed anxiety impairs the constitution; for she must wear a cheerful face, or be dismissed. The being dependent on the caprice of a fellow-creature, though certainly very necessary in this state of discipline is yet a very bitter corrective, which we would fain shrink from. (Mary Wollstonecraft, *Thoughts on the Education of Daughters*, 1787, pp. 69–71)

10

[Of Preston]
This town subsists . . . by many families of middling fortune who

live in it, and it is remarkable for old maids, because their families will not ally with tradesmen, and have no sufficient fortunes for gentlemen. (Dr Richard Pococke, *The Travels through England of Dr Richard Pococke*, Camden Society, 1888–9, Vol. 1, p. 12)

11

Those places where the manufactures flourish, draw, like a loadstone, the neighbouring inhabitants, and abound with males of the lower orders, so that we often behold a wife of sixteen; but Derby, having no internal commerce to retain her sons, they were diminished by emigration, or the military service; and the girls were left longing for husbands. (William Hutton, *The History of Derby*, 1791, p. 189)

12

. . . Girls who have been thus weakly educated are often cruelly left by their parents without any provision, and, of course, are dependent on not only the reason, but the bounty of their brothers. These brothers are, to view the fairest side of the question, good sort of men, and give as a favour what children of the same parents had an equal right to. In this equivocal humiliating situation a docile female may remain some time with a tolerable degree of comfort. But when the brother marries – a probable circumstance – from being considered as the mistress of the family, she is viewed with averted looks as an intruder, an unnecessary burden on the benevolence of the master of the house and his new partner.

Who can recount the misery which many unfortunate beings, whose minds and bodies are equally weak, suffer in such situations – unable to work, and ashamed to beg? The wife, a cold-hearted, narrow-minded woman – and this is not an unfair supposition, for the present mode of education does not tend to enlarge the heart any more than the understanding – is jealous of the little kindness which her husband shows to his relations; and her sensibility not rising to humanity, she is displeased at seeing the property of *her* children lavished on a helpless sister.

. . . The consequence is obvious; the wife has recourse to cunning to undermine the habitual affection which she is afraid openly to oppose; and neither tears nor caresses are spared till the spy is worked out of her home, and thrown on the world, unprepared for its difficulties; or sent as a great effort of generosity, or from some regard to propriety, with a small stipend, and an uncultivated mind, into joyless solitude. (Mary Wollstonecraft,

Vindication of the Rights of Woman [1792], ed. Miriam Kramnick, 1978, pp. 157–8)

13

Mrs. Sarah Spencer was the daughter of a gentleman in Sussex; her brother having once been high sheriff of the county. But, her family possessing only a competent landed estate, and being neither engaged, nor in circumstances to engage, in any lucrative profession, like too many others in this age of universal commerce insensibly dwindled to nothing; and though she had been well, and genteely, educated, and with such views as are common to people in her sphere of life, yet, on the demise of her father, she found her whole fortune did not amount to quite £300. Her sister Mary, a woman of perhaps not inferior goodness of heart, though certainly of very inferior abilities, was left in a similar predicament.

Their persons, though not uncomely, were not so attractive as to flatter them that, without fortunes, they could marry advantageously; and a mere clown was not much more likely to be happy with them, than they could have been with him. They either had no relations, on whom they would have been permitted to quarter themselves; or they thought such a state of dependence but a more specious kind of beggary. Yet, living in an age and country, in which well-educated women not born to fortunes are peculiarly forlorn; with no habits of exertion, not even of a rigid frugality; they soon found, that being thus unable to work, and ashamed to beg, they had no prospect but that of pining to death in helpless and hopeless penury.

It may be questioned, perhaps, whether even the most resolute spirits have virtue enough to embrace a life of labour, till driven to it by necessity: but it is no ordinary effort of virtue to submit to such a necessity with a becoming dignity. This virtue these sisters possessed: at a loss what else to do, they took a farm; and without ceasing to be gentlewomen, commenced farmers. This farm they carried on for many years, much to their credit and advantage; and, as far as example goes, in an instance where example is certainly of most effect, not less to the advantage of their neighbourhood. To this day the marks of their good husbandry are to be seen in the village of Rottington. (F. M. Eden, *The State of the Poor*, 1797, Vol. 1, p. 626 fn.)

14

There is sometimes seen in families an inmate, commonly a female relation of the master or mistress of the house, who, though admitted to live in the parlour, is in truth, an humble dependant, received either from motives of charity, or for the sake of being made more useful in the conduct of domestic affairs, or of being a companion to her protectoress when the latter is not otherwise engaged or amused. Have you such an inmate? Let your behaviour to her be such as she ought to experience. Pretend not to call her a friend, while you treat her as a drudge. If sickness, or infirmity, or a sudden pressure of occupation, disqualifies you from personally attending in detail to the customary affairs of your husband, avail yourself of her assistance. But seek it not from an indolent aversion to trouble, nor from a haughty wish to rid yourself of the employment. While you have recourse to it, receive it as an act of kindness, not as the constrained obedience of an upper servant. Teach the inferior parts of your family to respect her, by respecting her yourself. Remember the awkwardness of her situation, and consult her comfort . . . Rather dismiss her with some small pittance of bounty to search in obscurity for an honest maintenance, than to retain her to learn hypocrisy and to teach you arrogance, to be corrupted and to corrupt.

. . . of the women who pass through life without entering into a connubial engagement, there are probably, very few who have not had, earlier or later, the option of contracting it. If then, from a wise and delicate reluctance to accept offers made by persons of objectionable or of ambiguous character; from unwillingness to leave the abode of a desolate parent, struggling with difficulties, or declining towards the grave; from a repugnance to marriage produced by affection surviving the loss of a beloved object prematurely snatched away by death; if in consequence of any of these or of similar causes a woman continues single, is she to be despised?

Let it also be observed, that in the situation of the persons in question there are peculiarities, the recollection of which will produce in a generous mind impressions very different from scorn. They are persons cut off from a state of life usually regarded as most desirable. They are frequently unprovided with friends, on whose advice or assistance they can thoroughly confide. Sometimes they are destitute of a settled home; and compelled by a scanty income to depend on the protection, and bear the humours, of supercilious relations. Sometimes in obscure streets, solitary, and among strangers, they wear away the hours of sickness and age, unfurnished with the means of procuring the assistance and comforts which sinking health demands. Let no unfeeling derision be added to the difficulties, which it has perhaps been impossible to avoid, or virtue not to decline. (Thomas Gisborne, *An Enquiry into the Duties of the Female Sex* (1797), 1798, pp.291–3, 426, 428)

15

Among the higher classes of people, the superior distinctions which married woman receive, and the marked inattentions to which single women of advanced age are exposed, enable many men, who are agreeable neither in mind nor person, and are besides in the wane of life, to choose a partner among the young and fair, instead of being confined, as nature seems to dictate, to persons of nearly their own age and accomplishments. It is scarcely to be doubted that the fear of being an old maid, and of the silly and unjust ridicule, which folly sometimes attaches to this name, drives many women into the marriage union with men whom they dislike, or at best to whom they are perfectly indifferent. Such marriages must to every delicate mind appear little better than legal prostitutions. (T. R. Malthus, *An Essay on the Principle of Population,* [1798], 1973, bk 4, p. 184)

(b) Widows

16

[Stout's father died in 1680 leaving his mother a widow. Her death occurred in 1716]

[1709] My dear mother was now about seventy six years of age, and dwelt with my brother Josias as his housekeeper, and was become very infirm and uneasy with the care of the house, and was urgent on him to marry, he not being willing to keep house with a servant. And thereupon, with his mother's consent and approbation, he married Sibill Green, daughter of Thomas Green of Boulton Holmes, a neighbour. My brother Josias was about forty eight years of age, and his wife about thirty years of age, and my mother seemed well satisfied with the marriage. But when the young wife came to house keeping, my mother thought to have some direction in that, more than the young wife (who had been her father's housekeeper) would allow; which made their mother uneasy. And in a year's time my brother Josias desired me to entertain her, which I freely offered to do. So she came to me and my sister, and dwelt with us in much content and unity till the time of her death, which was about eight years, without any consideration except what my said brother Josias would freely offer.

[1716] She continued to spin till within four months of her death. Her disposition was always affable and courteous, and very neighbourly and charitable to the poor, or to such as so pretended; minded her own affairs, and not talkative in matters not concerning her. (*The Autobiography of William Stout of Lancaster, 1665–1752*, ed. J. D. Marshall, 1967, pp. 159, 175)

17

[In 1720 Bonham Hayes died. To his second son Richard the house was left plus 220 acres, etc. To this son he confided the care of his widow.]
I do hereby direct and appoint that my loving wife shall have the use and benefit of the little parlour chamber and my little parlour below stairs in my said mansion house in Cobham aforesaid and all the furniture in the same rooms during her natural life and her board gratis with my said son Richard Hayes if she thinks fit to take and accept the same. (Ralph Arnold, *A Yeoman of Kent : An Account of Richard Hayes (1725–1790) of Cobham*, 1949, p. 94)

18

[Of widows who are left ignorant of their husband's trade through pride]
. . . as the tradesmen's ladies now manage, they are generally above the favour, and scorn to be seen in the counting-house, much less behind the counter; despise the knowledge of their business, or act as if they were ashamed of being tradesmen's wives, and never imagined to be tradesmen's widows.
. . . This pride is indeed the great misfortune of tradesmen's wives; for as they lived as if they were above being owned for the tradesman's wife; so when he died, they live to be the shame of that tradesman's widow; they know nothing how he got his estate when he was alive, and they know nothing where to find it when he is dead. This drives them into the hands of lawyers, attorneys, and solicitors, to get in their effects; who, when they have got it, often run away with it, and leave the poor widow in a more disconsolate and perplexed condition than she was in before . . .
If she has been one of those gay, delicate ladies, that values herself upon her being a gentlewoman, and that thought it a step below herself when she married this mechanic thing called a tradesman, and consequently scorned to come near his shop or warehouse, and acquainting herself with any of his affairs, her folly calls for pity now, as her pride did for contempt before; . . .
The only remedy she has here, is, if her husband had e'er a servant

or apprentice who was so near out of his time as to be acquainted with the customers and with the books, and then she is forced to be beholden to him to settle the accounts for her, and endeavour to get in the debts; in return for which she is obliged to give him his time and his freedom, let him into the trade, make him master of all the business, set him up in the world, and, it may be at last, with all her pride, lets the boy creep to bed to her. And when her friends upbraid her with it, that she should marry her prentice boy, when, it may be, she was old enough to be his mother, her answer is, Why, what could I do? I must have been ruined else.

I am not for a man setting his wife at the head of his business, and placing himself under her like a journeyman; but such and so much of the trade only as may be proper for her, not ridiculous in the eye of the world, and make her assisting and helpful, not governing to him, and which is the main thing I aim at, such as should qualify her to keep up the business for herself and children if her husband should be taken away, and she be left destitute, as many are. (Daniel Defoe, *The Complete English Tradesman* (1726–7) from *The Novels and Miscellaneous Works of Daniel Defoe*, 1840–1, Vol. 1, pp. 213–15, 220–1)

19

Jo Story, a blacksmith at Belford, having courted the daughter of Mrs Eleanor Elliott, widow, near Haggerton, going one day to her house to ask for his sweet-heart, found none but the old woman, who told him her daughter was not at home, but asked him why he courted her daughter, who could not bring him above 20 1. and if he would please her, she would help him to one of 500 1. On which he replied, he would ever with gratitude acknowledge the favour. Then I am the person, (says she) if you'll accept of the offer: on which a bargain was struck immediately, and on Tuesday se'nnight they were married at Killo. The bridegroom is only 18 years of age, and the bride 64. (*Annual Register,* 14 February 1767, pp. 59–60)

20

. . . widowhood, when tolerable circumstances are annexed to it, is, of all other female states, the most eligible; being free from that guardianship and control, to which the sex are subject while virgins, and while wives. (William Alexander, *The History of Women,* 1779, Vol. 2, pp. 309–10)

Part 8   Crime and Punishment

'Now we are even' quoth Steven,
When he gave his wife six blows to one.
                   (Jonathan Swift)

any man may have his wife . . . confined for life, at a
certain stipulated price. (W. Pargeter, *Observations on Maniacal Disorders*, 1792, pp. 126–8)

Introduction

The virtual lack of a legal identity in women often made it
difficult, if not impossible, to obtain any legal redress for
wrongs committed against them. The successful case of
breach of promise quoted here **(1)** was unusual.

In cases of seduction, women were denied any legal means
of obtaining reparation for injury. Only their father could take
legal action. The success of such action depended on his
ability to prove either that his daughter's seduction had
effectively deprived him of her services as a servant, or that
her seducer had trespassed on his property. In other words, it
was the father's injury that was recognised by the law and not
her's **(2)**.

The case brought by a butcher for defamation of his
daughter's character **(3)** is exceptional, both because evidence of very few such cases exists and also because it was
successful. As Blackstone makes clear, women enjoyed little
or no protection against anyone who, for whatever reason,
wished to blacken their character.

Rape was a frequent occurrence throughout the eighteenth
century and there is no lack of evidence here. What is,
however, lacking is any case where successful action had
been brought on behalf of the woman, except in cases of
child rape where the victim was under consenting age. The
extract from Defoe is included here for its recognition – very
unusual in the eighteenth century – that rape was as possible
within a married relationship as without **(5)**.

There is no evidence of large numbers of husbands committing their wives to mad-houses or prisons in order to enjoy

a mistress and their wife's fortune unhindered (**12**). But that the practice existed at all is significant. The number of unlicensed and uninspected asylums that sprang up around London in the course of the century, and the rumours of their inmates that reached the public caused sufficient alarm in the 1760s to result in urgent legislation to make licences essential and to provide for regular inspection. What is frightening is the ease with which sane women could apparently be confined, the slender chance of their remaining sane under the conditions that existed in such institutions, and the very rare occasions when such women managed to escape and legally achieve their freedom. The case of the wife confined to prison by her husband (**16**) suggests the ease with which the law could be manipulated against women, and the difficulty of reversing the process. Behind eighteenth-century criminal law was the theory that savage sentences for trifling offences acted as a deterrent to crime and were necessary to the maintenance of law and order in the absence of a police force. There were a vast number of minor offences for which death was the penalty. They included theft of property worth more than 12 pence. In respect of petty theft the law was no more stringent in its application to women than to men but it was more often the woman who, bearing the main responsibility for feeding and clothing her family, and impelled by their needs, was led to resort to stealing. Those caught were rarely hardened criminals nor was the crime usually premeditated. The robbery occurred because of the combination of opportunity and urgent necessity.

In a society where chastity was seen as the most essential virtue in women, its loss, particularly when it resulted in the birth of illegitimate children, constituted a serious crime. Even more serious were attempts to conceal such births. Proof of infanticide was almost always difficult to establish, unless there were witnesses or accomplices who later talked. The law, recognising such difficulty, concentrated not on the actual killing of the bastard child, but on the concealment of the body. The punishment for such concealment was death unless evidence was available from witnesses, that the child had been born dead. There is evidence (**22**) of a mother being executed for infanticide as late as 1763, but this was exceptional. Although the law was not repealed until 1803, towards the end of the century far greater leniency was shown by the courts and very few cases of convictions for infanticide are found.

The motives for infanticide were many and urgent: the

disgrace and social stigma attached to unmarried mothers and bastards, the consequent fear of loss of livelihood and the loss of the support of family and of friends, the sheer pressure of poverty and the daunting prospect of having to feed another mouth – all of these made infanticide the most common crime among women. (See also Part 9e.)

The almost certain lack of reliable methods of birth control, the expense and dangers of primitive methods of abortion, combined with the vulnerability of women, especially those of the labouring poor, and more particularly servant maids (see Part 12), made for a high incidence of illegitimacy. Just how high we do not know. Because infanticide was regarded by so many contemporaries, including both Defoe and Mandeville, as a horrific and unnatural crime, those cases which came to light were often reported in the local press. There is thus abundant evidence of reputed infanticides but far less evidence of the subsequent trials and the verdicts.

We know only of those cases which were discovered, but there must have been far more cases where attempted concealment was successful. Of those cases reported, the majority of the women concerned were unmarried mothers of the poorer classes, and a high proportion of them seem to have been domestic servants. As is suggested in the frequent warnings to female servants in Part 12, this group of women were particularly vulnerable to seduction, and lived in circumstances where concealment was difficult and where discovery could mean immediate dismissal with little hope of re-employment. (See, for example, Parson Woodforde's frequent dismissal of pregnant servant maids in Part 12d).

In other areas, the law upheld the double standard between the sexes. As Blackstone shows (**23**) the crime of a wife killing her husband was far more serious than that of a husband killing his wife. Even in the case of coining the same distinction of punishment according to the sex of the offender operated – at least until towards the end of the century.

The section on women in prisons and bridewells, is included here not because conditions in prison were usually any worse for women than for men, but because far less is heard of female prisoners. They were always a minority, but not an insignificant one. Eighteenth-century prison conditions were almost universally bad despite the efforts of a handful of reformers in the second half of the century. Prisons were invariably grossly overcrowded, filthy, insanitary and disease-ridden places in which no separate provision for women existed and where no attempt was made to separate hardened criminals from those who had committed minor offences. Promiscuity was encouraged by the ease with which drink could be obtained and by the fact that pregnancy constituted grounds for delaying the execution of women condemned to death (**31**). The treatment of women prisoners in both gaols and bridewells was often brutal, as is suggested by the evidence of the common use of heavy irons on women prisoners (**36**), and, as William Hone suggests (**33**), women were subjected to particularly severe punishments in both.

(a) Breach of Promise, Seduction and Defamation of Character

1

[Friday, 5 June 1747]
At the court of Common Pleas was try'd a cause between Miss Davids of Castle-yard, Holborn, plaintiff, and Rev. Dr. Wilson, prebendary of Worcester, canon of Lincoln, and vicar of Newark upon Trent, defendant. The action was laid for 10,000 1. on a breach of promise of marriage, when, after a trial of almost a day, the jury gave a verdict for the plaintiff, with 7,000 1. damages. – It was proved by several witnesses and letters, that the Dr. had frequently promised to marry her, and prevailed on her to promise him: That they both had declared the same publicly in a solemn manner: And that he afterwards having deny'd his making such a promise, and the lady having refused the addresses of a gentleman on account of her engagement, and being liable to the law, if she married another, this action was brought, to justify her reputation. (*Gentleman's Magazine,* vol. 17, June 1747)

2

. . . Female virtue, by the temporal law, is perfectly exposed to the slanders of malignity and falsehood; for any one may proclaim in conversation, that the purest maid, or the chastest matron, is the most meretricious and incontinent of women, with impunity, or free from the animadversions of the temporal courts. This female honour, which is dearer to the sex than their lives, is left by the common law to be the sport of an abandoned calumniator.

It appears to be a remarkable omission in the law of England . . . that it should have afforded so little protection to female chastity. It is true that it has defended it by the punishment of death from force and violence, but has left it exposed to perhaps greater danger from the artifices and solicitations of seduction. In no case whatever, unless she had a promise of marriage, can a woman herself obtain any reparation for the injury she has sustained from the seducer of her virtue. And even where her weakness and credulity have been imposed upon by the most solemn promises of marriage, unless they have been overheard or made in writing, she cannot recover any compensation, being incapable of giving evidence in her own cause. Nor can a parent maintain any action in the temporal courts against the person who has done this wrong to his family, and to his honour and happiness, but by stating and proving, that from the consequences of the seduction his daughter is less able to assist him as a servant, or that the seducer in the pursuit of his daughter was a trespasser upon his premises. Hence no action can be maintained for the seduction of a daughter, which is not attended with a loss of service or an injury to property. (Sir William Blackstone, *Commentaries on the Laws of England* (1753), 1793, Vol. 1, p. 445; Vol. 3, p. 142 fn.)

3

The same day was tried at the Old Bailey, an indictment brought by a butcher in Whitechapel against a young gentleman of the cleaver, for publishing a libellous ballad, reflecting in the grossest manner on the chastity of the prosecutor's daughter, to whom the defendant paid his addresses, which not meeting with success, he in revenge made a song, that in direct terms charged the object of his affections with being a strumpet. He employed a man to sing this curious ditty in the open market . . . the attempt to turn the whole case into a trifling, unguarded step of his client, failed, as the Recorder, in his charge, considered it in an alarming point of view, as a preconcerted scheme to ruin the young woman, and destroy the happiness of the family. He was found guilty, paid 20 l. costs of the prosecution, asked pardon in court, and agreed to recant his reflections in the public prints. (*Annual Register,* 10 July 1779, pp. 219–20)

4

. . . when a man seduces a woman, it should, I think, be termed a left-handed marriage, and the man should be legally obliged to maintain the woman and her children, unless adultery, a natural divorcement, abrogated the law. And this law should remain in force as long as the weakness of women caused the word seduction to be used as an excuse for their frailty and want of principle; nay, while they depend on man for a subsistence, instead of earning it by the exertion of their own hands or heads. But these women should not, in the full meaning of the relationship, be termed wives, or the very purpose of marriage would be subverted, and all those endearing charities that flow from personal fidelity, and give a sanctity to the tie, when neither love nor friendship unites the hearts, would melt into selfishness. The woman who is faithful to the father of her children demands respect, and should not be treated like a prostitute . . .

I have before observed, that men ought to maintain the women whom they have seduced; this would be one means of reforming female manners, and stopping an abuse that has an equally fatal effect on population and manners. (Mary Wollstonecraft, *Vindication of the Rights of Woman* (1792), ed. Miriam Kramnick, 1978, pp. 164–5, 250)

(b) Rape

5

. . . there are yet a numberless variety of violences, as I may call them, committed like rapes upon nature, in which nothing is more frequent than for a husband to press a wife to such and such things as morality and modesty forbids . . .

It frequently does, or at least may happen, that when a young couple come together their constitutions may, as too often their tempers may and do, differ from one another, with respect to those things, to the greatest extreme; one is weak, faint, the spirits low, Nature unable to answer what is expected; another perhaps is reduced by child-bearing, too thick and too long together, by accidents in often hard and difficult travels, injuries received by unskilful hands, or many other incidents and circumstances not to be named; by these, I say, the person is reduced, debilitated, and render'd unfit to give the satisfaction which has formerly been found . . .

. . . What wretched work does this cause between the ill-match'd couple? I can openly say I know a beautiful young lady after bringing her husband several children, yet actually destroyed, I might have said murdered, by these conjugal violences, to say no worse of them . . . (Daniel Defoe, *Conjugal Lewdness*, 1727, pp. 79–82)

6

A destitute girl applied for assistance at a public house, and three young fellows under pretence of helping her to a lodging decoyed her into a hayloft, where they all severally lay with her and robbed her of what little she had. The three were committed to gaol.

A most shocking scene of brutal passion near Bath.
A band of thirteen or fourteen miscreants fell on a young man and his sweetheart on the road. They beat him, and carrying her to a by-lane about nine or ten successfully used her ill, when she was rescued by two gentlemen. The unhappy girl has since made oath against them, but they have escaped. (*Gentleman's Magazine*, 26 December 1763; 11 May 1765)

7

Oct 26, . . . the Revd. Benjamin Russen master of the charity school at Bethnal Green and who has a wife and six children; was tried at the Old Bailey for a rape on the body of one Anne Mayne only ten years of age, of which he was convicted and received sentence of death. Three more indictments found against him on other children. (Revd James Woodforde, *Diary of a Country Parson, 1758–1802*, ed. John Beresford, 1924–31, Vol. 1, p. 213)

(c) Wife-Beating and Male Tyranny

8

. . . the case of the women in England is truly deplorable, and there is scarce a good husband now to twenty that merited that name in former times; nor was beating of wives ever so much the usage in England, as it is now; the difference is manifest, and they tell me, that 'tis so frequent now, especially among the meaner sort of people, that to hear a woman cry murther now, scarce gives any alarm; the neighbours scarce stir at it, and if they do, if they come out in a fright, and ask one another what's the matter, and where is it that they cry murther? the common answer to one another is only thus; 'tis nothing neighbour, but such a one a beating his wife; O dear, says the other, is that all? and in they go again, compos'd and easy, as hearing a thing of no great consequence, that has no great novelty in it, nor much danger, and what, if it had, they don't much care to meddle with. (Daniel Defoe, *The Great Law of Subordination*, 1724, pp. 6–7)

9

And now I have mentioned the villainy of some husbands in the lower state of life, give me leave to propose, or at least to wish, that they were restrained from abusing their wives at that barbarous rate, which is now practised by butchers, carmen, and such inferior sort of fellows, who are public nuisances to civil neighbourhoods, and yet nobody cares to interpose, because the riot is between a man and his wife.

I see no reason why every profligate fellow shall have the liberty to disturb a whole neighbourhood, and abuse a poor honest creature at a most inhuman rate, and is not to be called to account because it is his wife; this sort of barbarity was never so notorious and so much encouraged as at present, for every vagabond thinks he may cripple his wife at pleasure; and it is enough to pierce a heart of stone to see how barbarously some poor creatures are beaten and abused by merciless dogs of husbands.

It gives an ill example to the growing generation, and this evil will gain ground on us if not prevented; it may be answered, the law has already provided redress, and a woman abused may swear the peace against her husband, but what woman cares to do that? It is revenging herself on herself, and not without considerable charge and trouble.

There ought to be a short way, and when a man has beaten his wife, which by the by is a most unmanly action, and great sign of cowardice, it behoves every neighbour who has the least humanity or compassion, to complain to the next justice of the peace, who should be empowered to set him in the stocks for the first offence; to have him well scourged at the whipping-post for the second; and if he persisted in his barbarous abuse of the holy marriage state, to send him to the house of correction till he should learn to use more mercy to his yoke-fellow.

How hard it is for a poor industrious woman to be up early and late, to sit in a cold shop, stall, or market, all weathers, to carry heavy loads from one end of the town to the other, or to work from morning till night, and even then dread going home for fear of being murdered? (Daniel Defoe, *Augusta Triumphans*, (1728) 1840–1, pp. 20–2)

10

The husband . . . (by the old law) might give his wife moderate correction. For, as he is to answer for her misbehaviour, the law thought it reasonable to intrust him with this power of restraining her, by domestic chastisement, in the same moderation that a man is allowed to correct his apprentices or children; for whom the master or parent is also liable in some cases to answer. But this power of correction was confined within reasonable bounds, and the husband was prohibited from using any violence to his wife . . .

But . . . in the politer reign of Charles the Second, this power of correction began to be doubted: and a wife may now have security of the peace against her husband; or, in return, a husband against his wife. Yet the lower rank of people . . . still claim and exert their ancient privilege: and the courts of law will still permit a husband to restrain a wife of her liberty, in case of any gross misbehaviour. (Sir William Blackstone, *Commentaries on the Laws of England* (1753), 1793, Vol. 1, p. 65)

11

. . . a wife cannot recover damages for the beating of her husband, as she hath no separate interest in any thing during her couverture. (Anon., *The Laws respecting Women*, 1777, p. 59)

(d) Confining Women to Mad-Houses – and to Prison

12

. . . this leads me to exclaim against the vile practice now so much in vogue among the better sort as they are called, but the worst sort in fact; namely, the sending their wives to madhouses, at every whim or dislike, that they may be more secure and undisturbed in their debaucheries; which wicked custom is got to such a head, that the number of private madhouses in and about London are considerably increased within these few years . . .

How many ladies and gentlewomen are hurried away to these houses, which ought to be suppressed, or at least subject to daily examination, as hereafter shall be proposed?

How many, I say, of beauty, virtue and fortune, are suddenly torn from their dear innocent babes, from the arms of an unworthy man, whom they love, perhaps, but too well, and who in return for that love, nay probably an ample fortune and a lovely offspring besides, grows weary of the pure stream of chaste love, and thirsting after the puddles of lawless lust, buries his virtuous wife alive, that he may have the greater freedom with his mistresses?

If they are not mad when they go into these cursed houses, they are soon made so by the barbarous usage they there suffer; and any woman of spirit, who has the least love for her husband, or concern for her family, cannot sit down tamely under a confinement and separation the most unaccountable and unreasonable.

Is it not enough to make any one mad to be suddenly clapped up, stripped, whipped, ill-fed, and worse used? To have no reason assigned for such treatment, no crime alleged, or accused to confront? And what is worse, no soul to appeal to but merciless creatures, who answer but in laughter, surliness, contradiction, and too often stripes? (Daniel Defoe, *Augusta Triumphans,* (1728), 1840–1, pp. 22–3)

13

It appears, that at a mad-house kept by one Turlington, at Chelsea, all persons who were brought, were admitted without enquiry; . . . that one Mrs. Smith was received into the house and confined merely at the desire of her husband, who did not pretend she was a lunatic, but only that the neighbours were afraid she would set the house on fire, and that six guineas a quarter were paid for her maintenance. The others were admitted for drunkenness, and other reasons of the same kind, alleged by those who brought them.

It appears also, that the persons confined in this house, were denied the use of pen, ink and paper, and secluded from all commerce with the world, being constantly denied, if any enquiry was made after them at the house . . . Dr. Battie declared . . . that he has frequently seen persons confined who were not, nor were pretended to be lunatics; that upon expostulating with the husband of one such person brought to a house under the Doctor's direction, he frankly declared, that he considered the house as a kind of bridewell, or house of correction. (*Gentleman's Magazine,* 1763, p. 126)

14

Jan. 24, 1761, a motion was made for an Habeas Corpus to the keeper of a private madhouse, commanding him to bring up the body of Mrs. Deborah D'Vebre, who was confined there by her husband. But the court thought fit to order a previous inspection of her by proper persons, physicians and relations, and then to proceed as the truth should come out upon such inspection. A rule was accordingly made, that Dr. Monro, Peter Bodkin, her nearest relation, and Edmund Kelly, her attorney, should at all proper times, and seasonable hours, respectively be admitted, and have free access to Mrs. Deborah D'Vebre, the wife of Gabriel D'Vebre, at the madhouse kept by Robert Turlington, at Chelsea, in order to consult with, advise and assist her. –

On the 26th an affidavit of Dr. Monro was read, which set forth, that he had seen and conversed with the woman, and examined her nurse, and saw no sort of reason to suspect that she was or had been disordered in her mind: on the contrary, he found her to be very sensible, and very cool and dispassionate. The doctor personally attended in court. Lord Mansfield thereupon ordered a writ of Habeas Corpus, by virtue of which Mrs. D'Vebre was brought up to court by Mr. Turlington. She appeared to be absolutely free from the least insanity. She was prepared to swear articles of the peace against her husband, and they were offered in court reading engrossed but not being stamped, they could not be read. – She was permitted to go with her attorney to his house, he undertaking to produce her the next morning. She desired not to go back to the madhouse, and the court would not permit the husband to take her under the circumstances of danger then apprehended from him. – The reporter says, the matter was afterwards compromised, and a separation by agreement took place. (Anon., *The Laws respecting Women*, 1777, pp. 74–5)

15

A lady of fashion, who last week exhibited articles of the peace against her husband, for confining her in a mad-house, had a public hearing in Westminster Hall; and after a long examination of herself and several witnesses, she was deemed by the court to be sane in mind. (*Gentleman's Magazine*, 1766, p. 245)

16

[Of Carlisle County Gaol]
Here was a prisoner, lately the widow of an old gentleman, who left her an estate of £300 per annum and £7000 in mortgages. She was afterwards married in Scotland to a Mr. Milbourne of this city, who soon spent £4000, but upon some disagreement she refused to give up the mortgages of the other £3000. By an attachment from the court of chancery her husband sent her to the common gaol, which confinement prevented her compliance with an order for appearance at that court in fifteen days of St Hilary's term next ensuing. At first she was on the master's side, but the late gaoler, after cruelly seizing her clothes etc. for chamber-rent turned her to the common side. Her room (nine feet and a half by eight and a half) has no fire-place. She, not having the county allowance, supports herself by spinning and knitting, and the occasional

kindness of her late husband's relations, while her present husband is living and rioting on her estate.

. . . for above two years, Mr. Milbourne did not give her one farthing, her subsistence being wholly on occasional charities, and the small earnings of spinning, at which employment she could not get more than 4d. but now by practice and extremely close application (when health permits) can earn 10d. a week. In March last her husband sent her twenty shillings, and in October 1788 (twenty-seven weeks after) the same sum. The justices last quarter sessions commiserating her hardships, have allowed her the county bounty. (John Howard, *An Account of the Principal Lazarettos in Europe*, 1789, p. 200 fn.)

(e) Illegitimacy and Infanticide

17

It is commonly imagined, that she who can destroy her child, her own flesh and blood, must have a vast stock of barbarity, and be a savage monster, different from other women; but this is likewise a mistake, which we commit for want of understanding nature and the force of passions. The same woman that murders her bastard in the most execrable manner, if she is married afterwards, may take care of, cherish and feel all the tenderness for her infant that the fondest mother can be capable of: All mothers naturally love their children. (Bernard de Mandeville, *The Fable of the Bees*, (1714), 1724, Vol. 1, p. 67)

18

The young Woman committed to Newgate for the Murder of her Child, (a girl about a Month old) was Servant to a Tallow Chandler in Cheshunt Street, from which Service she was dismissed on the Discovery of her being with Child by the Apprentice; and though the Officers of that Parish had obliged him to give Security to indemnify them, yet no Care was taken of her; and the Extremity she was reduced to, 'tis thought, deprived her of her Senses. It is said, that after she had cut off the Child's Head, she buried the Body in a Field near Dunance in Endfield Highway, but took it up again, and shewed it about, telling every one what she had done, and being carry'd before Justice Marsh of Green-Street, she signed to a Confession of the Murder: the Child's Head is not yet found, and she being examined about it, said *she saw the Devil fly away with it.* (*Ipswich Journal*, 15 August 1730)

19

On Saturday last was brought to the high gaol for the county of Devon, Mary Light, for that too common and most unnatural crime of murdering her own illegitimate infant. She is about 21 years of age, and lived as servant to one farmer Kerswell at a village near Modbury in this county, where, she says, a young fellow, servant also in the same house, courted her, to whose importunities she yielded, and became pregnant by him. Her condition was suspected by her mother, who charged her strictly with it, but she still denied it, concealing it also from all except her seducer, who on her acquainting him with it, left her and his service. About five weeks ago she was in bed seized with great pains, and was delivered of a living female child, without the knowledge of two girls who lay in the same room. She gathered up her infant, and got again into bed, wrapping the babe in one corner of the rug, and rising at her wonted hour, went about her household work. Her mistress going into her chamber, found the child stifled. (*Northampton Mercury*, 8 March 1756)

20

[16 April 1756]
Yesterday morning a woman, that lodged near the King's Arms at Stangate, was by herself delivered of a child, which she wrapped in a cloth and threw into a ditch, where the infant was found smothered, and the inhuman mother immediately secured and sent to Lambeth workhouse, to be taken care of till her recovery, when it is hoped she will meet her just fate. (*Jackson's Oxford Journal*, 17 April 1756)

21

[3 May 1757]
On Saturday morning a woman, servant to a linendraper in Cheapside, was by herself in her room delivered of an infant, which she murdered, and wrapt in an apron, and laid under her bed. But her delivery being, by some symptoms, discovered, she owned it. The Coroner's Inquest brought in their verdict Wilful Murder; and the woman was, by the Coroner's warrant, immediately committed to Newgate. (*London Chronicle*, 1757, Vol. 1, p. 417)

22

At assizes at Durham, a girl received sentence of death for the murder of her bastard child, and was executed accordingly. (*Gentleman's Magazine,* 1763, p. 409)

(f) Other Crimes and their Punishment

23

. . . the word baron, or lord, attributes to the husband not a very courteous superiority. But we might be inclined to think this merely an unmeaning technical phrase, if we did not recollect that if the baron kills his feme, it is the same as if he had killed a stranger, or any other person; but if the feme kills her baron, it is regarded by the law as a much more atrocious crime; as she not only breaks through the restraints of humanity and conjugal affection, but throws off all the subjection to the authority of her husband. And therefore the law denominates her crime, a species of treason, and condemns her to the same punishment as if she had killed the king. And for every species of treason, (though in petit treason the punishment of men was only to be drawn and hanged,) till the 30. Geo. III. c. 48., the sentence of women was to be drawn and burnt alive.

By the 30. Geo. III c. 48. women shall no longer be sentenced to be burnt, but in all cases of high and petit treason they shall be condemned to be drawn and hanged, . . .

In the case of coining, which is a treason of a different complexion from the rest, the punishment is milder for male offenders; being only to be drawn and hanged by the neck till dead. But in treasons of every kind the punishment of women is the same, and different from that of men. For, as the decency due to the sex forbids the exposing and publicly mangling their bodies, their sentence (which is to the full as terrible to sensation as the other) is to be drawn to the gallows, and there to be burned alive.
Footnote: But now by the statue 30. Geo. III. c. 48. women convicted in all cases of treason, shall receive judgement to be drawn to the place of execution, and there to be hanged by the neck till dead. (Sir William Blackstone, *Commentaries on the Laws of England,* (1753), 1793, Vol. 1, p. 445 (ed. footnote), Vol. 4, pp. 204 (ed. footnote), Vol. 4, p. 92 and footnote)

24

Wed. 7 March . . . At the assizes at Monmouth, a girl about 18 was found guilty of the wilful murder of her mistress, and is to be burnt. (*Gentleman's Magazine*, 1764, p. 144)

25

Mary Norwood for pois'ning her husband received sentence of death, and is to be burnt at Ivelchester on the 8th of May. (*Gentleman's Magazine*, 1765, p. 198)

26

At Shrewsbury assizes, . . . two women for shop-lifting . . . received sentence of death. (*Gentleman's Magazine*, 1766, p. 295)

27

April 24. 1774. A woman was committed . . . for the murder of a man with whom she had cohabited for nineteen years, and had bore him eleven children. She cut his throat in a fit of jealousy, and that not putting an immediate end to his life, she dashed out his brains with a poker. Her resentment was so strong, and she was so far from denying the fact, on her examination, that she owned, if the deed could be recalled, she would again repeat it. (*Gentleman's Magazine*, 1774, p. 4)

28

Sarah Evans. For stealing a loaf of bread, the property of George Bolton, of Witney, to be imprisoned in the Bridewell there till next Thursday, and then publicly whipped. (*Jackson's Oxford Journal*, 14 January 1786)

29

The woman for coining was brought out after the rest were turned off, and fixed to a stake and burnt, being first strangled by the stool being taken from under her. (*Gentleman's Magazine*, 1789, p. 272)

30

Monday last the General Sessions of the peace for the city [Salisbury] was held . . . when Martha Dew, wife of William Dew, convicted of stealing six ounces weight of worsted, was ordered to be privately whipt; Ann Butt, wife of George Butt, for stealing one white cotton petticoat, to be privately and severely whipt.

Yesterday morning upwards of 50 female convicts were removed from Newgate in waggons, in order to be put on board the transport fleet off Portsmouth bound to Botany Bay. (*Salisbury and Winchester Journal*, 27 July 1789; 16 November 1789)

(g) Women in Prison

31

The women or wenches that are condemn'd to death, never fail to plead that they are with child, (if they are old enough) in order to stop execution till they are deliver'd. Upon this they are order'd to be visited by matrons; if the matrons do not find them quick, they are sent to swing next execution-day: But very often they declare that they are with child, and often too the poor criminals are so indeed; for tho' they came never so good virgins into the prison, there are a set of wags there that take care of these matters. No doubt they are diligent to inform them the very moment they come in, that if they are not with child already, they must go to work immediately to be so; that in case they have the misfortune to be condemn'd, they may get time, and so perhaps save their lives. Who would not hearken to such wholesome advice? (M. Misson, *Memoirs and Observations in his Travels over England*, 1719, pp. 329–30)

32

[Of the King's Bench Prison in 1762]
There appeared nothing of what I conceived to be a prison except the door of admission, and high walls. There was a coffee-room and a tap-room, both filled with persons drinking, though it was Sunday, and I had never before seen such a number of profligates and prostitutes, unabashed, without fear, without blushes. (Thomas Joseph Pettigrew, *Memoirs of the Life and Writings of the late John Cockley Lettsom*, 1817, Vol. 2, p. 194)

33

[Of Liverpool Bridewell, 1766]
In the Bridewell I saw a ducking-stool . . . A standard was fixed

for a long pole, at the extremity of which was fastened, a chair, on this the woman was placed, and soused three times under water till almost suffocated . . . but why in a prison this wanton and dangerous severity was exercised on women and not on men, I could no where learn . . . This, however, was not the only cruel punishment used at this Bridewell, for the women were flogged weekly at the whipping-post. (William Hone, *Everyday Book of Popular Amusements,* 1826–7, Vol. 2, p. 197)

34

Vagrants and disorderly women of the very lowest and most wretched class of human beings, almost naked, with only a few filthy rags almost alive and in motion with vermin, their bodies rotting with the bad distemper, and covered with itch, scorbutic and venereal ulcers; and being unable to treat the constable even with a pot of beer to let them escape, are drove in shoals to gaols, particularly to the two Clerkenwells and Tothil-fields; there thirty, and sometimes near forty of these unhappy wretches are crowded or crammed together in one ward, where in the dark they bruise and beat one another in a most shocking manner.

Men and women, felons and disorderly people, are crammed together in one ward in the day, and at night lie on dirty boards in filthy holes, almost unfit for swine. In this prison riot, drunkenness, blasphemy, and debauchery, echo from the walls; sickness and misery are confined within them.

There are at this time 52 prisoners in the Fleet, 46 children, and 25 wives: . . . The inconvenience from permitting prisoners to bring their wives and children to gaol are many and obvious. (William Smith, *State of the Gaols in London, Westminster, and the Borough of Southwark,* 1776, pp. 9–10, 32–3, 62–3)

35

The whole prison was much out of repair, and had not been white-washed for many years . . . There is no separation of the women, or of the bridewell prisoners. The licentious intercourse of the sexes is shocking to decency and humanity. Many children have been born in this gaol. (John Howard, *The State of the Prisons,* 1777)

36

[Of Newgate]
In three or four rooms there were near one hundred and fifty women crowded together, many young creatures with the old and hardened, some of whom had been confined upward of two years: . . . There were four sick in the infirmary for women, which is only fifteen feet and a half by twelve, has but one window, and no bedsteads . . .

[Of the county gaol at Warwick]
The felons were sadly overcrowded . . . In two rooms (seven feet and a half by six and a half) with apertures only in the doors, there lay fourteen women, almost suffocated.

[Of the county gaol at Hereford]
Women convicts continue in this and other gaols longer than the men – some even four or five years. I found that most of the women felons were in heavy irons . . .

[Of the county gaol at Morpeth]
Here a woman, committed for receiving a stolen handkerchief, though lately brought to bed, was in heavy irons . . .

[Of Exeter High Gaol]
There were three women in their sick room, and I was surprised at finding with them a shoe-maker at work at his trade. On inquiring into the cause, I was informed that he was the husband of one of the women who was committed Sept. 1st 1785, and on the 20th March 1786 was sentenced to be transported for seven years for stealing a calf's skin. In Nov. 1786 she was ordered to the hulk at Plymouth, but on account of lameness contracted by a fever in the gaol, she could not be removed: a fine child, which is her fifteenth, was born in the prison. Her husband persisted in declaring he would never leave her, but would go abroad with her. Such constancy of affection in prisoners is very uncommon in men, though I have frequently found it in the other sex – . . . the woman received a free pardon Dec. 27th, 1787.

[Of Bridewells]
Each sex has a work-room and a night-room. They lie in boxes with a little straw, on the floors.

[Of Dartford Bridewell]
. . . only one room for women whether sick or well: no coverlets:

employment, beating hemp. Allowance, a twopenny loaf a day (weight 19½ oz) and a halfpenny in money.

[Of Oxford City Bridewell]
Two rooms on the second floor; that for the women only seventeen feet by nine, and seven feet high, in which were seven prisoners, and frequently there were many more . . . prisoners never let out but for a few minutes. Allowance, two quartern loaves a week. No employment: no coals: no bedding. (John Howard, *An Account of the Principal Lazarettos in Europe,* 1789, sect. 8, pp. 12, 158, 176, 199, 185–6, 127, 145, 171)

Part 9   The Female Poor

guilty of no crime but poverty. (Sir John Fielding,
the Bow Street magistrate)

Introduction

Poverty in the eighteenth century was not confined to
women. Yet, for a number of reasons, conditions bore more
heavily on women than on men. Among women, widows and
single women, whether spinsters, unmarried mothers or
abandoned wives, fared worst.

If the contraction of opportunities for productive work in
agriculture for the wives of farm labourers could make all the
difference between subsistence, if at a low level, and dependence on the parish, how much more devastating were the
consequences of such change for single women and widows.
Many such women had been wholly dependent for a living on
common rights and a little spinning. Even where employment
was available to them the wages they received were inadequate for their subsistence. Now as common rights were whittled away, and spinning, along with other domestic industry,
declined, these women found themselves with no means of
support. Often they were forced upon the parish.

There was great reluctance among poor women to become
dependent on poor relief. Many chose to starve rather than
become so dependent. Some took to the road in the hope of
finding employment in London or other towns. Some became
permanent vagrants fleeing from the clutches of the overseers of the poor. A great number were reduced to begging
(see Section a). The depth of their degradation is seen in their
willingness to exploit young children in order to attract the
charity of the rich (2).

Those women who migrated to the towns were to find a
vast mass of urban poverty, with which after fruitless
attempts to get employment, they soon merged. Conditions
among urban paupers were horrifying. The newspaper
account of the women who lived and died in Stonecutter
Street (5) was a rare-enough incident to have been thought

newsworthy. Three dead women was remarkable. But many other women who died in poverty must have passed unnoticed. When the choice of entering the workhouse seemed preferable to maintaining their independence, it did not always follow that conditions were necessarily much better (**7**).

Particularly hard were the circumstances in which many widows were left (see Part 7**b**). Widows tend to predominate in the lists of those in receipt of poor relief (**11**), as well as those who were inmates of workhouses. Widows in the eighteenth century made up as much as 8 or 9 per cent of the whole population (see R. W. Malcolmson, *Life and Labour in England 1700–1780*, 1981, pp. 79–80). They were far less likely to remarry than widowers, particularly if they had dependent children. A combination of pride and determination kept many of them from relying on poor relief (**9, 11, 16**).

Towards the end of the century, to the decline of domestic industry and the diminishing opportunities for productive labour in agriculture, there was added the rise in the cost of living as a new factor in the lives of the female poor. For married women, the wages of their husbands may well have risen too but by no means sufficiently to meet the increase in prices. In such circumstances budgeting called for the utmost exertion and ingenuity of wives if they were to retain their independence of poor relief. Some were able to earn a little from spinning (where it survived) or by taking in washing (**14, 16**). The majority lived on the very margins of subsistence with nothing to fall back on if illness struck, nothing to spare for schooling and often confined to the house for much of the time by their lack of clothing (**15**).

There are constant criticisms of the female poor for their indolence, their inability to make their own clothes and their habit of drinking tea, a luxury it was felt, they could ill afford. With no opportunity for productive labour despondency and despair set in. Without the money to buy the materials for making their own clothes they were forced to buy from shops (on those rare occasions when new clothes were seen as essential). Tea drinking was the only comfort, and indeed, often the only liquid sustenance many women received (**3**).

To the difficulties of survival in such conditions was added the hardships imposed by the Settlement Laws. Under the Act of Settlement of 1662 parishes had the right to remove any person likely to become chargeable. A watchful eye was kept on those who came into this category. Poor families with a number of children held out a future threat to parish relief. Cottages were destroyed in order to prevent farm labourers from marrying, having large families and, it was thought, coming on the parish for relief. One consequence of the law was an increase in the number of illegitimate children born. Single women constituted a particular risk to parishes, especially if they became pregnant. The terrible consequences of parishes' efforts to avoid such women becoming chargeable are seen in Sections (e) and (f).

Women who had difficulty enough in feeding themselves could view such illegitimate children only as another mouth to feed. 'Dropping' of children was a frequent occurrence (**17, 19, 21**). The account of the opening of the Foundling Hospital in London suggests the conflict many women suffered between their desire to give their children some hope of survival and their equal desire not to part with them (**20**).

(a) Female Beggars

1

She says that she does not know very well how old she is, but appears to be between 13 and 14 years of age. That her father and mother were named Richard and Sarah Johnson, and that her father was a miller and lived in the parish of Wirksworth, in the county of Derby, in which parish the deponent was born, as she had often been told by her father and mother. That her father owing more money in and about Wirksworth than he was able to pay and afraid of being thrown into prison, some years ago (but how many deponent cannot tell) together with his wife and deponent, left the parish of Wirksworth and went from thence to the City of London where after they had been some time deponent's mother died, and the same summer the father also died. Ever since his death she had lived by begging, and some times had earned some small wages by keeping of sheep and cows in the fields belonging to the several parishes and counties through which she had wandered. (*Bedfordshire County Records*, ed. W. J. Hardy and W. Page, 1907, Vol. 1, p. 10)

2

. . . The female beggars generally hire infants from those who are poorer than themselves, to rouse, by that means, the charity of the passengers. They pay various prices for these children, from sixpence to two shillings a day, according as they are more or less deformed. A child that is very crooked and distorted generally earns three shillings, and sometimes even more. I happened once to overhear the conversation of two women who were talking concerning their profession. One of them informed the other that she paid two shillings for the child in her arm: 'What!' replies her companion, 'are you a fool? Two shillings for that charming baby! – I would not give more for a monster.' (J. W. von Archenholz, *A Picture of England*, 1791, p. 73)

(b) How the Poor Lived and Died

3

. . . even a common washerwoman thinks she has not had a proper breakfast without tea and hot buttered white bread . . . being the other day at a grocers, I could not forbear looking earnestly and with some degree of indignation at a ragged and greasy creature, who came into the shop with two children following her in as dismal a plight as the mother, asking for a pennyworth of tea and a halfpennyworth of sugar, which when she was served with, she told the shopkeeper: Mr. N. I do not know how it is with me, but I can assure you I would not desire to live, if I was to be debarred from drinking every day a little tea. (Charles Deering, *Nottinghamia Vetus et Nova*, 1751, p. 72)

4

We have an Account from Cumberland that Corn is so scarce that People actually die for Want of Bread, and that a poor Widow and two Children, after living some time on Grain and Bran were found dead one Morning; the Children had Straw in their Mouths . . .

We are informed that a poor Woman in Buckinghamshire, with nine Children, and big with a Tenth, was so far distressed as not to have had, for some Days, any kind of Sustenance, either for herself or Family. A Person accidentally giving her Six-pence, she bought a Calf's Pluck to make into Broth; but while she was gone out to get a few Sticks, the Children fastened on it, raw as it was, and ate it up every Bit, Gullet and all, before their Mother's Return . . . (*Ipswich Journal*, 16 April 1757, 28 May 1757)

5

[The following incident occurred in November 1763]
A Mr. Stephens, of Fleet-market, was commissioned to show
some empty houses in Stonecutter Street intended for sale, and
one day accompanied a gentleman to them, who had thoughts of
purchasing the estate on which they were situated. On entering a
room on the first floor, an object of horror attracted their
attention, a naked female corpse! Stephens, alarmed beyond
expression, fled from the scene; but the other more courageous
ascended to the next floor, where he was soon after joined by his
terrified attendant, and they discovered a second and third woman
dead, and nearly destitute of clothing; pursuing this dreadful
research, they found in the upper storey, two women, and a girl
about eighteen years of age, one of whom, and the latter,
appeared emaciated beyond description, but their companion in
misery was in better condition, . . . the survivors were taken into
custody, and the ensuing particulars were related by them before
the Coroner and his Jury.

It appeared on the inquisition, from the evidence of Elizabeth
Stanton, one of these women, that on the Wednesday preceding
the inquiry she came from Westminster, and being in want of
lodging, strolled to this house, and laid herself down on the
ground-floor, where she saw nobody; that about eleven that
evening the woman in good condition (Elizabeth Pattent) a
stranger to her, came into the room where she (Stanton) had laid
herself down, and by treading on her awakened her, at the same
time crying out 'Who is there?'. To which Stanton replied, 'No
person that will hurt you, for that she was going away in the
morning'. Pattent therefore advised her to go up to the garret with
her, which she did, and stayed there all that night, and the
following day and night, and until she was taken into custody in
the garret upon the above discovery.

Pattent, being out of place, attended the Fleet-market as a
basket-woman; where she became acquainted with the deceased
women, who were basket-women, and both known by no other
names than Bet. Pattent, being destitute of lodging was recommended to this ruinous house by the deceased women, who had
lived, or rather starved, there for some time. Pattent, in the
daytime, used to go to her late mistress's, who kept a cook-shop in
King-Street, Westminster, and worked for her victuals, and lodged
in this house at night, where she continued till she was taken into
custody. About the middle of the week preceding the inquisition,
the deceased women were taken ill; and on Saturday the 12th
instant, Pattent pawned her apron for sixpence, and bought some

beef and plumb-pudding at a Cook's-shop in Shoe-lane, and both the deceased women on Saturday and Sunday ate heartily thereof, and on Sunday night she heard the deceased women groan. One had the itch, and the other a fever; and being fearful of catching the one or the other, she did not go to them any more; nor did she know of their deaths till taken into custody.

Elizabeth Surman, the girl, was the daughter of a deceased jeweller in Bell-alley, Coleman Street; her parents died when she was about six years of age, and she was taken care of by Mrs. Jones a next door neighbour, with whom she lived about four years; Mrs. Jones then dying, Surman was left destitute; and on being informed she could get employment in Spitalfields, she went there, and assisted a woman winding quills, but she retiring into the country, Surman was again left destitute; however, she found employment in Spitalfields market, with Mrs. Bennett, in winding silk, but, not pleasing her, was discharged in a week. She then went to Mrs. Roach's in that market, who took in washing and nursed children, where Surman continued six years, and until she was taken ill, on which account she was discharged her service. She then went to the churchwarden of the parish where her father had been housekeeper many years, to desire relief; but he refused, without so much as expostulating with her about her legal settlement, or informing her she had gained a settlement by servitude. She being very ill and weak, lay all night at the churchwarden's door, but it had no effect on him; and this girl was obliged to lie about the streets until she was informed of this empty house, where she lay every night for near two months; the deceased women being there when she came, and both then lying on straw in the two pair of stairs room. For the first week of Surman's being there, she lay in the room with them on straw, all which week she was ill with ague, and had no sustenance whatever; that then Elizabeth Pattent relieved her; and as Surman grew better, she went abroad and received alms, returning at night, and delivering her money to Pattent, who bought her victuals. Surman was afterwards received into St. Andrew's workhouse, where she continued a week; and, about a fortnight ago, she returned to this empty house, and lodged in the garret; and being very ill, was assisted by Pattent, when she, with the two other women were found in the garret, and taken into custody, and never saw or heard, all that time, anything of the deceased women till she was apprehended.

. . . There were no marks of violence about the deceased women, but they appeared as if starved. (J. P. Malcolm, *Anecdotes of the Manners and Customs of London during the 18th century*, (1807), 1810, pp. 59–63)

6

On Monday evening a poor woman with a little boy in her hand, and another on her back, travelling from Salisbury to Blandford, and mistaking her way in the heaviness of the snow, as is supposed, perished with her two miserable infants, and was discovered by a shepherd's dog, covered with snow very early the next morning. She had three farthings in her pocket, a bit of bread and cheese, and a rusty thimble. (*Annual Register*, 19 January 1767)

7

[Of D—— in Hertfordshire]
It appeared upon the examination of witnesses examined on oath relative to the death of the four persons found dead in the Poor-house here, as mentioned in our paper of Saturday last, that no fire had been seen in the house for upwards of ten days previous to their being found dead. One of the witnesses said that about ten days ago she saw the poor woman, with a kettle, attempt to fetch some water from a puddle near her door, but that after filling it, she fell down, left the kettle, and crawled on all-fours again to her wretched habitation. (*Kentish Gazette*, 1 February 1769)

8

In my way from Royston to Baldock, passing a village I saw a couple of cottages which seemed very miserable. Alighted therefore and entered one. The woman said she was very unhappy. I enquired why? Her daughter was now dead in the house. How old? Thirty-eight. Married to a glazier in London. She had been down with her mother some time for health in a decline, and died two days ago. 'I hope she died a good Christian'. 'I hope so', replied the woman, who seemed to feel very little. And it is the blessing of God that they do not – they cannot afford to grieve like their betters . . . The husband was expected soon, and the woman has a son, a miller, who keeps her, a cow, and she had a good pig feeding at the door.

. . . the cottage almost tumbling down, the wind blowing through it on every side. On a bed, which was hardly good enough for a hog, was the woman very ill and moaning; she had been lately brought to bed, and her infant was dead in a cradle by the bedside . . . She had four children living; one, a little girl, was at home, and putting together a few embers on the hearth. (Arthur Young,

The Autobiography of Arthur Young, ed. M. Betham-Edwards, 1898, pp. 330–1, 331–2)

(c) Poor Widows

9

The widow of a timber-merchant, who had lived in affluence, finding herself, by the premature death of her husband, reduced to a very forlorn situation, took refuge in a small, though neat cottage, built upon the edge of a common, and supplied with a little flower garden, which was nicely cultivated in the days of her prosperity . . . At her husband's death she retired to it, as the only habitation she could call her own; the companion of her distress, was a daughter the widow of a sea lieutenant, with her child, a girl about eight years of age, and this daughter's pension of thirty pounds constituted their whole revenue. For some years they lived with an appearance of decency, though totally sequester'd from all communication, till the daughter died, and all the resources of her mother were cut off. She, nevertheless, appeared at Church with her grandchild in mourning, and the girl having now attained her thirteenth year afforded the promise of a very agreeable person . . . she rejected all advances that were made to her by her charitable neighbours; she was observed to pawn her household furniture, and her wearing apparel piecemeal; she no longer came to church and her granddaughter gradually put on the appearance of want and misery. During this last hard winter, no baker was ever seen at her door, no firing was carried into her lonely hut, and scarce any smoke issued from her chimney. The Overseers of the Poor were desired to visit and assist her; she met them on the threshold in wretched attire, declined their assistance, and told them they were set upon her by her enemies to affront her. At length the boards that formed a little fence to her yard, were torn down for fuel; the granddaughter became more meagre, and more naked, and her piteous moanings were often over-heard by passengers . . . I went to the cottage, accompanied by two honest tradesmen of my acquaintance, I knocked at the door, and after some delay, was admitted by such a melancholy spectre of misery as I could not behold without shedding tears. It was the wretched damsel, wrapped in an old, tattered blanket, exhibiting in her countenance the marks of famine, grief, horror, and despair; when I entered the place, nothing was to be seen but bare walls, except in one corner where the grandmother lay expiring upon straw . . . (*London Chronicle*, vol. 1, 1757, p. 403)

10

[Of Alf-Piddle parish, Dorset]
Mary Chilcott, a widow, with four children, the eldest nineteen years of age, the youngest six . . . She earns nothing, except in harvest. Fuel and 2s. 6d. a week allowed by the parish, with house-rent, but no garden, which is a hard circumstance. She has been used to the spinning of harn, (the refuse of flax) for which there is no call here, and she cannot spin worsted. To the flour also is added what barley she consumes. Clothes she cannot afford to buy; the children have had the father's, and the parish has promised further assistance in linen, so this charge must be set very low, say 15s. The boys' loss of work and sickness, at a medium three weeks, £1. 0s. 3d. Sum £1. 15s. 3d. (David Davies, *The Case of Labourers in Husbandry,* 1795, pp. 149–50)

11

Anne Hurst was born at Witley in Surrey; there she lived the whole period of a long life, and there she died. As soon as she was thought able to work, she went to service; there, before she was twenty, she married James Strudwick, who like her own father, was a day-labourer. With this husband she lived a prolific, hard-working, contented wife, somewhat more than fifty years. He worked more than three-score years on one farm; and his wages, summer and winter, were regularly a shilling a day. He never asked more; nor was ever offered less. They had between them seven children; and lived to see six daughters married, and three of them the mothers of sixteen children, all of whom were brought up, or are being brought up to be day-labourers. Strudwick continued to work till within seven weeks of the day of his death; and at the age of four-score, in 1787, he closed, in peace, a not inglorious life; for, to the day of his death, he never received a farthing in the way of parochial aid. His wife survived him about seven years, and though bent with age and infirmities, and little able to work, except as a weeder in a gentleman's garden, she also was too proud either to ask or receive any relief from her parish. For six or seven of the last years of her life, she received twenty shillings a year from the person who favoured me with this account, which he drew up from her own mouth. With all her virtue, and all her merit, she yet was not much liked in her neighbourhood; people in affluence thought her haughty; and the paupers of the parish, seeing, as they could not help seeing, that her life was a reproach to theirs, aggravated all her little failings. Yet, the worst thing they had to say of her was, that she was proud; which, they said, was manifested by the manner in which she buried her husband. Resolute, as she owned she was, to have the funeral, and everything that related to it, what she called decent, nothing could dissuade her from having handles to his coffin, and a plate on it, mentioning his age. She was also charged with having behaved herself crossly and peevishly towards one of her sons-in-law, who was a mason; and went regularly, every Saturday evening to the alehouse, as he said, just to drink a pot of beer. James Strudwick, in all his life, as she often told this ungracious son-in-law, never spent five shillings in any idleness; luckily (as she was sure to add) he had it not to spend. A more serious charge against her was, that, living to a great age, and but little able to work, she grew to be seriously afraid, that, at last, she might become chargeable to the parish, (the heaviest, in her estimation, of all human calamities), and that thus alarmed, she did suffer herself more than once, during the exacerbations of a fit of distempered despondency, peevishly, (and, perhaps, petulantly), to exclaim that God Almighty, by suffering her to remain so long upon earth, seemed actually to have forgotten her.

[Of the Warwick poor receiving poor relief]
The poor who are regular pensioners, are enumerated in the following list.
A. S. aged 50; a little insane, was formerly employed in needle-work; has been chargeable some years: the parish allows 4s. weekly; for her maintenance.
M. B. a widow, aged 45; has received parochial aid, about 10 years: her allowance is £2 a year, which added to her earnings by spinning, and working for farmers, is sufficient to maintain her, and her children.
M. B. a widow, aged 40 years, has been chargeable 5 years: she receives 3s. a week. Her husband was a weaver, but in consequence of bad health was obliged to apply for assistance from the parish, which since his death, has been continued to his widow, and children.
M. W. aged 60; a widow, with a small family; has received parochial aid for 20 years; her present allowance is £2 a year; her own endeavours were not sufficient for their support: her husband rented a small farm in the parish.

The following is an account of a widow and her family: she has eight children, viz. 5 boys, 18, 17, 13½, 12 and 2½ years old; and three girls, 16, 9 and 6½ years old. The eldest son only contributes 6d. a week towards the support of his mother's family; which sum he pays them for washing and mending his clothes: the remainder of his earnings he applies to his own maintenance: he is a bricklayer, and earns 1s. 8d. a day. The second son is settled at some distance from home. The third boy earns 3s. a week, when employed, but is not always certain of work: the fourth boy 2s. a week. The mother, and two eldest girls, by spinning, earn 4s. a week; but their receipts are by no means regular, as work of this kind cannot always be procured.

Weekly Receipts	s. d.	*Weekly Expenses*	s. d.
From the eldest son	0 6	Barley flour	8 3
Earnings of third and		Yeast 2d., salt 3d.	0 5
fourth son	5 0	Tea, 2 oz.	0 6
Earnings of mother		Butter, 2 lb.	1 8
and two daughters	4 0	Cheese	0 7½
Allowance from the		Soap and blue	0 4¼
parish	5 0	Candles	0 7
		Thread – Worsted	0 3
		Coals	1 0
		Garden stuff chiefly	
		Potatoes	0 9
	14 6		14 4¾

In this instance the receipt and expenses nearly balance each other: but during last summer, when the family did not bake barley bread at home, they expended 13s. or 14s. a week in bread. The late reduction in the price, may, perhaps, enable them to use wheat instead of barley: but if wheat was only 5s. the bushel, still their income would not provide them with shoes, shifts, shirts, and many other necessaries, which are not set down under the head of expenses, and which they could give no account of. Their rent, amounting to £2 a year, is paid by the parish. The mother is a decent, frugal, and industrious woman.

[Of the parish of St Peters, Derby]
The following is a list of the out-pensioners belonging to the parish:

	Age	Weekly Allowance
An unmarried woman; subject to fits;	58	1. 0
A widow, and three children	40	3. 0
A bricklayer's widow;	70	1. 0
A soldier's widow;	70	1. 0
A stocking-weaver, and his wife; both infirm, both about	66	1. 0
A stocking-weaver's widow, and 1 child;	40	1. 0
A widow;	75	1. 0
A stocking-weaver, and 2 children;	70	1. 0
A soldier's wife and 2 children;	—	1. 0
A joiner's wife, lame, with three children;	30	1. 0
A labourer's widow, with 2 children;	40	1. 0
An orphan, under 7 years of age;	—	1. 0
A blind man;	30	1. 0
A soldier's child;	—	1. 0
A stocking-weaver, and his wife;	70	1. 0
A silk-twiner's widow;	65	1. 0
A labourer's widow;	60	1. 0
2 lame children;	—	2. 0
A lame man, and his wife; each about	70	1. 0
An infirm woman;	25	1. 0
A widow, and 3 children;	50	1. 0
A blind woman;	—	1. 0
A butcher's widow; with 3 children;	45	2. 6
A labourer's widow; with 2 children;	22	3. 0
A seaman's wife, and one child;	23	1. 0
A labourer's widow; sick;	60	1. 0
A soldier's wife; and 4 children;	28	4. 0
A bricklayer's widow; and 3 children;	38	2. 0
A woman, deserted by her husband; with 1 child;—		1. 0
An innkeeper's widow;	74	1. 6
A shoemaker's widow;	80	1. 6
The family of a disorderly person who has absconded;	—	1. 6
Carried over –		£2. 4. 0

(F. M. Eden, *The State of the Poor,* 1797, Vol. 1, p. 579 fn.; Vol. 2, pp. 92–3; Vol. 3, p. 797; Vol. 2, p. 125)

(d) Making Ends Meet

12

I have not known anywhere in the country, that a husband, his wife and three children, have ask'd any relief from the parish, if the whole labour of such a family could procure twenty pounds per annum. So that four pounds per head is the common annual subsistence of working people in the country . . . ('The cost of living', *British Merchant,* 1713, Vol. 1, p. 237)

13

[How the rising cost of living affected town dwellers]
Sir, – I am the wife of a poor journeyman, whose wages are 19s. per week, which makes a great sound, and I am well satisfied is as much as his honest master can afford to give. We have five children my husband gives me every farthing of his wages, every Saturday night; he frequents no alehouse, nor scarce goes in one from year's end to another . . . We eat eight quartern loaves, and a quartern of flour, in a week, two pounds and a half of meat, at 4½d and 5d. per pound, comes near 7s. more, for small beer 1s. 3d. milk 8d. coals and candle 2s. soap, butter and cheese 1s. 9d. Greens 7d. which makes 19s. 4d. per week; so that what little I get myself is not sufficient to pay our unreasonable house-rent, and cloathe our children from the cold . . . (*Public Advertiser*, 24 June 1768)

14

[The father of Francis Place lost all his money on a state lottery in 1790]
There remained of the family my father my mother and my youngest sister, these were to be clothed fed and lodged and washed for. My brother who was still an apprentice, was also to be provided for in clothes and washing.

No human being can conceive, the distress of my poor mother, plunged as she and the rest of the family were all at once into what for a moment seemed irremediable poverty and misery. She had never been used to hard work of any kind, for not withstanding she was laborious and industrious to the greatest possible extent still she had not been used to the mere drudgery of household work to any considerable extent, but she was a woman who on important occasions could decide at once and act on her decision . . . Without saying a word to my father lest he should oppose some obstacle to her intention she went into the neighbourhood she had left, told her tale to some of the housekeepers, and showed the necessity there was for her doing something by which to procure the means of maintaining her family, and requested them to give her their clothes to wash which they did not usually wash at home, they all instantly complied with her request and regretting her condition gave her their clothes to wash and thus when nearly sixty years of age she became a washer-woman.

1791 my net weekly earnings did not exceed fourteen shillings. My wife used to go, two and sometimes three days in the week to help my mother to wash and iron, this she did without direct pay, my mother was indeed too poor to be able to pay her, . . . But we . . . would take nothing from her, but my wife's board, and an occasional present of small value, which we could not refuse. What we really received could not exceed three shillings a week in value, and this made our income seventeen shillings a week. From this we had to pay, for lodging three shillings and sixpence a week, and on an average one shilling and sixpence a week for coals and candles, thus we had only twelve shillings a week for food and clothes and other necessaries. (*The Autobiography of Francis Place (1771–1854)*, ed. Mary Thale, 1972, pp. 98, 105–6)

15

[In the parish of Barkham, Berks., Easter 1787]
Weekly expenses of a family consisting of a Woman, whose husband is run away, and six children, the eldest 16 years of age, the youngest 5: four of the children are too young to earn anything.

	s.	d.
Flour for bread, 6 gallons, at 10d. per gallon	5	0
Ditto ½ gallon for puddings, and thickening the children's messes	0	5
Yeast for the bread, 2d; – salt 1½d.	0	3½
Bacon, 2 lbs at 8d. (with sometimes a sheep's head)	1	4
Tea, 1½ ounce, 4d.; – sugar, ½lb. 4d.; – butter, ½lb. 4d	1	0
Soap, something more than ¼ lb. at 9d. per lb.	0	2½
Candles ⅓ lb. one week with another, at 9d. per lb.	0	3
Thread, worsted, etc.	0	3
Total	8	9

Weekly Earnings of this family, with the Parish
Allowance

This family receives from the parish weekly	5	0
The eldest boy earns per week	2	6
The next, aged 13 years, earns, but not constantly	1	6
The mother, whilst an old woman looks after the younger children, earns, one week with another, about	1	6
The amount, supposing none of them to lose any time is	10	6

But some deduction must be made from this sum, because they are
an unhealthy family, one or other of them being often laid up with
the ague or rheumatism; disorders to which poor people, from low
living and working in the wet, are very subject. The woman
assures me that their earnings with the parish allowance do not
exceed 9s. per week on an average; therefore deduct

	1	6
Total of earnings, with the parish allowance	9	0
Surplus of Earnings	0	3

[Of Berks.]
Clothing . . . The wife's: wear of gown and petticoat 4s.; one shift
3s. 6d.; one pair of strong shoes 4s.; one pair of stockings 1s. 6d.;
two aprons 3s.; handkerchiefs, caps, etc. 4s. Sum £1 – The
children's: their clothing is (usually) partly made up of the parents'
old clothes, partly bought at second-hand: what is bought (supposing three children to a family) cannot well be reckoned at less than
£1:
(Note. Very few poor people can afford to lay out this sum in
clothes; but they should be enabled to do it: some cottagers breed
a few fowls, with which they buy what sheets and blankets they
want: but those who live in old farmhouses are seldom allowed (to
use their own words) to keep a pig or a chick)

. . . it is but little that in the present state of things the belly can
spare for the back. Even such persons as may have been provident
enough when single, to supply themselves with a small stock of
clothes, are after marriage, from inability to buy more, soon
reduced to ragged garments. And then the women spend as much
time in tacking their tatters together, as would serve for manufacturing new clothing, had they the skill to do it, and materials to do

it with. One bad consequence of this meanness of dress is, that many of the poor are ashamed to appear among decent people at our churches; they either neglect the duty of public worship altogether, or they assemble at places where they are sure of meeting with people as ill-clothed as themselves. (David Davies, *The Case of Labourers in Husbandry,* 1795, pp. 9, 15–16, 28)

16

[Of High Walton, in the parish of Runcorn, Cheshire]
The poor have a weekly allowance at home . . . The following are the weekly poor;

	Weekly Allowance	
	s.	d.
A labourer's widow; aged 55;	2	0
A labourer's widow; aged 45;	2	6
A family deserted by their father;	2	0
A poor woman;	0	6
	7	0

5 house-rents are paid; and several persons have occasional relief.

The following is a statement of the earnings and expenses of a woman aged sixty-one, and is an instance of Cumberland economy among many others that might be pointed out

	£.	s.	d.
She spins wool for her neighbours about 15 weeks a year, and earns 4d. a day and victuals	1	10	0
The remaining 37 weeks she spins lint at home for a manufacturer, and earns 13½d. a week	2	1	7½
Total Earnings	3	11	7½
Interest of £10	0	10	0
Total Income	4	1	7½

Expenses	£.	s.	d.
House rent, 10s.; fuel (peat and turf) 7s.	0	17	0
Barley, 2½ bushels at 5s.	0	12	6
Oatmeal, 6 stone at 2s. 4d.	0	14	0
Butter, 8 lbs. at 8d., 5s. 4d.; milk, 220 qts., 5s. 6½d.	0	10	10½

She gets 3 pecks of potatoes planted for her; her turf

ashes produce about 9 bushels, balance of expense about	0	2	0
Tea not used; sugar and treacle	0	4	0
Clogs (one pair in two years), 1s. 6d.; shoes (one pair in seven years), 6d.	0	2	0
Butchers' meat 1s. 6d.; wheaten bread, 1s.	0	2	6
Shifts, 2s. 9d.; other clothes, etc., 10s.	0	12	9
Total Expenses	4	1	7½

This woman's earnings are small; but she makes her expenses correspond. She seems perfectly happy, content and cheerful, and always takes care to avoid debt. Her father rented a small farm of only £8 a year, and as he was very lame she was obliged to do the greatest part of the work. On his death she disposed of the stock, etc., and after discharging all his debts and funeral expenses, a surplus of £10 remained, which she placed in the hands of her land-lord; the interest of which pays her rent. When she was able to reap in harvest she earned a little more money, yet, not withstanding her present scanty income, she has no thought of applying to the parish: She receives no assistance whatever from her friends. Her common diet is hasty pudding, milk, butter and potatoes. She was brought up in a most frugal manner, and feels no inconvenience from being obliged to live so abstemiously. She never had a teapot in her house at any period of her life.

[Of Cumberland]
In the article of clothing, great economy is used in this part of the world: the parents often make the few they possessed when they were married, (clogs, shirts, shifts, etc., excepted) last them till their children are able to earn their own maintenance, and in summer the children go without many articles of dress. In such a family . . . it requires the most rigid parsimony, to spare anything towards putting a child to school.

There are two sisters, (Spinsters,) who live upon 3s. 6d. a week: 1s. 6d. of which is allowed by the Parish to one, that is confined to her bed the greatest part of the year: the other sister, (although in good health,) being obliged to devote much of her time to her sister, cannot earn more than 2s. a week, by spinning. From the whole of their receipts, 6d. a week is paid for lodging. (F. M. Eden, *State of the Poor*, 1797, Vol. 2, pp. 40, 75–6, 107; Vol. 3, pp. 798–9)

(e) **Unwanted children**

17

Whereas a child near a year old, tho' not much bigger than a child of a month old, having all his fore teeth, and a sore head, was left near the Tower on Sunday morning last: Whoever can discover who left the said child, shall have the reward of 40s. to be paid by Mr. Johnson, Overseer of the Poor on Tower-Hill. (*Daily Courant,* 12 February 1714)

18

. . . not a session passes but we see one or more merciless mothers tried for the murder of their bastard children; . . .

Those who cannot be so hardhearted to murder their own offspring themselves, take a slower, though as sure, a way, and get it done by others, by dropping their children, and leaving them to be starved by parish nurses. (Daniel Defoe, *Augusta Triumphans,* (1728), 1840–1, p. 7)

19

On Monday night last, a male child about three or four days old, was dropped at a nobleman's door in Grosvenor Square, with an inscription on a paper pinned to his breast; the infant was sent to the workhouse of St. George's Hanover Square.

And on Thursday night another male child about a month old in a basket was laid at a clergyman's door near St. James; the infant was neatly dressed, bearing a direction for the clergyman. It was sent to St. James's Workhouse. (*Daily Post-Boy,* no. 7958, 3 October 1735)

20

At eight o'clock the lights in the entry were extinguished, the outward door was opened by the porter, who was forced to attend at that door all night to keep out the crowd. Immediately the bell rung and a woman brought in a child the messenger led her into the room on the right hand, and carried the child into the stewards room where the proper officers together with Dr. Nesbitt and some other Govrs were constantly attending to inspect the child . . . The child being inspected was received number'd, and the billet of its description enter'd by three different persons for greater certainty. The woman who brought the child was then dismissed . . . Immediately another child was brought and so continually till 30 children were admitted.

About twelve o'clock, the house being full the porter was order'd to give notice of it to the crowd who were without . . . And the Govrs. observing seven or eight women with children at the door and more amongst the crowd desired them that they would not drop any of their children in the streets where they most probably must perish but to take care of them till they could have an opportunity of putting them into the hospital; . . .

On this occasion the expressions of grief of the women whose children could not be admitted were scarcely more observable than those of some of the women who parted with their children. ('Minutes of the Meeting of Incorporation of the Foundling Hospital, 25 March 1740,' quoted from R. Paulson, *Hogarth: His Life, Art and Times,* 1971, Vol. 2, p. 39)

21

At Hicks-hall a woman was convicted of dropping a child in St. George's parish, Hanover Square, and sentenced to a month's hard labour in Bridewell. Since Christmas last 12 children have been dropt in that parish, and there are but 20 orphans in the foundling hospital. (*Gentleman's Magazine*, 7 July 1743)

22

London, May 28th. Yesterday a female child, about a week old, tied up in a brown silk handkerchief, was taken out of the Thames near Chelsea. (*Jackson's Oxford Journal,* 29 May 1756)

(f) The Settlement Laws

23

1722. To a big bellyd woman several days & nights at nursing at Robinsons, & conveying her to Chigivell after she had gathered strength to prevent her lying in here, she fell to pieces in 2 or 3 days there . . . 17.7d.

1723 for removing of foure big bellyd women out of ye parish when like to be chargeable . . . 16.00d.; 1724 Gave her to go off with her great belly . . . 16.00d;

1731 for maintaining a poor woman found in the forest in labour
who afterwards died . . . 2–0–0 . . . 1733 To cost for nursing ye
woman delivered at the stocks . . . 2–0–0. (J. Kennedy, *History of
Leyton,* 1894, pp. 148, 152, 159)

24

On Saturday morning early a poor woman who had been shifted
from parish to parish, for fear of a charge, was brought to bed at a
door in Pater-noster Row, without any assistance.

Bristol, Sept. 5. This week one White, his wife, and a child about
four years old, were sent away from Salisbury by a Pass, to a parish
in this city. The poor woman was far advanc'd in her pregnancy,
and was so very ill as to be obliged to be carried on a man's back to
the cart, in which they were to be pass'd. Her illness on the road
increasing, the husband intreated the drivers to make a small stop,
in order to procure some relief: But the harden'd miserable men
disregarding their cries and intreaties, drove on more hastily than
before, 'till at length she miscarry'd on the cart: And tho' the
husband held up the child to a farmer passing by, thinking thereby
to draw him to their assistance, yet all would not melt the stony
hearts of the drivers so that the poor creature expir'd between
Fordhill and Marchfield in the cart: and was brought in this
condition to the Bridewell without Lawford's Gate, and the body
lying exposed for a considerable time in the cart, waiting for the
Coroner's Jury. – One of the carmen is fled, but the other is taken.
– Tho' these villains are out of reach of that justice they so richly
deserve, it being impossible to convict them of murder, yet let it
serve as a warning to those in authority, that they show tenderness
and compassion to their fellow creatures in distress, and avoid the
appellation of brute beasts. (*Northampton Mercury,* 5 June 1738, ⸙
14 September 1741)

25

[28 June 1750]
On Sunday morning last a poor woman (who had been harrassed
the evening before, and refused relief by the parish-officers, at a
town east of London, and not many miles from the sea) was found
dead in a gravel-pit in the neighbourhood, together with an infant,
of which 'tis supposed she was there delivered. (*Salisbury and
Winchester Journal,* 2 July 1750)

26

On Tuesday last began the General Quarter Sessions for this county, at which a remarkable case came before the bench, upon an appeal to an order for removing Elizabeth the widow of Edward Haynes, and her six children from the parish of Cowley in this country, to the place of her settlement when a single woman; upon a presumption that the children were illegitimate, and her marriage illegal. – Upon examination of evidence it appeared, that previous to the late Act for preventing clandestine marriages this wedding had been solemnised in a church by a layman, and the parties had cohabited for sixteen years as man and wife, in the parish of Cowley, the place of settlement of the deceased: When after many learned arguments by the council retained on each side, the determination was adjourned to next sessions, the bench being equally divided in their opinions. (*Jackson's Oxford Journal*, 13 January 1770)

27

134 Ann How, wife of Michael How who hath lately run away and left her. 27 Mar. 1786.

About twenty years ago she was married at Stone, Bucks., to her husband Michael How, who was and is as she believes (and as he informed her since their marriage) a legal inhabitant of Woburn, Beds., by being a yearly servant there, but with whom she doth not know. The place of her last legal settlement before such marriage was in Wadstone, Bucks., by living a full year as a servant with Mr. Jo. Woodman a farmer there. She hath 3 children by her said husband, namely Eliz. aged 15 years, Ann 13 years and Michael upwards of 2 years. [Mark]

Ordered to endeavour to find her husband as she cannot be removed to her maiden settlement while he is living, and it is doubtful whether she was married.

207 Eliz. wife of Ja. Chilman. 22 Dec. 1798.

19 years ago Ja. Chilman hired himself as a servant to the Earl of Donegal in East Acton, Middx. at wages of £12. 12s. and served him 11 mths and was then discharged for deafness but duly received his year's wages. 13 years ago she was married at Banstead and has 3 children, Abigail 12 years, Ja., 2 yrs 3 mths, Mary 7 weeks. He has deserted her.

[sig.] [Copy]

Removal order for wife and 3 children, 22 Dec. 1798. (*Mitcham Settlement Examinations, 1784–1814,* ed. Blanche Berryman, 1973, Surrey Record Society, Vol. 27, pp. 36, 84)

Part 10 Women and Agriculture

> Women, by the day, earn, sometimes 6d., but
> mostly 4d., for weeding corn, hoeing turnips, etc., in
> harvest 10d., in hay-making, 6d. (F. M. Eden, *State
> of the Poor*, 1797, Vol. 2, p. 73)

Introduction

In the course of the eighteenth century, changes occurred
which were to influence women's productive work in agriculture. Whether the wives of large or small farmers, female
servants in husbandry or the wives of agricultural labourers,
women's work tended to diminish.

Of course, these agricultural changes – the growth of
bigger farms, greater agricultural specialisation, more capita-
listic organisation of farming and marketing of farm products,
the speeding up of the process of enclosure and the consequent erosion of common rights – all occurred at very
different times and rates in different regions of the country.

The role of many women in agriculture at the beginning of
the century approximated to one of a working partnership
with their husbands. That it was not an equal partnership is
clear, but wives of farmers, smallholders, and even of cottagers, were able to contribute something towards the family
income. Such work as they did was not wage-earning, but in a
variety of ways it enabled women to contribute to the subsistence of the family – and often towards the rent of the farm,
smallholding, or cottage. What exactly that function was
varied according to the size of the farm, holding, or garden.

The work of farmers' wives could involve the supervision
and training of a body of living-in farm servants. The number
involved varied with the size of the farm, but as many as
twenty or more might well be employed. The particular
spheres of the farm work for which the wife was normally
responsible were the dairy (**2, 5**), all cheese- (**4**) and butter-
making, the care of the poultry and pigs (**1**), the kitchen
garden and orchard, and the marketing of the products
involved in these spheres (**13**), the general supervision of the
household, often spinning and the making of the family

clothes, as well as brewing and baking. Very often the job of the accounts was also her responsibility. How far the work involved was actual manual work, and how far supervisory, depended on the size and prosperity of the farm. The smaller the farm, the more essential was the labour of the farmer's wife and daughters to run it.

The withdrawal of such women from agricultural labour was both voluntary and enforced. The work involved was demanding, and when circumstances made it less necessary, many must have been only too glad to relinquish the duties involved. At least this must have been true of some of the more prosperous farmers' wives. It is difficult to decide which was more important as a motive for the withdrawal of labour, notions of gentility, or the changing organisation of farming and marketing of farm produce. Both factors may well have operated together. The consequence for the wives and daughters of farmers was lamented by many contemporary writers (see Section **b**), particularly the decline of home baking and brewing, and the spinning of yarn for the making of the family's clothing. Indicative of the role such women were seen as playing – at least by their husbands – was the whole notion of 'pin money' (**1**). Was it so very dissimilar from the modern housewife who economises on the house-keeping money in order to have a little financial independence from her husband? Yet perhaps this is to underestimate its importance, for many wives contributed a large portion of the farm's rent by their efforts. It also provided her with the satisfaction of knowing that she was making a contribution to the family income.

As smallholders were squeezed out by the process of enclosure and higher rents, their wives became indistinguishable from the wives of farm labourers dependent on wage labour. Yet earlier in the century such wives and, indeed, even the wives of mere cottagers, had been enabled to contribute something to the subsistence of the household (**22**). Now many cottages were shorn of their garden plots and, with the erosion of common rights, such wives were reduced to being housewives and, when the opportunity presented, engaging in seasonal wage-labour.

One other consequence of the changes in farming was the decline in the number of living-in servants on farms. The role of female servants in husbandry was not clearly defined. Often they ended up as maids of all work. If their main work was out of doors, at least in the early part of the century when their work was barely distinguishable from that of male servants, they were also expected to undertake household work and to spend their 'idle hours' in spinning (**10**). We know little about their lives on farms (but see, Ann Kussmaul, *Servants in Husbandry in Early Modern England*, 1981). All were agreed on the tough qualities demanded of such women (**11, 12**). In the south-west, where the practice persisted longest, pauper children were apprenticed to farmers in order to train them as servants in husbandry. Charles Vancouver describes the work expected of girls of 10 and 12 years of age (**15**). Some saw the work as physically harmful to women – a conclusion confirmed by the 1843 Commission Report on the Employment of Women and Children in Agriculture.

The need for living-in servants grew less as farming methods changed – and specialisation was extended. Hiring labour annually or, and more often, by the month or year, was cheaper and less demanding of the farmer's wife. So specialisation contributed to the shrinking of the agricultural work traditionally done by women. In the east and much of the south of the country, the tendency to concentrate on corn production meant less work for women in dairying and hay-making. So women's wages in such areas declined relatively to men's. With such a trend went the decline of much cottage industry. Whether or not such a decline was fully compensated for by domestic industries such as lace-making and straw work, seems doubtful (see K. D. M. Snell, 'Agricultural seasonal unemployment, the standard of living, and women's work in the south and east, 1690–1860', *Economic History Review*, 2nd ser., vol. 34, August 1981). The work in agriculture that remained for women to do is illustrated in Section **d**; the sowing of beans and peas, the setting of wheat and potatoes, picking stones from the fields, hop-picking, weeding and hoeing, the picking of fruit and the gathering of vegetables. A far wider range of agricultural activity still existed in the west and north. In Northumberland, at the end of the century, women were still engaged in reaping and winnowing wheat (**26**). In the west the traditional role of women in dairying continued.

Female migrant workers (see Section **f**) were perhaps a symptom of the declining work for women available in many parts of the country and where no other source of employment presented itself. As London grew, its demand for food led to a mushrooming of market-gardens in many of the surrounding villages in Kent and Middlesex, and in the outlying suburbs of London itself. Seasonal labour from

Wales and the Welsh borders, from Shropshire and the Midlands, and even as far afield as Ireland, was attracted to the work it offered. Most of this labour was female. It was not only the picking and gathering of fruit and vegetables that was done by women, but much of the carrying of heavy loads of such produce into Covent Garden or for sale in London shops (**35, 36**). Such carrying often involved women in travelling considerable distances on foot and with heavy loads on their backs. All this was done for a net wage of about 5s per day at very best. Much of the hay-making and harvesting around London was also done by such labour, as well as the picking of hops (**33, 34**). Annual wages for female servants in husbandry and those of milkmaids averaged about £3 to £6, the day-rate for women's work in agriculture varied between 3d and 1s, according to the job. The best-paid work was harvesting. In general a woman's earnings averaged about half of what a man would earn doing the same job (see Section **g**).

One other kind of women's work in agriculture deserves mention – that of 'leasing' or gleaning (see Section **e**). This customary right of the poor – and more particularly of the female poor – to glean after the harvest was over had a long history. It was accepted practice for farmers to avoid too close reaping, at the edges and corners of fields, for example, in order to leave sufficient corn to make gleaning worthwhile. The gradual questioning of this custom in the course of the century deserves closer study. Blackstone makes it clear in 1753 that 'by the common law and customs of England' such gleaning did not constitute trespass (**29**). Yet, by the end of the century, it was possible by a threat of legal proceedings to stop Margaret Abree and her family from any further gleaning (**31**).

Despite Marshall's comments (**30**), it is clear that gleaning was widely practised throughout the century (**28, 32**), and that it was a customary right of vital importance to the poor. It also enabled women to make a contribution to the subsistence of their families. Only towards the end of the century was there an increasing questioning and withdrawal of this right.

(a) Farmers' Wives: their Contribution to the Family Income

1

Poultry and their eggs come more immediately under the care and management of our country housewife, than any other outward part of the farmer's business; and accordingly many farmers think it their interest to let their wives have all the profit of their eggs and poultry, for raising money to buy what we call common or trivial necessaries in the house, as sugar, plumbs, spices, salt, oatmeal, etc., etc. . . . (William Ellis, *The Country Housewife's Family Companion*, 1750, p. 152)

2

I shall insert here the method of conducting a dairy, pursued by a farmer's wife in this neighbourhood, who for thirty years was reckoned an excellent manager . . .
. . . Begin to milk in summer at half an hour after four o'clock in the morning.
Begin in the afternoon before six.
The dairy maid should always be up in the morning between three and four o'clock.
For twenty-two cows, Mrs. How (who gave this intelligence) was in her dairy regularly with her maid from between three and four o'clock in the morning, and had not finished till twelve at noon, sometimes with two maids. (Arthur Young, *A Six Weeks' Tour through the Southern Counties of England and Wales*, 1772, pp. 57–8)

3

With respect to veal, pork, lamb, and sometimes mutton, a singular practice prevails in Norfolk; most especially at the Norwich market, which is supplied with the above articles entirely by the farmers; who for fifteen or twenty miles round, are most of them capable of dressing a calf, a lamb, or a sheep; which, with poultry made ready for the spit are carried weekly by themselves, their wives, their daughters, or other servants, to Norwich market; which, whether for plenty or neatness, is I believe, beyond all comparison, the first in the kingdom.
. . . Whether viewing the neatness of the market-women themselves, the delicacy of their wares, or the cleverness which, through habit, many of them are mistresses of in the disposal of

them, the Saturday's market of Norwich exhibits a very agreeable sight.

Poultry of every species are sold, in the market, ready picked and skewered fit for the spit; and are, in general, so well-fatted, and dressed up in such neatness and delicacy, as show the Norfolk housewives to be mistresses in the art of managing poultry. (William Marshall, *The Rural Economy of Norfolk*, 1787, Vol. 1. pp. 195–6, 375)

4

The management or immediate superintendence of a large dairy, especially one of which cheese is the principal object, is not a light concern. It requires much thought, and much labour. The whole of the former, and much of the latter, necessarily falls on the immediate superintendent, who, though she may have her assistants, sees, or ought to see, herself, to every stage of the business; and performs, or ought to perform, the more difficult operations.

This arduous department is generally undertaken by the mistress of the dairy; especially on middlesized and small farms. In some cases, an experienced dairy maid is the ostensible manager . . .

With respect to cleanliness, the Gloucestershire dairywomen stand unimpeachable . . .

Cleanliness implies industry. A Gloucestershire dairywoman is at hard work, from four o'clock in the morning until bed time.

One general remark, respecting the dairywomen of the district. It is customary, even in the larger dairies for the ostensible manager whether mistress or maid, to perform the whole operation of making cheese; except the last breaking, etc., and the vatting; in which she has an assistant. But this, in a dairy of eighty or ninety cows, is too great a labour for any woman: it is painful to see it. (William Marshall, *The Rural Economy of Gloucestershire*, 1796, Vol. 1, pp. 263–5; Vol. 2, p. 156, fn.)

5

On the management of Suffolk dairies, Mrs. Chevalier of Aspal, thus communicates: – In the year 1784 I made from five cows to the amount of £42, besides the milk and cream consumed by a family fourteen in number nor was that a more productive year than common; for I have done it more than once; and I am informed that £7 per cow is very common in this country, large dairies, through, on an average. (Arthur Young, *A General View of the Agriculture of the County of Suffolk*, 1797, p. 186)

(b) Their Declining Role

6

[A Devon farmer on how times had changed]
Formerly, . . . we were all happy and healthy, and our affairs prospered, because we never thought about the conveniences of life: now, I hear of nothing else. Our neighbour, for I will not mention names, brings his son up to go a shooting with gentlemen; another sends his to market upon a blood horse, with a plated bridle; and then the girls, the girls! – There is fine work, indeed; they must have their hats and feathers, and riding-habits; their heads as big as bushels, and even their hind-quarters stuck out with cork or pasteboard; but scarcely one of them can milk a cow, or churn, or bake, or do any one thing that is necessary in a family . . .

. . . my wife was bred up under a notable mother, and, though she must have her tea every afternoon, is, in the main, a very good sort of woman. She has brought her daughters up a little better than usual; but I can assure you she and I have had many a good argument upon the subject. Not but she approves their milking, spinning, and making themselves useful; but she would fain have them genteel, Master Merton: all women now are mad about gentility; and, when once gentility begins, there is an end of industry. (Thomas Day, *Sandford and Merton*, 1786, pp. 301–3)

7

[On the small farmers under the open-field system as compared with the larger, richer farmer after enclosure]
. . . The lands in their former state were let to five times the number of tenants, and at about half their present rent, which rent was to be raised by dint of industry, as they were not opulent, and were obliged to make money of everything they could sell; therefore the markets were fully stocked; and to supply the markets, the farmers' wives used all their industry and care to raise all manner of poultry and eggs and to make the best of their dairies, out of which they used to supply the house with all manner of goods from the shops, and the remainder used to sink into their own pockets as a kind of pin-money, to buy themselves and children such necessary little articles as they required, without

applying to their husbands for every trifling penny they might want to lay out . . .

On the other hand, the farmers are reduced to one fourth of their number, and they, very opulent, generally having enough to support themselves and families without any kind of business; . . . As to dress, no one that is not personally acquainted with the opulent farmer's daughter can distinguish her from the daughter of a Duke by her dress, both equally wishing to imitate something, they know not what. View the farmer before the land was enclosed . . . in a coat of the growth of his flock, and spun by his industrious wife and daughters, and his stockings produced from the same quarter of his industry, and his wife and daughters clad from their own hands of industry, and the growth of their own flock their best attire – their outward covering being a neat camblet, faced with a small quantity of silk in colour according to the choice of the wearer. (Anon., *Cursory Remarks on Enclosures . . . by a Country Farmer*, 1786, pp. 19–22)

8

We have no longer our markets filled with Pork, Pigs, Geese, Poultry, and Butter as formerly, for little of these articles is produced by large farmers, other than for the use of their own families; and a farmer, now become a gentleman, by swallowing up the farms of his neighbours, would be much effronted to have it even supposed that he would concern himself about such small matters, and the fine lady, his wife would faint at the idea of attending at market, like her mother or grandmother, with a basket of butter, pork, roasting pigs, or poultry, on her arm. Hence all our butter and cheese comes from grass farms only, through the medium of the monopolisers; and a scanty supply of pork, pigs, and poultry, is produced by a new set of persons unknown to our ancestors, who raise and feed them with corn purchased from the rich farmers. (J. S. Girdler, *Observations on the Pernicious Consequences of Forestalling, Regrating and Engrossing*, 1800, p. 9)

9

By the appellation of farmer, was formerly understood a plain, industrious, frugal, honest man, who either cultivated a farm of his own or rented one of a gentleman . . . Whether these good old-fashioned yeomen occupied a considerable or an inconsiderable quantity of land, they vested all their capital in farming stock, and they and their families dedicated the greater part of their thoughts and time to farming business. These worthy people *pitched* in the markets corn, cattle, pigs, bacon, butter, cheese, poultry and eggs; and after they had disposed of their commodities at *fair* prices returned home with satisfied minds to their afternoon employments . . . Their houses were nurseries and schools for industrious husbandman, notable housewives, good servants, and quiet subjects.

Now . . . these farmers' daughters . . . instead of dishing butter, feeding poultry, or curing bacon, the avocations of these young *ladies* at home are, studying dress, attitudes, novels, French, and music, whilst the fine ladies their mothers sit lounging in parlours adorned with the fiddle-faddle fancy-works of their fashionable daughters . . . We see not now the farmers' wives and daughters jogging to the towns in little carts for the purpose of selling the productions of their cartons and dairies; but we see them rattling in their spruce gigs to the milliners and perfumers, in order to lavish in fripperies part of the enormous gains extorted by their fathers and husbands from the groaning public. (*Gentleman's Magazine*, 1801, pp. 587–9)

(c) Female Living-In Farm Servants

10

Judith Carpenter . . . lived in the house of the said William Carpenter [in 1723] and used to do all manner of work as a servant, as in all the time of harvest she used to go every day with the tithe cart into the fields, and to rake after the cart, and at other times used to do all the commercial business of the house, as looking after the dairy, dressing the fowls for market, and if the business of the house was over she used to spin . . . (Norfolk Record Office, DEP/60)

11

She may be known by her red plump arms and hands, and clumsy fingers; for in most great dairies they are forced to milk their cows abroad, great part of the year; I may say, almost all the year, even in frosts and snows, while their fingers are ready to freeze in the action; and sometimes they stand in dirt and water . . . And indeed it may be justly said of these, that their work is never done; for where twenty or thirty cows are kept, they must begin about four o'clock in the summer time to milk, and at the same hour next morning; and between these times they have enough to do, to scald and scour their utensils, and make butter and cheese; and thus are constantly employed throughout the year. A good dairy-maid is a very valuable servant; I mean, one that readily rises betimes; is diligent and skilful in making the best butter and cheese; is cleanly in the performance of it, making the most of her milk, and doing all in her power to promote her master's interest . . .

. . . if we about Gaddesden want maid servants, several of our farmers go to Aylesbury Statute, because in Aylesbury Vale, there are great dairies carried on, that employ considerable numbers of these useful females, who, if rightly chosen, commonly prove more hardy, more strong, and more diligent than our country wenches, that are brought up more tenderly, and more unskilful in the business of husbandry . . .

[Of Oxfordshire]
About twenty or thirty years ago, women in some parts of this country, as well as in many more, would exert their strength and skill in husbandry affairs, more than they do now; for then they would reap corn, fill dung carts, drive a team, and now and then, for making haste, would mount a horse and ride away with the same to mill or otherwise. (William Ellis, *The Modern Husbandman*, 8 vols (1750), Vol. 5, p. 92; William Ellis, *The Modern Husbandman*, 1744, Vol. 1, October 1743, p. 140; December 1743, p. 77)

12

It is painful to one . . . to behold the beautiful servant maids of this county toiling in the severe labours of the field. They drive the harrows, or the ploughs, when they are drawn by three or four horses; nay, it is not uncommon to see, sweating at the dung-cart, a girl, whose elegant features, and delicate, nicely-proportioned limbs, seemingly but ill accord with such rough employment. (A. Pringle, *General View of the County of Westmorland*, 1794, p. 265)

13

On the dairy farms one woman servant is generally kept to every ten cows, who is employed in winter in spinning and other household business, but in milking is assisted by all the other servants of the farm. (J. Aikin, *A Description of the Country from Thirty to Forty Miles round Manchester,* 1795, p. 47)

14

[Of Cumberland]
The wages of men-servants in husbandry who are hired from half-year, are from 9 to 12 guineas a year; whilst women, who here do a large portion of the work of the farm, with difficulty get half as much. It is not easy to account for so striking an inequality; and still less easy to justify it. (F. M. Eden, *The State of the Poor,* 1797, Vol. 2, p. 47.)

15

[Of parish apprentices sent out as female servants in husbandry]
The manner . . . in which the females are sometimes treated, requires that some further regulations should be made to soften the severity of their servitude. Scraping the roads, lanes and yards, turning over mixings and filling dung-pots, is at best but a waste of time, and a feeble effort of infantile strength. What can a female child at the age of ten or twelve years be expected to perform with a mattock or shovel? or how will she be able to poise, at the end of a dung-fork, any reasonable weight, so as to lift it into the dung-pots slung upon the horses' backs, for hacking out the manure to the distant parts of the farm? Even driving the horses after they are loaded is by no means an employment proper for such girls, being altogether incompatible with the household and more domestic duties they ought early to be made acquainted with. (Charles Vancouver, *General View of the Agriculture of the County of Devon,* 1808, p. 360)

(d) Wives of Farm Labourers

16

A . . . way to improve a crop of horse-beans in the Chiltern country, as I have seen it performed between Watford and Hempstead, is: They set them in a gravelly, loamy, inclosed field, that was plowed hollow, by the short dibber, made with the upper part of the handle of a shovel or spade, cut off within five or six inches of the hollow handle into a small round point, which is shod with iron about three inches in length; this women jab into the ground, and then immediately drop into the hole a horse-bean, and so they proceed in a very quick manner, making the holes by a line, perhaps fifteen or twenty yards long: and, when one row is finished, the line is moved at a foot or eighteen inches distance, and so they move on throughout a field, till the whole is completed. Thus, the women work, for ninepence setting every peck of horse-bean seed, which they carry in an apron before them, and with great agility take out and set by this dibber; the latter in the right hand, and the other in the left, at three inches asunder each hole. Afterwards they harrow all the ground, and, when the beans have got a few inches above the earth, they handhoe them. (William Ellis, *The Modern Husbandman*, 1744, Vol. 2, February 1744, p. 14)

17

[23 September 1762]
The pickers had as fine a time as ever was known both for the weather and the goodness of the hops. I never saw them so large in general and of fine beautiful colour. N.B. One woman in particular (G. Medhurst) earned 6½d. above 12s. per week. (Ralph Arnold, *A Yeoman of Kent: An Account of Richard Hayes (1725–1790) of Cobham*, 1949, p. 177)

18

[East Kent, Becksbourne]
They have no manufacture for the women and children; picking hops the only employment, except drinking tea and brandy very plentifully. (Arthur Young, *The Farmer's Tour through the East of England*, 1771, Vol. 3, p. 48)

19

[1775]
. . . my farm contains six hundred acres. As I now consider it an amazonian land, I affect to consider the women as capable of assisting in agriculture as the men. They weed my corn, hoe my turnips, and set my potatoes; and by these means promote the prosperity of their families. (Dr Doran, *A Lady of the Last Century (Mrs. Elizabeth Montagu)*, 1873, pp. 210–11)

20

[Stone-picking]
Seven or eight women boys and girls, one man, one horse and a

light cart, have run over just forty acres in three days and three
quarters. Four women at 10d. is 3s. 4d. – four boys or girls, at 6d.
is 2s. – the man, 1s. 8d. – the horse 15d. – wear and tear, 9d. –
Together, 8s. a day . . . 30s. for forty acres, or 9d. an acre for
picking and carrying it off! . . . The pickers in this practice have
nothing to do but fill their baskets. (William Marshall, *Minutes of
Agriculture made on a Farm of 300 acres . . . near Croydon,
Surrey,* 1778)

21

[Of planting peas in Wiltshire]
With a plough, drawn by one horse, they make three shallow
furrows in the dressed land, about eighteen or twenty inches
asunder; into which women following, throw the peas very regularly at proper distances. A man coming after, covers the earth by
means of his foot, or a hoe, according as the land requires.
(Samuel Rudder, *A New History of Gloucestershire,* 1779, p. 22)

22

[Cases of wives of farm labourers who kept]
. . . two or three milch cows, two or three calves a rearing: forty or
fifty sheep, two or three hogs, and poultry consisting of chickens,
ducks, geese and turkies: to the amount in number of fifty to one
hundred in a year, according as they may have had success . . . By
this means I have known instances of herself and her children in
haytime, and harvest, etc., produce nearly as much money in the
course of the year, as her husband by all his labour during the
same time. (Anon., *A Political Enquiry into the Consequences of
Enclosing Waste Lands,* 1785, pp. 44, 46)

23

[On women's role in 'dibbling wheat', 27 October 1781]
One man and one woman dibbled, while three women and three
girls dropped.
   They proceeded thus: The man was followed by one woman,
taking the first flag, and three girls taking among them the
remaining two. The woman was followed by two other women,
each of them taking a flag. When the weather holds fair, the set do
about three quarters of an acre a day, at ten shillings and sixpence
an acre. (Willliam Marshall, *The Rural Economy of Norfolk,* 1787,
Vol. 2, p. 53)

24

In this country, an instance of practice occurred to me, which is well entitled to a place in this register: that of employing a woman to follow the plough especially in fallowing, to pick up the root weeds exposed in the furrow; more particularly the Dock. When root weeds are abundant, the practice is evidently eligible: the expense is no object, and the benefit, in some cases, may be almost invaluable. (William Marshall, *The Rural Economy of the Midland Counties*, 1790, Vol. 1, p. 211 fn.)

25

[On hoeing]
Hence women and children may, with sufficient safety, be trusted with hoes among wheat, and where the soil is tolerably free from rootweeds, soon become sufficiently expert.

If the soil be tolerably free, the season kind, and the crop taken in a proper state as to growth, not withstanding it may be foul with seed weeds, there are women will hoe half an acre, a day. Such a crop is not infrequently done, at 2s. an acre.

[The setting of pulse]
Pulse, whether beans or peas, separate or mixed, are, in the ordinary practice of the district, planted by women, and hoed by women and children once, twice, and sometimes thrice . . .

In theory, a line appears to be necessary; Women, who have been long in the habit of setting without one, are able to go on, pretty regularly, by the eye alone; and the young ones are trained up, by putting one of them between two who are experienced . . .
. . . In setting the women walk sideway, to the right, with their faces toward the ground which is set: the last row, therefore is immediately under the eye, and the difficulty of setting another row, nearly parallel with it, is readily overcome by practice. An expert hand will set with almost inconceivable rapidity.
  The price of setting – sixteen to eighteen pence a bushel: costing from 3s. 6d. to 4s. 6d. an acre.

[The gathering of apples and pears in Herefordshire]
The ordinary method which I have seen used, and which is, I believe, the prevailing practice of the country, is to send men with long slender poles or rods, – provincially 'polting lugs', to beat the trees; and women with baskets, to pick up the fruit. I have seen

two men and eight women thus employed, as a set; with an ox wain, and a boy to drive it, to receive the apples as they were collected; clearing the trees as they went. (William Marshall, *The Rural Economy of Gloucestershire*, 1796, Vol. 1, pp. 121, 124, 140, 143–4; Vol. 2, p. 285)

26

[Of the corn harvest]
Two men and three women will winnow, dress and measure up into sacks, 250 bushels of oats or 150 bushels of wheat per day, – the expense 3s. 8d.

Most of the corn is cut with sickles, by women; seven of whom, with a man to bind after them, generally reap two acres per day (J. Bailey and G. Culley, *General View of the County of Northumberland*, 1797, pp. 55, 95)

27

Some employments are particularly inimical of the female poor; among which may be included field labour of every kind, where women are obliged to mix indiscriminately with men of good and bad character; many of whom have often no reputation at stake in the neighbourhood, being strangers, who have travelled from distant parts, for the purpose of finding work during a particular season. (Priscilla Wakefield, *Reflections on the Present Condition of the Female Sex* (1798), 1817, p. 141)

(e) Gleaning: a Customary Right

28

Leasing or gleaning of wheat . . . is of such importance, that many poor families supply themselves with bread by it the most part of the year after . . . (William Ellis, *The Modern Husbandman*, 1744, Vol. 4, August 1744, pp. 34–35)

29

Also it hath been said, that by the common law and customs of England the poor are allowed to enter and glean on another's ground after harvest without being guilty of trespass . . . (Sir

William Blackstone, *Commentaries on the Laws of England* (1753), 1793, Vol. 3, p. 212)

30

Gleaning ought . . . to be considered, as an exclusive privilege of children, cripples, and superannuated reapers . . .

In Yorkshire, all the wheat, generally speaking, is reaped by women. A young healthy woman, there, would be ashamed to be seen gleaning; and the actual disgrace is equal, in any other country. (William Marshall, *The Rural Economy of the Midland Counties,* 1790, Vol. 2, p. 159)

31

[A gleaner, in 1791, makes a formal apology and promise to the owner of the land who objected to her gleaning and threatened legal proceedings against both her and her husband]

Whereas I, Margaret Abree, wife of Thomas Abree, of the city of New Sarum, blacksmith, did, during the barley harvest, in the month of September last, many times wilfully and maliciously go into the fields of, and belonging to, Mr. Edward Perry, at Clarendon Park, and take with me my children, and did there leaze, collect and carry away a quantity of barley . . . Now we do hereby declare, that we are fully convinced of the illegality of such proceedings, and that no person has a right to leaze any sort of grain, or to come in any field whatsoever, without the consent of the owner; and also truly sensible of the obligation we are under to the said Mr. Perry for his lenity towards us, inasmuch as the damages given, together with the heavy cost incurred, would have been much greater than we could possibly have discharged, and must have amounted to perpetual imprisonment as even those who have least disapproval of our conduct, would certainly not have contributed so large a sum to deliver us from the legal consequences of it. And we do hereby faithfully promise never to be guilty of the same, or any like offence in future.

Thomas Abree, Margaret Abree. [Her + Mark] (*Annals of Agriculture,* (1784–1804), Vol. 17, p. 293)

32

[Of Rode in Northants.]

. . . several families will gather as much wheat as will serve them for bread the whole year . . .

[Of Yardley Goben]
Women do very little out of doors except during harvest when they go out to glean in great numbers. (F. M. Eden, *The State of the Poor,* 1797, Vol. 2, pp. 547–8)

(f) Immigrant Women in Agriculture and Market-Gardening around London

33

So it is the case with those from Wales that they earn their money also on this side of England in Kent, for towards the hay-making season, the folk come from thence in very large numbers down to the country parts of Kent to work for wages; . . . there come mostly only women and girls . . . all well, cleanly and very neatly clad. These perform nearly all the summer cropping in Kent, both of hay and grain. They also take down and pluck off the hops. They remake the hop gardens. They gather the various kinds of beautiful fruits which Kent produces. (Pehr Kalm, *Account of his Visit to England on his Way to America in 1748,* trans. Joseph Lucas, 1892, pp. 82–3)

34

During the summer season, great numbers of women are employed by the gardeners. They principally come from the neighbourhood of Shrewsbury and Dudley. They receive 6s. per week in summer, and 5s. in winter. This working in the open air is found conducive to their health, and much preferable to the spinning in which the sex are employed in other parts of the kingdom. Mowing barley or oats costs 5s. per acre. Reaping and stocking wheat from 10s. to 12s. In summer they begin to labour at 5 in the morning, and end at 7 in the evening. They are allowed an hour for breakfast, and another at dinner. On the whole, it cannot be said that the price of labour is high, for a country in which the metropolis of so great an empire happens to be situated. (Thomas Baird, *General View of the Agriculture of the County of Middlesex,* 1793, p. 21)

35

Above three hundred acres of land on the parish of Battersea are occupied by the market gardeners . . . These gardeners employ, in the summer season, a considerable number of labourers . . . The wages of the men are from ten to twelve, of the women from five to seven shillings by the week. Most of the women travel on foot from Shropshire and North Wales in the spring; and, as they live at a very cheap rate, many of them return to their own country much richer than when they left it.

[Of fruit women in Isleworth]
There are now 14 acres occupied by nurserymen, and about 430 by market gardeners. Some of the gardeners raise great quantities of raspberries, which are sold principally to the distillers, and conveyed to town in swing carts, but fruit for the table is carried in head-loads by women, who come principally from Shropshire, and the neighbourhood of Kingsdown in Wiltshire. The fruit is gathered very early in the morning, 12 women being employed to gather a load which is 12 gallons, (of three pints each). The pay for gathering is a penny halfpenny per gallon. One of the gatherers carries the load to Covent Garden market (a distance of about 10 miles) for which she has 3s. 6d. It is needless to say that they perform but one journey in the day, the Hammersmith women perform three, and receive 8d. for each journey, over and above their day's work. At Kensington they are paid sixpence, and frequently go four times in the day. These women usually go at the rate of about five miles an hour. (Daniel Lysons, *The Environs of London*, 1796, Vol. 1, pp. 27, Vol. 3, pp. 81–2)

36

The high vegetable season in summer, as well as peculiar crops at other times, calls for exertions of labour, or rather of slavery, scarcely paralleled by any other classes of people. Thus, in the strawberry season, hundreds of women are employed to carry that fruit to market on their heads; and their industry in performing this task is as wonderful, as the remuneration is unworthy of the opulent classes who derive enjoyment from their labour. They consist, for the most part, of Shropshire and Welsh girls, who walk to London at this season in droves, to perform this drudgery, just as the Irish peasantry come to assist in the hay and corn harvests. I learnt that these women carry upon their heads baskets of strawberries, or raspberries, weighing from forty to fifty pounds, and make two turns in the day from Isleworth to market, a distance of thirteen miles each way; three turns from Brentford, a distance of nine miles; and four turns from Hammersmith, a distance of six miles. For the most part, they find some conveyance back; but even then these industrious creatures carry loads from twenty-four to thirty miles a-day, besides walking back unladen some part of each turn! Their remuneration for this unparalleled slavery is from 8s. to 9s. per day; each turn from the distance of Isleworth being 4s. or 4s. 6d.; and from that of Hammersmith 2s. or 2s. 3d. Their diet is coarse and simple, their drink, tea and small-beer; costing not above 1s. or 1s. 6d.; so that their net gains are about 5s. per day, which, in the strawberry season, of forty days, amounts to 10 l. After this period the same women find employment in gathering and marketing vegetables, at lower wages, for other sixty days, netting about 5l. more. With this poor pittance they return to their native country, and it adds either to their humble comforts, or creates a small dowry towards a rustic establishment for life. Can a more interesting picture be drawn of virtuous exertion? . . . Their morals too are exemplary; and they often perform this labour to support aged parents, or to keep their own children from the workhouse! . . . They live hard, they sleep on straw in hovels and barns, and they often burst an artery or drop down dead from the effect of heat and over-exertion. (Sir R. Phillips, *A Morning Walk from London to Kew,* 1817, pp. 226–9)

(g) Women's Wages in Agriculture

37

[Of Oxford]
Dairy maids, £3. 10s. . . . Women per day in hay-time, 6d. and beer.

[Of Henley on Thames]
Women per day in harvest, 1s. and beer. In hay-time, 6d. and beer.

[Of Maidenhead]
Dairy maids, £4 . . . Women per day in harvest, 1s. and beer. In hay-time, 8d. In winter, 6d.

[Of Harmondsworth]
Maids, £3 to £3. 10s. Women per day in harvest, 1s. and board. In hay-time, 8d. and beer.

[Of St Albans]
Maids £4 to £5. 10s. Women per day in harvest, 1s. In hay-time, 10d. In winter, 6d. (Arthur Young, *A Six Months' Tour through the North of England,* 1770, Vol. 3, pp. 5, 8, 11, 13, 24)

38

Maid-servants, by the year. In some farmers' families, where they are hard worked, maid-servants receive £6 a year. Their ordinary wages in other families may be about £4. 10s. or, perhaps, £5. When they do not change their service, if strangers in the parish, care is taken to vary their wages every six months, to prevent them from acquiring a settlement.

By the month. In hay-time and harvest, when hired for a month, they get from 16s. to 24s. and board.

By the day. When hired by the day, in harvest and hay-time, they receive 8d. or 10d., and victuals. At other seasons they are paid from 8d. or 10d. or 1s. a day. Their time of entry, and of leaving off work, their hours of labour and of rest, are very various. (A. Pringle, *General View of the County of Westmoreland*, 1794, p. 293)

39

In Gloucestershire, the average earnings of a labourer's wife were given as 6d. a week by spinning for 39 weeks, and a total of £2. 11s. 6d. for the other 13 weeks employed in agriculture. Her time was spent in the following manner:

	£	s.	d.
Bean or pease setting, for 3 weeks at 7d. a day		10	6
Fruit picking, 2 weeks at 4d.		4	0
Hay-making, 2 weeks at 4d.		4	0
Gleaning, or leasing 6 bushels at 5s. 6d. per bushel	1	13	0
	2	11	6

(David Davies, *The Case of Labourers in Husbandry*, 1795, p. 162)

Part 11 Women in Industry and Other Occupations

> The poor women of this country are generally employed in spinning flax and wool, which turns out to be but very little advantage. (David Davies, *The Case of Labourers in Husbandry*, 1795, p. 189)

> The sphere of feminine action is contracted by numberless difficulties . . . (Priscilla Wakefield, *Reflections on the Present Condition of the Female Sex* (1798), 1817, p. 6)

> Women are not less capable than men of filling the employments in society! (Anon., *Female Rights Vindicated*, 1758, p. 74)

Introduction

Work in textiles was always the traditional employment of women. Clothing the family tended to be the responsibility of the wife, and involved her in every process from shearing the wool off the sheep's back to the assembly of the finished garment. In the eighteenth century the most widespread employment among women and children was the spinning of silk, linen, cotton and wool. By far the most important of these was wool-spinning. Hardly a household was without its spinning wheel, spinning appears to have been an almost universal occupation. Yet already there was a concentration of the woollen industry in three areas – East Anglia, the south-west and Yorkshire. Early in the century, Defoe is found drawing a distinction between the 'manufacturing' and the 'unemployed' counties where spinning was not apparently the common occupation of both women and children (2).

While spinning was the most important branch of the industry as far as women were concerned, it was by no means the only branch. They were also employed in weaving, carding, combing, and, indeed, in all other processes of the woollen manufacture (2). The nature of that employment, and the variety of the work involved, varied between the three main concentrations of production. Where, as in the south west, it was already organised on a capitalist basis, women workers – mainly spinners – were wage-earners collecting their work from local factors who in turn gathered up the spun yarn from them in their homes. On the other hand, in Yorkshire where the small independent producer predominated, women contributed to a family wage by involvement in almost every process of the industry – from the buying of the raw wool to the selling of the finished product in the local market (**3**). Only at the end of the century were some of these processes becoming concentrated in local mills.

For women the clothing industry was a by-employment. Those to whom it represented a full-time occupation were a minority. The wives of agricultural labourers, for example, could do a little spinning to supplement their husbands' wages. In farming households a certain amount of spinning was done – if not for marketing, then for the use of the family. Wherever women were employed in spinning in the home this had to be combined with the work of the household and the care of their children. In some ways the nature of domestic industry had great advantages for a woman in that it enabled her both to contribute to the family income and to carry out household work and look after her children, something that was impossible under the factory system (**6**). On the other hand, because it was seen as supplementary employment, it was underpaid and had the additional effect of depressing the wages of men.

Any comparison of wage rates for spinning shows just how subject to local fluctuations was the trade, and how irregular the employment. Over the century, as a whole, wage rates declined. Defoe's claim that the high wages for spinning were denuding the country of dairy maids is consistent with a boom in the wool trade, but it was not to last (**1**). What is always emphasised is that spinning was an occupation for the female poor (**4, 6, 7**). By the 1770s the effect of machinery was beginning to depress wages (**7**). The same trend is seen in weaving and other branches of the wool trade.

While cotton-spinning, as a far more localised employment for women, had existed throughout the eighteenth century and before, the cotton industry only emerged as a major branch of textiles at the end of the century when it became the focus for the first stage of the process of industrialisation. To one writer the effect of the new inventions was seen as a great gain for women's earnings (**9**). Wage rates certainly appear to have risen – at least temporarily – until they attracted other workers to spinning, and until more complex and expensive machines led to a decline in hand-spinning as a home industry. By the 1780s domestic cotton-spinning was virtually at an end.

The way in which factory employment affected women's traditional skills is seen in Aikin's comment of 1795 (**11**). Mill employment was said to have had bad effects on the health and morals of women workers (**13**).

Eden emphasises that women could earn higher wages in the cotton mills than in woollen manufacture (**12**). By the end of the century the cotton industry was a factory industry and expanding rapidly, while in the woollen industry the transition to a mechanised industry had begun but the process was far slower and more haphazard than in cotton.

If textiles provided the bulk of women's work in home industry, there were other smaller domestic industries which relied largely on the labour of women. Glove manufacture, button-making, framework knitting, straw work and lace manufacture all employed large numbers of women, but they were far more highly localised industries than textiles. By far the most important of them was lace manufacture which, although concentrated in Buckinghamshire, Northampton-shire and Bedfordshire, was also carried on in other localities over a wide area. At the end of the seventeenth century it was estimated to have given employment to 100,000 persons (**15**). Defoe certainly suggests that it was an expanding industry in the early eighteenth century (**16**), and by 1780 a lace manufacturer estimated that three counties employed as many as 400,000. Most of these were women. From early on, the industry was rigidly controlled by local lace manufactur-ers who provided the thread, supervised the work and col-lected the finished product from the lace-workers' homes or the small workplaces in which some were housed. Like most other domestic industries, trade was irregular and subject to fluctuations in demand. So while, in good times, women's earnings appear to be higher than in other trades, employ-ment was irregular. Many writers emphasised the unhealthi-ness of the work both from its sedentary nature and from the overcrowded and ill-ventilated conditions in the small work-shops (**20**). If really skilled, women lace-workers could earn as much as 1s to 1s 6d a day, the average wage was 8d to 10d – and out of these earnings the thread had to be purchased. Yet when other women's work in domestic industries was in decline – particularly spinning – lace manufacture may well have served to fill the gap in certain localities, at least for a period. At the end of the century, wages were at their highest in lace manufacture as a result of war involving a ban on foreign imports of lace. Yet it was to be only a temporary boom. From the end of the French Wars the industry went into decline.

A less highly organised industry was the plaiting of straw for the making of hats and baskets. It had long been a casual by-employment among farmers' families (**22**). It seems to have slowly increased in importance, but at the end of the eighteenth century it rapidly expanded. It was concentrated in much the same areas of the country as lace-making – Buckinghamshire, Bedfordshire and Hertfordshire. As with lace, the French Wars and the cessation of imports of Italian straw hats gave a fillip to the industry here. Eden suggests that women could earn wages that were high compared with those they could earn elsewhere (**27**). Many saw it as an answer to the unemployment of the female poor all over the country and attempts were made by parish officers and others to introduce it in new areas by providing instructors. Despite such efforts, straw work could not compensate for the loss of women's employment in other domestic industries and agriculture.

The great variety of other occupations in which women were employed is illustrated in Section **e**. What they have in common is that they were all poorly paid jobs.

All women's work underground in mines was said to have ended well before the end of the century; but the 1842 Commission – appointed to investigate the employment of children underground – was extended to women when it was revealed how many were still working underground.

For most of the eighteenth century the employment of women underground seems to have been taken for granted, and was not cause for comment. Yet what is strange is the difficulty of finding any evidence, except the scantiest, of that employment. It is only when the attention of the public was drawn to the conditions of women bearers in Scotland, and the nature of women's employment in the Whitehaven pits (**31, 32**) that evidence of their employment can be found. Yet clearly they were so employed underground throughout the eighteenth century, as well as on the surface around mines washing ore and breaking or chipping it into small pieces (**36, 37**). The grounds on which women's work in the mines or in the nail-making trade (**33**) was criticised was quite as much because the work deprived women of their femininity and that the close proximity in which men and women worked encouraged immoral behaviour, as that the work involved was hard.

Women also worked as street-traders selling milk, vegetables and fruit, flowers, fish, poultry and rabbits, as shoe-cleaners and ballad vendors (**40, 41, 42**), as washer-women, and even, on occasion, as highway-women (**38**). Many worked alongside their husbands in shops (**47**). Some assisted in their husbands' trades (**41**). Widows are often found as shop- or inn-keepers, taking over the business at their husbands' death (**46**).

Contemporary writers were very conscious of how restricted were the employment opportunities for women (**56**). David Davies, at the end of the century, lamented the declining work opportunities for the wives of labouring men (**54**). Other writers recognised how few were the 'genteel' openings for the daughters of the middle class faced with the need to earn their living (**48, 50, 51**). They could apprentice themselves to milliners, mantua-makers, or some other branch of the clothing trade (**39**). These were considered suitably 'genteel', and for those possessed of capital offered some of the few possibilities of setting up in business for themselves. For the majority, there were no such prospects. As with the work of governesses and teachers – those other 'genteel' employments – all were poorly paid. In trades in which both sexes worked, the rates for women were always much lower than for men (**55**). The Society for the Encouragement of Arts, Manufactures and Commerce vainly tried to promote new openings for women (**52**). Among those putting forward ideas for enlarging opportunities, Priscilla Wakefield urged that many trades hitherto monopolised by men should be opened to women. Arguing for more 'liberal' employments for women, Mary Wollstonecraft asked why they should not be as capable of becoming physicians as they were of becoming nurses (**53**). For well over fifty years the question remained unanswered.

(a) The Woollen Industry

1

The rate for spinning, weaving and all other manufacturing work, I mean in wool, is so risen, that the poor all over England, can now earn or gain near twice as much in a day, and in some places, more than twice as much as they could get for the same work two or three years ago: Particularly in Essex, Suffolk, and Norfolk, eastward; and in Wiltshire, Somerset and Devon, west; the poor women now get 12d. to 15d. a day for spinning, . . .

. . . the farmers' wives can get no dairy maids . . . and what's the matter? truly the wenches answer, they won't go to service at 12d. or 18d. a week, while they can get 7s. to 8s. a week at spinning. (Daniel Defoe, *The Great Law of Subordination*, 1724, pp. 83–6)

2

In these unemploy'd counties [where no employment existed for women and children], you see the women and children idle, and out of business; these sitting at their doors, and those playing in the streets; even in the market towns, and the most populous villages, where they might be supposed to be employ'd, the poor by the rich, yet there 'tis the same, much more in the single scattering villages, where they have no business but their own.

Whereas, in the manufacturing counties, you see the wheel going almost at every door, the wool and the yarn hanging up at every window; the looms, the winders, the combers, the carders, the dyers, the dressers, all busy; and the very children, as well as women, constantly employed . . . a poor labouring man that goes abroad to his day work, and husbandry, hedging, ditching, threshing, carting, etc. and brings home his week's wages, suppose at eight pence to twelve pence a day, or in some counties less; if he has a wife and three or four children to feed, and who get little or nothing for themselves, must fare hard, and live poorly; 'tis easy to suppose it must be so.

But if this man's wife and children can at the same time get employment, if at next door, or at the next village there lives a clothier, or a bay-maker, or a stuff or drugget weaver; the manufacturer sends the poor woman comb'd wool or carded wool every week to spin and she gets eightpence or ninepence a day at home; the weaver sends for her two little children, and they work by the loom, winding, filling quills, etc., and the two bigger girls spin at home with their mother, and there earn threepence or fourpence a day each; so that put it together, the family at home gets as much as the father gets abroad and generally more.

This alters the case extremely the family feels it, they all feed better, are cloth'd warmer, and do not so easily nor so often fall into misery and distress. (Daniel Defoe, *A Plan of the English Commerce*, 1728, pp. 67–9)

3

Day labourers, who whilst they are employed abroad themselves, get 40 or 50 pounds of wool at a time, to employ their wives and children at home in carding and spinning, of which when they have 10 or 20 pounds ready for the clothier, they go to market with it and there sell it, and so return home as fast as they can: the common way the poor women in Hampshire, Wiltshire and Dorsetshire, and I believe in other counties, have of getting to market (especially in the winter-time) is, by the help of some farmers' waggons, which carry them and their yarn . . . During the time the waggons stop, the poor women carry their yarn to the clothiers for whom they work; then get the few things they want, and return to the inn to be carried home again . . . As to those who may live in or near the market town, there will be in market time 3 or 400 poor people (chiefly women) who will sell their goods in about an hour. (Anon., *Remarks upon Mr Webber's Scheme and the Drapers' Pamphlet*, 1741, pp. 21–2)

4

[Of Sir George Strickland's woollen manufactory at Boynton, near Cleveland]
In this country the poor have no other employment than that what results from a most imperfect agriculture; consequently three-fourths of the women and children were without employment. It was this induced Sir George to found a building large enough to contain on one side a row of looms of different sorts, and on the other a large space for women and children to spin. The undertaking was once carried so far as to employ 150 hands, who made very sufficient earnings for their maintenance; but the decay of the woollen exportation reduced them so much, that now those employed there are, I believe, under a dozen. (Arthur Young, *A Six Months' Tour through the North of England*, 1770, Vol. 1, pp. 239–40)

5

When our woollen manufactory flourishes, the wives and children of small farmers, cottagers, and labouring men can earn nearly as much money by spinning at the wheel as the man can get by his industry in the field; should he then fall sick or lame, the family will work with double diligence to keep him from the parish until his health returns; but when our woollen manufactory declines, the man alone must wield the labouring oar. Women and children in harvest only are wanted in the field, if some trifles are excepted that may be done by boys: therefore, should misfortunes then attend the man, he and the family all together must fall upon the parish, and what was heretofore thought a great discredit, now ceases to be disreputable from its melancholy frequency. (Francis Moore, *The Exhorbitant Price of Provisions*, 1773, p. 58)

6

Humble Petition of the Poor Spinners, which on a very moderate calculation consist of Eighteen Thousand, Five Hundred, employed in the Town and Country aforesaid.

Sheweth, that the business of *Spinning*, in all its branches, hath ever been, time out of mind, the peculiar employment of women; insomuch that every single woman is called in law a *Spinster*; to which employment your Petitioners have been brought up, and by which they have hitherto earned their maintenance. That this employment above all others is suited to the condition and circumstances of the *Female Poor;* inasmuch as not only single women, but married ones also, can be employed in it consistently with the necessary cares of their families; for, the business being carried on in their own houses, they can at any time leave it when the care of their families requires their attendance, and can re-assume the work when family duty permits it; nay, they can, in many instances, carry on their work and perform their domestic duty at the same time; particularly in the case of attending a sick husband or child, or an aged parent . . .

It is therefore with great concern your Petitioners see that this antient employment is likely to be taken from them – an employment so consistent with civil liberty, so full of domestic comfort, and so favourable to a religious course of life. This we apprehend will be the consequences of so many spinning mills, now erecting after the model of the cotton mills. The work of the poor will be done by these engines, and they left without employment. (Leicester, 1788, British Museum Tracts, B544 [10]. See appendix to B. L. Hutchins, *Women in Modern Industry*, 1915)

7

[Of South Tawton, Devon]

. . . the number of inhabitants is 2500: they are chiefly employed in the various branches of the serge manufacture, which is here carried on to a considerable extent. Nine tenths of the women in the parish, (all of the poorest class,) are spinners, and are regularly supplied by the serge-makers with constant employment. Their number may be estimated at 600 or 700 . . . spinners cannot earn above 6d. or 7d. a day.

As the chapelry consists almost entirely of dairy farms, and consequently affords very little employment in husbandry, except during the hay-harvest, the labouring poor are very dependent on the neighbouring towns where the cloth manufacture is carried on; but unfortunately, since the introduction of machinery, which lately took place, hand spinning has fallen into disuse, for these two reasons: the clothier no longer depends on the poor for the yarn which they formerly spun for him at their homes, as he finds that fifty persons (to speak within compass), with the help of machines, will do as much work as five hundred without them; and the poor, from the great reduction in the price of spinning, scarcely have the heart to earn the little that is obtained by it. From what they used to receive a shilling and one and twopence the pound for spinning, before the application of machinery, they now are allowed only fivepence, so that a woman in a good state of health, and not encumbered with a family, can earn two and sixpence a week, which is . . . the utmost that can be done; but if she has a family, she cannot earn more than twopence a day . . . The consequence is that their maintenance must chiefly depend on the exertions of the man (whose earnings have not increased in proportion to this defalcation . . .) and therefore the present dear times are very severely felt by all families, and even by single women who depend upon spinning for their support. (F. M. Eden, *The State of the Poor,* 1797, Vol. 2, p. 139; Vol. 3, p. 796)

(b) Cotton and Other Textiles

8

The silk-throwster, by a mill calculated for that purpose, throws the silk, and prepares it for the various uses of the weaver; he employs mostly women, to whom he gives but small wages: It is a very profitable business for the master, and requires but a small share of ingenuity. Spinning the hard silk and winding it employs a great number of female hands, who may make good bread of it, if they refrain from the common vice of drinking and sotting away their time and senses. (R. Campbell, *The London Tradesman,* 1747, p. 260)

9

What a prodigious difference have our machines made in the gain of the females of the family! Formerly the chief support of a poor family arose from the loom. The wife could get comparatively but little on her single spindle. But for some years a good spinner has been able to get as much as or more than a weaver. For this reason many weavers have become spinners, and by this means such quantities of cotton warps, twists, wefts, etc., have been poured into the country that our trade has taken a new turn. All the spinners in the country could not possibly have produced so much as this, as are now wanted in a small part of our manufacture. If it were true that a weaver gets less, yet, as his wife gets more, his family does not suffer. But the fact is that the gains of an industrious family have been upon the average much greater than they were before these inventions. (Anon., *Thoughts on the Use of Machines in the Cotton Manufacture,* Manchester, 1780)

10

. . . thousands of women, when they can get work, must make a long day to card, spin and reel 5040 yards of cotton, and for this they have fourpence or fivepence and no more. (*The Case of the Poor Cotton Spinners,* 1780)

11

[The effect of working in mills on the instruction of women]
The females are wholly uninstructed in sewing, knitting, and other domestic affairs, requisite to make them notable and frugal wives and mothers. This is a very great misfortune to them and the public, as is sadly proved by a comparison of the families of labourers in husbandry, and those of manufacturers in general. In the former we meet with neatness, cleanliness, and comfort; in the latter with filth, rags, and poverty; although their wages may be nearly double to those of the husbandman. It must be added, that the want of early religious instruction and example, and the numerous and indiscriminate association in these buildings, are very unfavourable to their future conduct in life.

[Of Oldham]
The manufactures of the place are the different branches of the cotton trade, especially the heavy fustians . . . The manufactures employ all the people, except some colliers, shop-keepers and husbandmen. The gains are from 2d. per day by young children, to 3s. 6d. and 4s. by grown people. Women will sometime earn 16 and 17s. per week by spinning with a Jenny! (J. Aikin, *A Description of the Country from Thirty to Forty Miles round Manchester,* 1795, pp. 220, 239)

12

[Of Manchester]
Women and children are employed in winding cotton, reeling, ending and mending, cutting fustian, picking cotton, managing the spinning jennies etc. Women can earn from 6s. to 12s. a week: their clear weekly earnings may be stated at 8s.

[Of Bury, Lancs.]
The inhabitants are employed in the cloth and in the cotton manufacture; but principally, in the latter, which is here carried on in most of its branches . . . The wages in the woollen are much lower than in the cotton manufacture. Women, by spinning wool, do not earn more than 3s. or 4s. a week.

[Of Newark, Notts.]
The cotton manufacture is the principal business of consequence carried on in this parish: a mill, for making cotton-thread for stockings, employs about three hundred hands; chiefly women and children: they earn, at present, from 1s. to 5s. a week. (F. M. Eden, *The State of the Poor*, 1797, Vol. 2, pp. 357, 294, 565)

13

[The effect of crowded factories on the health and morality of women]
. . . the savage debauchery of the men – the loss of every semblance of feminine modesty in the women – the initiation of the children in the nomenclature and theory of vices they are physically incapable of practising – the irreclaimable depravity of all. Beside this disgustful and afflicting picture, place the scene in which the workmanship of ten thousand labourers of luxury comes into use, and it will require no oracle to pronounce, whether the consumer gains what the artificer loses in happiness . . . (J. E. Stock, *Memoirs of the Life of Thomas Beddoes*, 1811, pp. 208–9)

14

[Samuel Crompton's account of his introduction to the cotton trade as a child related to French in May 1854]
. . . I recollect that soon after I was able to walk I was employed in the cotton manufacture. My mother used to bat the cotton wool on a wire griddle. It was then put into a deep brown mug with a strong ley of soap suds. My mother then tucked up my petticoats about my waist, and put me in the tub to tread upon the cotton at the bottom. When a second riddleful was batted I was lifted out and it

was placed in the mug, and I again trod it down. The process was continued until the mug became so full that I could no longer safely stand in it, when a chair was placed beside it, and I held on by the back. When the mug was quite full, the soap suds were poured off, and each separate dollop of wool well squeezed to free it from moisture. They were then placed on the bread-rack under the beams of the kitchen and left to dry. My mother and my grandmother carded the cotton-wool by hand, taking one of the dollops at a time on the simple hand-cards. When carded they were put aside in separate parcels ready for spinning. (Gilbert J. French, *The Life and Times of Samuel Crompton*, 1868, pp. 78–9)

(c) Lace and Straw Work

15

[A petition against the proposal to repeal the Act prohibiting the import of foreign lace]
. . . there are now above one hundred thousand in England who get their living by it, and can earn by mere labour £500,000 a year, according to the lowest computation that can be made; and the persons employed in it are, for the most part, women and children who have no other means of subsistence . . .
. . . The lace manufacture in England . . . maintains a multitude of people, which otherwise the parishes must, and that would soon prove a heavy burthen, even to those concerned in woollen manufacture. On the Resolution, which shall be taken in this affair depends the well-being, or ruin of numerous families in their country. Many laws have been made to set the poor on work, and it is to be hoped none will be made to take away work from multitudes who are already employed (*Petition of Lace Manufacturers to House of Commons*, 1698)

16

[Of bone lace manufacture]
The improvement and increase of it within about 20–30 years past is such, and so visible, that he must be utterly ignorant of trade that is not convinc'd of it . . . In a word, this manufacture is so much increased in England, that it employs many thousands of our people more than ever; and if I may credit the report of the country where 'tis chiefly made, where one was employ'd by it 30 years ago, above 100 are employ'd by it now, and those of the most idle, useless and burthensome part of our people (I mean such as

were so before) are the principal hands employ'd, viz. the younger women, and female children. These were a real charge upon the diligent laborious poor, such as the husbandmen, the farmers, and the handicrafts of other trades; and are now made able to provide for themselves, and ease their parents and parishes of a dead weight, which was in many cases insupportable; . . . In short, 'tis believed there are above an hundred thousand women and children employ'd, and who get their bread by this manufacture, more than did formerly . . . (Daniel Defoe, *A Plan of the English Commerce*, 1728, p. 216)

17

[Between Henley and Maidenhead]
The employment of the poor women and children is a little spinning, but much lace making, at which the women earn 10d. or 1s. a day; girls from 4d. to 6d. (Arthur Young, *A Six Months' Tour through the North of England*, 1770, Vol. 3, p. 9)

18

[In April, 1780, there was a threat to remove the tariff on Irish goods which worried the Olney lace-makers]
I am an eye-witness of their poverty, and do know that hundreds in this little town are upon the point of starving, and that the most un-remitting industry is but barely sufficient to keep them from it. I know the bill by which they would have been so fatally affected is thrown out, but Lord Stormont threatens them with another; and if another like it should pass, they are undone. We lately sent a petition from hence to Lord Dartmouth. I signed it, and am sure the contents are true. The purport of it was to inform him that there are very near 1200 lace-makers in this beggarly town, the most of whom had reason enough, while the bill was in agitation, to look upon every loaf they bought as the last they should ever be able to earn – I can never think it good policy to incur the certain inconvenience of ruining 300,000 in order to prevent a remote and possible damage, though to a much greater number. The measure is like a scythe and the poor lace-makers are the sickly crop that trembles before the edge of it (*Correspondence of William Cowper*, Letter to J. Hill, 8 July 1780, ed Thomas Wright, 1904, Vol. 1, p. 210)

19

Yon cottager, who weaves at her own door,

Pillow and bobbins all her little store;
Content though mean, and cheerful, if not gay,
Shuffling her thread about the livelong day –
Just earns a scanty pittance, and at night
Lies down secure, her heart and pocket light.
(From 'Truth', *Verse and Letters of William Cowper*, ed. Brian
Spiller, 1968, p. 230)

20

In the course of a late journey into Buckingham and North-
amptonshire, the frequent sight of deformed and diseased women
in those counties drew my attention; . . . these diseased women,
who are generally workers of lace . . . are deformed . . . and many
more are diseased, seemingly owing, in a great measure, to their
inclined posture while working, which prevents their lungs having
a free play; and from the same cause the blood does not circulate
freely in the liver . . . The interrupted circulation in the several
bowels cannot fail to bring on difficulty of breathing, pains in the
region of the stomach, bad digestion, jaundice, and many other
complaints . . .
. . . The rooms where these people generally work are small,
low and close, in which many sit together. . . . (*Gentleman's
Magazine*, 1785, pp. 938–9)

21

[Of lace-makers in Bedfordshire in the neighbourhood of Harrold]
The women, who are mostly lace-makers, can, if expert in this
business, maintain themselves, even in the present dear times.
Ordinary lace-makers earn 6s. a week: and boys and girls from 3s.
to 4s. (F. M. Eden, *The State of the Poor*, 1797, Vol. 1, p. 566)

22

. . . farmers' wives, children and servants do at their spare hours
earn some 10, some 20 and some £30 per annum by manufacturing
their own straw which is a good article towards paying their rent.
(*The Case of the Poor Straw Hat Makers in the Counties of
Hertford, Bedford, Buckingham etc.*, 1719)

23

[Of the basket-maker]
Apprentices must have some robustness but not much ingenuity
. . . There are numbers of women employed in all the classes, and

all things considered earn as much money as at trades that make a greater figure in the world. Journeymen have from nine to fifteen shillings a week. (R. Campbell, *The London Tradesman*, 1747, p.244)

24

[Of Hertfordshire]
The greater number of the English women in this district trouble themselves very little about such domestic duties as in other countries form a great part of the occupations of women, but that they had laid most of the burden of that on the men. I saw, however, in some places some part of the women afford proof that they are not wanting in ability for various things, if only the custom of the country had not freed this sex from such. Here were several women who were very busy making straw hats which they afterwards sent hither and thither to be sold. (Pehr Kalm, *Account of his Visit to England on his Way to America in 1748*, trans. Joseph Lucas, 1892, pp. 337–8)

25

Canker – A girl, about twelve years of age, that being daily employed to sew straw hats (which is most of the women's work in our part of Hertfordshire) used to put her brass thimble into her mouth, which bred many white cankering blisters on her tongue, gums and lips was cured by anointing the outside of her jaws, chin and lips, three days together, with stale goose grease, and binding a rag of the same over the parts. (William Ellis, *The Country Housewife's Family Companion*, 1750, p. 288)

26

The basket-makers are indeed decreased in this town, but many live in the neighbouring villages, who make not only common work, but are famed all over England for the curiosity of their workmanship in wicker-ware. (Charles Deering, *Nottinghamia Vetus et Nova*, 1751, p. 96)

27

[Of Dunstable in Beds, September 1795]
In the straw work, which is the staple manufacture of the place, a woman can earn from 6s. to 12s. a week; children, from 2s. to 4s. a week. This business has given employment, for the last twenty years, to every woman, who wished to work: and, for ten years

back, straw work has sold well, particularly in the spring. Earnings in this line, have, for the last four years, been exceedingly great, which, in some measure, perhaps, accounts for the Poor's Rates not having risen during that period. The straw is chiefly manufactured into hats, baskets, etc. (F. M. Eden, *The State of the Poor*, 1797, Vol. 2, p 2)

28

[Of Dunstable 1801]
... went to meet a person who instructs people in plaiting straw, and I bargained with him at 30s. a week for a girl to be instructed – a month will do; that is 6 1d. and the journey there and back, about 4 1. so for 10 1. I shall be able to introduce the most excellent fabric among our poor. The children begin at four years old, and by six earn 2s. or 3s. a week; by seven 1s. a day; and at eight and nine, etc. 10s. or 12s. a week. (*Autobiography of Arthur Young*, ed. M. Betham-Edwards, 1898, p. 367)

(d) Mines and Metal Industries

29

But none of the poor need be compelled to the working against their wills in the mines, because the labour is not very hard, and 10d. a day for a man, 6d. for his wife and 4d. for his children, from 8 to 14 years old: makes it, if he have but two children, 14s. per week, out of which he may live well in those counties, and save money to buy cattle; and for this they may work industriously there, 6 or 8 hours, which is usually a miner's days work . . . and there is washing and knocking of ores, which are works that many good men's daughters are now glad to do, in many places of this kingdom, for bread for them and their children . . . (M. Stringer, *English and Welsh Mines and Minerals*, 1699, p. 16)

30

A woman employed in putting at South Biddick [was] riding up one of the pits [when] the other hook in passing, caught her clothes. The weight of the rope forced her out of the loop, and she fell to the bottom of the shaft. (*Newcastle Journal*, 8 February 1772)

31

When the coal is ready to be sent to the pit bottom, if women are employed as bearers, immense loads are put upon their backs, and these oppressed females, groaning under heavy burdens, travel to the pit, where they lay down the coals, and build them up in the place appointed for each collier, until their respective turn arrives for sending their coals to the hill.

Let a collier be ever so expert at his occupation, if his wife or daughters be indisposed, all his exertion goes for nothing, and it is certain much work is lost annually by this cause alone.

At present time there are four modes practised in Scotland, for transporting of coals from the wall-face to the hill . . . In the third mode the coals are carried by women, known by the name of Bearers, who transport them from the wall-face to the pit-bottom, from whence they are drawn by machinery to the hill.

The fourth and last mode is the most severe and slavish; for the women are not only employed to carry the coals from the wall face to the pit bottom, but also to ascend with them to the hill. . .

[It was customary for the men to go to work in the mines about 11 p.m.]
In about three hours after, his wife (attended by her daughters, if she has any sufficiently grown) sets out for the pit having previously wrapped her infant child in a blanket, and left it to the care of an old woman, who for a small gratuity, keeps three or four children at a time, and who, in their mother's absence, feeds them with ale or whisky, mixed with water . . .
The mother . . . descends the pit with her elder daughters, when each, having a basket of a suitable form lays it down, and into it the large coals are rolled; and such is the weight carried, that it frequently takes two men to lift the burden upon their backs: the girls are loaded according to their strength. The mother sets out first, carrying a lighted candle in her teeth; the girls follow, and in this manner they proceed to the pit bottom, and with weary steps and slow ascend the stairs, halting occasionally to draw breath, till they arrive at the hill or pit top, where the coals are laid down for sale; and in this manner they go for eight or ten hours almost without resting. It is no uncommon thing to see them when ascending the pit, weeping most bitterly, from the excessive severity of their labour; but the instant they have laid down their burden on the hill, they resume their cheerfulness, and return down the pit singing.

The weight of coals thus brought to the pit top by a woman in a day, amounts to 4080 pounds or above thirty-six hundred weight English, and there have been frequent instances of two tons being carried.

The wages paid them for this work, are eightpence per day! (R. Bald, *General View of the Coal Trade of Scotland*, 1812, pp. 48, 92, 127–9, 130–2, 134)

32

[Of the William Pitt Mine at Whitehaven]
While we were conversing here . . . on the possible accidents that might occur in ascending or descending in the basket, we were told of a poor woman who lately had an extraordinary escape. It was her business to attach the chain to the basket, and while she was in the act of doing this, her hand became somehow entangled, and the man at the engine setting it in motion before the proper time, she was pulled from the ground before she could extricate herself, and dragged up, as she hung by one arm, to the top of the pit, with no injury but a slight laceration of her hand.

Occasionally a light appeared in the distance before us, which did not dispel the darkness so as to discover by whom it was borne, but advanced like a meteor through the gloom, accompanied by a loud rumbling noise, the cause of which was not explained to the eye till we were called upon to make way for a horse which passed by with its long line of baskets, and driven by a young girl, covered with filth, debased and profligate, and uttering some low obscenity as she hurried by us. We were frequently interrupted in our march by the horses proceeding in this manner with their cargoes to the shaft and always driven by girls, all of the same description, ragged and beastly in their appearance, and with shameless indecency in their behaviour . . .

The people in the mines are looked upon as mere machinery, of no worth or importance beyond their horsepower. The strength of a man is required in excavating the workings, women can drive the horses, and children can open the doors; and a child or a woman is sacrificed, where a man is not required, as a matter of economy, that makes not the smallest account of human life in its calculations. In consequence of the employment of women in the mines the most abominable profligacy prevails among the people . . . If a man and woman meet in them, and are excited by passion at the moment, they indulge it, without pausing to enquire if it be father and daughter, or brother and sister, that are polluting themselves with incest.
    . . . They lose every quality that is graceful in woman,, and become a set of coarse, licentious wretches, scorning all kind of restraint, and yielding themselves up, with shameless audacity, to

the most detestable sensuality. (Richard Ayton, *A Voyage round Great Britain*, 1814, Vol. 2, pp. 153, 155, 159–60)

33

[Of nail-making in Birmingham]
When I first approached her from Walsall, in 1741, I was surprised at the prodigious number of blacksmiths shops upon the road; and could not conceive how a country, though populous, could support so many people of the same occupation. In some of these shops I observed one, or more females, stript of their upper garment, and not over-charged with their lower, wielding the hammer with all the grace of the sex. The beauties of their face were rather eclipsed by the smut of the anvil; or, in poetical phrase, the tincture of the forge had taken possession of those lips, which might have been taken by the kiss. Struck with the novelty, I enquired, 'Whether the ladies in this country shod horses'? but was answered, with a smile, 'They are nailers'. (William Hutton, *History of Birmingham*, (1781) 1806, p. 116)

34

[Of the iron collieries near Rotherham]
Near the town are two collieries, out of which the iron ore is dug . . . There are few women employed; and only in piling old bits of scrap iron . . . into the form of small pyramids, upon round pieces of stone, after which they are set into the furnace till they become of a malleable heat, and are then worked over again.

Sheffield contains about 30,000 inhabitants, the chief of which are employed in the manufacture of hardware. The great branches are the plating work, the cutlery, the lead works, and the silk mill . . . In the plated work some hundreds of hands are employed . . . Girls earn 4s. 6d. and 5s. a week; some even to 9s. No men are employed than earn less than 9s. (Arthur Young, *A Six Months' Tour through the North of England*, 1770, Vol. 1, pp. 73, 78)

35

[Of Gloucester]
the staple of which city is pins, which employs near 400 hands, of whom a great number are women and children: good hands at pointing and sticking earn from 10s. to 12s. and 15s. a week: children of 9, 10 and 11 years old earn 2d. . . .

[Of pin-making, near Bristol]
. . . employing a great number of girls, who with little machines, worked by their feet, point and head them with great expedition: and will each do a pound and a half in a day. The heads are spun by a woman with a wheel, much like a common spinning wheel, and then separated from one another by a man, with another little machine like a pair of shears. (Arthur Young, *The Farmer's Tour through the East of England*, 1771, Vol. 4, pp. 152, 172)

36

[Of the washing of lead ore by women in Derbyshire]
All the ore as it comes from the mine is beaten into pieces before it is sold. This business is performed by women, who can earn about 6d. per day. (J. Aikin, *A Description of the Country from Thirty to Forty Miles round Manchester*, 1795, p. 79)

37

There is always something interesting in the busy bustle of industry; but in copper works and iron works, it certainly presents itself to the eye under its most unfavourable appearances. One is more particularly disgusted with the soot and smoke of Neath, from seeing them so familiar with the faces of the women, who in all parts of Wales are employed in offices of the hardest and dirtiest drudgery like the men. On the banks of the canal I saw little companies of them chipping the large coals into small pieces for the furnaces, without shoes or stockings, their clothes hanging about them, released for the sake of ease, from pins and strings, and their faces as black as coals, except where channelled by the streams of perspiration that trickled down them. (Richard Ayton, *A Voyage round Great Britain*, 1814, p. 67)

(e) Other Work for Women
38

Monday 24 November. A butcher was robb'd in a very gallant manner by a woman on a side saddle, etc. near Romford in Essex. She presented a pistol to him, and demanded his money; he being amaz'd at her behaviour told her, he did not know what she meant; when a gentleman, coming up, told him he was a brute to deny the lady's request, and if he did not gratify her desire immediately, he would shoot him thro' the head; so he gave her his watch and six guineas. (*Gentleman's Magazine*, 1735, p. 680)

39

[Of the button-maker]
The silver and gold button-maker is a pretty ingenious business
. . . it requires no great strength, and is followed by women as well
as men, which has reduced the trade to small profits, and a small
share of reputation; the women are generally gin-drinkers, and,
consequently, bad wives; this makes them poor, and, to get
something to keep soul and body together, work for a mere trifle,
and hawk their work about the trade at an under-price . . .

[Of the milliner]
The milliner, though no male trade, has a just claim to a place on
this occasion, as the fair sex, who are generally bound to this
business, may have as much curiosity to know the nature of their
employment before they engage in it, and stand as much in need of
sound advice in choice of an occupation, as the youth of our own
sex.
    The milliner is concerned in making and providing the ladies
with linen of all sorts, fit for wearing apparel, from the Holland
smock, to the tippet and commode . . .
    The milliner must be a neat needle-woman in all its branches,
and a perfect connoisseur in dress and fashion . . . The most noted
of them keep an agent at Paris, who have nothing else to do but to
watch the motions of the fashions, and procure intelligence of their
changes . . . They have vast profits on every article they deal in;
yet give but poor, mean wages to every person they employ under
them: Though a young woman can work neatly in all manner of
needle-work, yet she cannot earn more than five or six shillings a
week, out of which she is to find herself in board and lodging.
Therefore, out of regard to the fair sex, I must caution parents, not
to bind their daughters to this business: The vast resort of young
beaus and rakes to milliners' shops exposes young creatures to
many temptations, and insensibly debauches their morals before
they are capable of vice . . .

[Of the Stay-maker]
. . . the work is too hard for women, it requires more strength than
they are capable of . . . The materials in stays are tabby, canvas,
and whale-finn commonly called Whale-bone: The Stay-maker
. . . cuts out the tabby and canvas by the shape in quarters, which
are given out to women to be stitched, at so much a pair of stays:
This part of the stay-making trade is but poor bread; a woman
cannot earn above a crown or six shillings a week let her sit as close
as she pleases.

[Of the mantua-maker]
Their profits are but inconsiderable, and the wages they give their
Journey-women small in proportion; they may make a shift with
great sobriety and economy to live upon their allowance; but their
want of prudence, and general poverty, has brought the business
into small reputation. If a young creature, when out of her time,
has no friend to advise with, or be a check upon her conduct, it is
more than ten to one but she takes some idle, if not vicious course,
by the many temptations to which her sex and narrow circumstances subject her.

[Of the hoop petticoat maker]
They are chiefly made by women: They must not be polluted by
the unhallowed hands of a rude male. These women make a
tolerable living by it: The work is harder than most needle-work,
and requires girls of strength. A mistress must have a pretty kind
of genius to make them fit well and adjust them to the reigning
mode . . . (R. Campbell, *The London Tradesman*, 1747, pp. 152,
206–9, 224–5, 227–8, 212–13)

40

[Of work at a Lime-kiln]
The baskets which the small pieces of chalk were cast into . . .
were carried by women to the lime-kilns . . .
    The fuel they use is . . . coal . . . A little way from the kiln lie
large heaps of coal, but before they are used they are broken with
an iron hammer into quite small pieces . . . Thus prepared the coal
is carried by women in the . . . baskets, and is set around the sides
of the kiln . . .
    At every kiln there are six persons, three men and three women.
Two of the carls have the charge of breaking the chalk loose, and
of hewing it into small pieces, as well as of lifting the baskets onto
the women's shoulders; but it often happens, nevertheless, that
the women also get helping to hack it into small pieces. Both the
carls and all three women help to fill the baskets with the bits of
chalk, when the carls commonly screen the bits of chalk in the
fiddle, and the women throw them into the baskets. The women
are obliged, almost alone, to carry the baskets on their heads and
shoulders from the place where the chalk is taken to the lime-kiln.
The third of the three carls is constantly at the lime kiln, where he
takes the chalk baskets from the women's heads and shoulders,
and throws the chalk into the kiln . . . Every woman always carries
three baskets each time, namely, she has a piece of board of about
8 inches broad and about 1 foot long, on which is a rope or band,

one end of which is fastened to one end of the piece of wood, and the other to the other. This band is laid by a noose over the upper part of the head, so that the piece of board comes to lie across the shoulders, when one basket is set to rest upon the piece of board, and the other two beside it on the head, whilst the woman inclines her head a little as she walks. On the head they have an old man's hat, and under the piece of wood and the band a bunch of hay, that the piece of wood and the cord may not injure the back . . .

The women receive each about eightpence a day, for which they work exceedingly hard, for they mostly labour like slaves.

They said they were paid in this way, that a woman gets one penny when she has carried sixteen baskets of chalk to the lime-kiln, and for this penny she had also broken up a good deal of chalk. The man who had charge of them, confirmed what the women had said, that they receive one penny for sixteen baskets carried, at which rate they can earn twelve, fifteen or eighteen-pence a day, according as they are industrious. The men get either nine or ten shillings a week.

I saw . . . old women and girls . . . walk or sit in the streets of London with baskets full of all kinds of flowers, bound in small bunches . . . which they offered to the passers-by, who also bought them in numbers.

In several places, especially in the larger streets, where the people stream backwards and forwards, there sit . . . old women with shoe-brushes, blacking, and such like, ready to clean shoes for anyone who may require their services. (Pehr Kalm, *Account of his Visit to England on his Way to America in 1748*, trans. Joseph Lucas, 1892, pp. 431–8 34, 62)

41

[Of Sutton near Birmingham]
There I met a woman chimney-sweeper and her children . . . This chimney-sweep told me her life story . . . Early in her married life her husband had been pressed into the army and she had lost him. She assumed him dead and had then earned a living as a servant in Ireland without anyone knowing she was married. During this time her chimney-sweep husband had returned to England and set up in business in Lichfield. As soon as he was firmly established there he inquired on all hands for his wife and at last found out where she was. He not only fetched her home to her rightful place, but organised a splendid feast in her honour, for all her neighbours

to welcome her. She lived with her husband in Lichfield . . .
respected by all and helping him with his work.

[Of a London shoe-cleaner]
The cleaning of shoes is not done in the house but by a woman in
the neighbourhood who makes this her trade. She collects the
shoes from the house every morning, cleans them and brings them
back for a fixed weekly payment. (Carl Philip Moritz, *Journeys of
a German in England in 1782*, trans. and ed. Reginald Nettel,
1965, pp. 146, 35)

42

[Of female ballad singers and vendors]
I beg leave to mention The Ballads, among the singularities to be
met within this nation. These, it is true, are also common in
France, but not sold publicly as in London.

It is usually females who are employed in this avocation. They
wander about the most populous streets of the capital, stop now
and then and draw a crowd around them, to whom they sing their
songs, which they sometimes accompany with music. In these witty
expressions and humorous sallies are often contained; and one is
sometimes sorry to see such talents as the writers must undoubtedly possess, employed in celebrating the trifling occurrences of the
day. The subject is generally some political event, which has
novelty and interest to recommend it. These ballads, being printed
on coarse paper, are sometimes sold for a farthing, and sometimes
for a halfpenny a piece; the quickness of the sale, however, amply
repays the printer, they are vended by thousands, if they happen
to be popular. (J. W. von Archenholz, *A Picture of England*, 1791,
p. 292)

43

[Of girls and women employed in Chelsea in the manufacture of
painted silk, varnished linen, etc]
In the year 1791 . . . natives of Holland . . . established . . . a new
and beautiful manufacture of painted silk, varnished linen, cloth,
paper, etc.,, for the most part stamped, some of the pieces are
very highly finished by hand. The linen is painted entirely by hand
and is done by girls from eight or nine to fourteen or fifteen years
of age; about forty of these have constant employ, and work in a
room, which is kept in a proper state of ventilation by an air pump,
to prevent any deleterious effects from the paint. (Daniel Lysons,
The Environs of London, 1796, Vol. 2, pp. 148–9)

44

[Of Port Isaac, Cornwall]
. . . a little creek, where vessels . . . are loaded with slate procured from a quarry in the neighbourhood. We saw a small sloop on the sand receiving her freight: the people employed to load her were principally women, two or three of whom stood in a cart, and as many on the vessel's deck, tossing the slates from one to another, with an energy that quite shamed their petticoats. Their labour is immoderately hard, they can accomplish as much in a given time as men can do, and yet they receive considerably less wages, because they are women. On all occasions the same injurious system of detraction is extended towards women, and whether it be as poets and philosophers, or servants of all work, they are equally obliged to submit to the deduction of a percentage on their sex.

At some distance from the pier, and at low water, you may occasionally see a company of industrious women with their petticoats considerably above the line of decency or their knees, gathering cockles and mussels among the rocks; but let me observe, to the credit of these ladies, that they resent all impertinent intrusion in a tone of indignation, and, if necessary with a power of fist, that few men would put themselves in the way of a second time. (Richard Ayton, *A Voyage round Great Britain*, 1814, vol 1 pp. 28, 71)

45

[Of Blandford, Dorset]
The women, and children, are chiefly employed in making thread and wire buttons for shirts, etc.

[Of a labourer's wife in Ellesmere, Shropshire]
His wife was formerly a laundry maid; and earns, by washing, 3s. a week: a sum that not one woman in 20, here, ever earns. (F. M. Eden, *The State of the Poor*, Vol 2, pp. 146, 621)

46

[Of women in trades and other occupations in Bedford in 1783]

Bookseller – Stationer	Anne Fletcher
Butcher	Widow Barker
Grocers	Widow Negus, Widow Butler, Widow Dennis

Ladies Boarding School	Miss Worral
Inns	Swan . . . . . Mary Thomas
	White Hart . . . . . Sarah Elger
	Red Lion . . . . . Elizabeth Sam-mons
	White Bear . . . . . Anne Page
	Peacock . . . . . Widow Butler

(Merchants' Miscellany and Travellers' Complete Compendium,
1785)

47

[Of the wife of a bookseller]
My . . . wife's attachment to books was a very fortunate circumstance for us both, not only as it was a perpetual source of rational
amusement, but also as it tended to promote my trade: her
extreme love for books made her delight to be in the shop, so that
she soon became perfectly acquainted with every part of it, and (as
my stock increased) with other rooms where I kept books, and
could readily get any article that was asked for. Accordingly, when
I was out on business my shop was well attended. (James
Lackington, *Memoirs of the Forty-Five First Years of the Life of
James Lackington* (1791), 1794, p. 206)

(f) Employment Opportunities

48

What business of life must daughters be brought up to? I must
confess, when I have seen so many of the sex who have lived well
in their childhood, grievously exposed to many hardships and
poverty upon the death of their parents, I have often wished there
were more of the callings or employments of life peculiarly
appropriated to women, and that they were regularly educated in
them, that there might be a better provision made for their
support. What if all the garments which are worn by women were
so limited and restrained in the manufacture of them, that they
should all be made only by their sex? This would go a great way
towards relief in this case: and what if some of the easier labours of
life were reserved for them only? (Isaac Watts, *The Improvement
of the Mind* (1725) 1819, pp. 345–6)

49

[Reasons for the reluctance of some tradesmen to let their wives learn their business]

1 The tradesman is foolishly vain of making his wife a gentlewoman, forsooth; he will have her sit above in the parlour, receive visits, drink tea, and entertain her neighbours, or take a coach and go abroad; but as to the business she shall not stoop to touch it; he has apprentices and journeymen, and there is no need of it.

2 Custom has made some trades not proper for the women to meddle in, such as linen and woollen drapers, mercers, goldsmiths, all sorts of dealers by commission, and the like. Custom, I say, has made these trades so effectually to shut out the women, that what with custom and the women's thinking it generally below them, we never or rarely see any women in such shops or warehouses.

3 Or if the trade is proper, and the wife willing, the husband declines it, and shuts her out; and this is the thing I complain of as an injustice upon the woman. But our tradesmen, forsooth, think it an undervaluing to them and to their business to have their wives seen in their shops; that is to say, that because other trades do not admit them, therefore they will not have their trades or shops thought less masculine, or less considerable than others; and they will not have their wives to be seen in their shops.

4 But there are two sorts of husbands more, who decline acquainting their wives with their business; and those are, first, those who are unkind, haughty, and imperious; who will not trust their wives, because they will not make them useful, that they may not value themselves upon it, and make themselves, as it were, equal to their husbands. A weak, foolish, and absurd suggestion! as if the wise were at all exalted by it, which indeed is just the contrary; for the woman is rather humbled and made a servant by it. Or, secondly, the other sort are those who are afraid their wives should be let into the knowledge of their business, lest they should come into the grand secret of all, namely to know that they are bankrupt, and undone, and worth nothing. (Daniel Defoe, *The Complete English Tradesman*, (1726–7), 1840–1 Edition citing that of 1745, Vol. 1, pp. 219–20)

50

[A letter to Archdeacon Sterne written in 1751 about Laurence Sterne's sister and the ways in which she might maintain herself, being a woman of good family]

. . . that if she would set herself to learn the business of a mantua-maker, as soon as she could get insight enough into it, to make a gown and set up for herself, that we would give her 30 pounds to begin the world and support her till business fill in. – Or if she would go into a milliner's shop in London, my wife engaged not only to get her into a shop where she could have ten pounds a year wages, but to equip her with clothes etc. properly for the place: or lastly if she likes it better, as my wife had then an opportunity of recommending her to the family of the first of our nobility – she undertook to get her a creditable place in it where she would receive no less than 8 or 10 pounds a year wages with other advantages. (*Letters of Laurence Sterne*, ed. Lewis P. Curtis, 1935, pp. 37–8)

51

'Tis the misfortune of this nation that the most part of our gentlemen and tradesmen bring up their daughters at a boarding school, where . . . time is, for the most part, employ'd in trifles, whilst the useful and becoming part of her education is wholly neglected, as her being taught to cut out and make up (her own and her family's) linen, and prudent management of household affairs, whereby she might become qualify'd for the government of a family, at her entrance into the married state.

But no sooner does the little creature leave school, furnish'd with all these trifling accomplishments, than the father and mother are for showing her off to get her a husband. This of course spoils the girl; for she now thinks of nothing but dress, receiving and returning visits, tea-drinking, and card-playing, which last is of the most fatal consequence . . . if this manner of life fails of getting her a husband, when young, and her parents are unable to give her a large fortune, she is obliged to live an old maid, and die useless to her generation. On the contrary, if her parents die, and leave her only a small fortune, she can't live upon the interest, and consequently must endeavour to marry for a livelihood; whence she becomes a prey to some designing mercenary fellow, or otherwise she spends her narrow income, and then what must she do for a support? Why she takes to ill courses; which makes so many women kept awhile, and then come upon the town, to the inevitable ruin both of soul and body.

. . . Let all gentlemen who have several daughters, and tradesmen, who can't give about 1000 or 1500 1. a piece to their daughters, and some who are able to give no more than two or three hundred pound . . . take care their daughters be taught the most useful part of needle-work, all the arts of economy, writing and book-keeping, with enough of dancing and French to give them a graceful easy freedom both of discourse and behaviour: And when they have acquir'd these necessary accomplishments in some degree of perfection, let them also at the age of fifteen or sixteen be put apprentices to genteel and easy trades, such as linen or woollen drapers, haberdashers of small wares, mercers, glovers, perfumers, grocers, confectioners, retailers of gold and silver lace, buttons, etc.

Why are not these as creditable trades for the daughters of gentlemen as they are for their sons?

. . . If women were train'd up to business from their early years, 'tis highly probable they would in general be more industrious, and get more money than men, and if so, what woman of spirit would submit to be a slave, and fling herself away, as many are forc'd to do, merely for a maintenance, because she cannot stoop to be a servant, and can find no reputable business to go into? . . .

As for tradesmen in particular, it would be much happier for them, if their wives and daughters knew how to keep their books, and be serviceable to them in their shops, than to have them walk through with that state and unconcernedness they usually do: They would then better know how to spend their husband's money, so as not to exceed his income . . .

. . . From the delicacy of their make, they are, indeed, unfit for certain laborious employments, which require considerable strength and robustness of body; but in all those where quickness of thought, activeness, dispatch, neatness, address, and a habit of pleasing are capital requisites, they would, I persuade myself, in no wise fall short of the men as are most remarkable for these qualifications. (*Gentleman's Magazine*, Vol. 9, September, 1739, pp. 525–6)

52

[Of the Society for the Encouragement of Arts, Manufacturers and Commerce]

The making of point lace . . . was . . . an art, which the society thought to deserve some encouragement. The working the flowers being the principal part of the labour, and performed by the hand, it was imagined, that the introduction of that manufacture would not only be a saving of the money sent abroad for this article . . . but employ a number of women of middling rank, who at present are supported by their relations, or struggle with difficulties from the smallness of their fortunes, and the present great expense of living. The Society was, moreover, particularly induced to lend attention to this matter, from the application of a milliner, who declared, she had assiduously employed herself to promote this matter, by instructing young gentlewomen to work flowers for point, and taking the produce of their labours, to be wrought into point lace, and disposed of in the course of her trade.

. . . the tediousness of the work, and the small price paid in proportion for the flowers, by those who are to finish the point and carry it to market, seem insurmountable impediments to establishing this manufacture in our country. (Robert Dossie, *Memoirs of Agriculture and Other Commercial Arts*, 1768, Vol 1, pp. 137–9)

53

But what have women to do in society? . . . Women might certainly study the art of healing and be physicians as well as nurses. And midwifery, decency seems to allot to them . . .

Businesses of various kinds, they might likewise pursue, if they were educated in a more orderly manner, which might save many from common and legal prostitution. Women would not then marry for a support, as men accept of places under Government, and neglect the implied duties; nor would an attempt to earn their own subsistence, a most laudable one! sink them almost to the level of those poor abandoned creatures who live by prostitution. For are not milliners and mantua-makers reckoned the next class? The few employments open to women, so far from being liberal, are menial; and when a superior education enables them to take charge of the education of children as governesses, they are not treated like the tutors of sons . . . But as women educated like gentlewomen, and never designed for the humiliating situation which necessity sometimes forces them to fill; these situations are considered in the light of a degradation . . .

. . . How many women thus waste life away the prey of discontent, who might have practised as physicians, regulated a farm, managed a shop, and stood erect, supported by their own industry, instead of hanging their heads surcharged with a dew of sensibility, that consumes the beauty to which it at first gave lustre . . . (Mary Wollstonecraft, *Vindication of the Rights of Woman* (1792), ed. Miriam Kramnick, 1978, pp. 260–2)

54

If constant employment were found for the wives and children of labouring men . . . the benefit public and private thence resulting would be great.

The greatest part of their time is unprofitably spent, because no care is taken to furnish them with work. (David Davies, *The Case of Labourers in Husbandry*, 1795, pp. 61, 83)

55

Another heavy discouragement to the industry of women, is the inequality of the reward of their labour, compared with that of men; an injustice which pervades every species of employment performed by both sexes.

In employments which depend on bodily strength, the distinction is just; for it cannot be pretended that the generality of women can earn as much as men, when the produce of their labour is the result of corporeal exertion; but it is a subject of great regret, that this inequality should prevail, even where an equal share of skill and application is exerted. Male stay-makers, mantua-makers, and hair-dressers, are better paid than female artists of the same professions; but surely it will never be urged as an apology for this disproportion, that women are not as capable of making stays, gowns, dressing hair, and similar arts, as men: if they are not superior to them, it can only be accounted for upon this principle, that the prices they receive for their labour are not sufficient to repay them for the expense of qualifying themselves for their business; and that they sink under the mortification of being regarded as artisans of inferior estimation . . .

Besides these employments which are commonly performed by women, and those already shown to be suitable for such persons as are above the condition of hard labour, there are some professions and trades customarily in the hands of men, which might be conveniently exercised by either sex. – Watchmaking requiring more ingenuity than strength, seems peculiarly adapted to women; as do many parts of the business of stationer, particularly, ruling account books or making pens. The compounding of medicines in an apothecary's shop, requires no other talents than care and exactness; and if opening a vein occasionally be a indispensable requisite, a woman may acquire the capacity of doing it, for those of her own sex at least, without any reasonable objection, – cupping is an art which wants neither strength in the performance, nor medical judgement in the application, as that depends upon the direction of the physician, and might, under the restriction just mentioned with regard to bleeding, be exercised by women – Pastry and confectionery appear particularly consonant to the habits of women, though generally performed by men: perhaps the heat of the ovens, and the strength requisite to fill and empty them, may render male assistants necessary; but certain women are most eligible to mix up the ingredients, and prepare the various kinds of cakes for baking. – Light turnery and toy-making depend more upon dexterity and invention than force, and are therefore suitable work for women and children.

There must be public houses for the reception of travellers, and labourers who are single and have no homes . . . without recommending it as an eligible employment for women, reasons may be urged for the widows of publicans, or even other women of a certain age, engaging in it; as houses of this description, which are under female management, are generally the most orderly, and the most successful.

Farming, as far as respects the theory, is commensurate with the powers of the female mind: nor is the practice of inspecting agricultural processes incompatible with the delicacy of their frames if their constitution be good. (Priscilla Wakefield, *Reflections on the Present Condition of the Female Sex* (1798), 1817, pp. 114, 115, 125–7)

56

. . . it were much to be wished that women were somewhat more attended to, in the distribution of fortune. This attention to their worldly comfort, is the more reasonable, that they are debarred by the tyranny of fashion . . . from availing themselves of their talents and industry, to promote their interests and independence. However high the sphere of life in which a man is born, if his fortune be not equal to his birth or his ambition, there are a thousand different ways by which he may advance himself with honour in the world; whereas women of a certain rank, are totally excluded from a possibility, even of supporting that style of life to which they have been accustomed, if they are left without competent fortunes. But what is infinitely worse – because it leads to want, or infamy, or both – few, very few are the employments left open even to women of the inferior classes, by which they can secure independence: . . . want of fortune, and want of appropriate employment . . . likewise unfit them, for being proper wives to men in their own station, who in general can scarcely afford to marry, without some assistance either in industry or money.

Indeed the businesses appropriated by custom for women, are so very few in proportion to the number of candidates, that they are soon monopolized. (Mary Hays, *Appeal to the Men of Great Britain in Behalf of Women*, 1798, p. 278)

Part 12 Female Domestic Servants

[The inmates of a fashionable boarding school question a new arrival – the daughter of a clergyman]
I was interrogated by many of the young ladies as to
the station of my father, or rather respecting the
figure he made in the world. 'Does your papa keep a
coach?' – 'No' – 'How many servants have you?' –
'Four' – 'Dear: only think. Miss's papa does not keep
a coach, and they have only four servants' (*Memoirs
of the Life of the late Mrs Catherine Cappe*, 1824, p.
40)

Introduction

One consequence of the growth of a middle class with
aspirations to gentility, was the increased demand for servants. It was a demand which spread downwards in the social
scale. It led to a frenzied competition from those of the upper
classes who had always employed servants, to employ more
and better-dressed servants, in order to distance themselves
from their social inferiors.

The distinction in the countryside between female domestic servants and female servants in husbandry is by no means
always a clear one. Those recruited as servants in husbandry
were often expected to work, for at least a part of the time, in
the house (see Part 10c). On the other hand, female domestic
servants in the countryside usually combined their work in
the house with labour outside – help at hay-time and harvest,
work with the poultry and in the dairy.

In the first half of the century the daughters of small
farmers, as well as agricultural labourers, provided the main
source of supply of servants (**4**). With the decline of small-
holdings and the reluctance of farmers to continue to employ
living-in servants in husbandry, such local employment
opportunities for girls declined. Hiring fairs or statutes which
had long been the traditional way to hire such servants also
became less frequent (**3**).

The shrinking of employment opportunities for country
girls, the pressure of rural poverty and the fear of becoming
chargeable to the parish (**5**) all acted as an incentive to look

elsewhere for employment. The demand for country-bred female servants in London, combined with the higher wages they could earn in the metropolis, led to a steady exodus of girls from the country. By far the greatest demand for female domestic servants came from London. Patrick Colquhoun, the magistrate, estimated that there were rarely less than 10,000 servants of both sexes out of a place in the capital (*A Treatise on the Police of the Metropolis* (1796), 1797, p. 423n.)

There may well have been some basis for Defoe's questioning of the real motives for girls leaving their homes in the countryside to come to London (2). The attitude of the Settlement Laws to pregnant women often must have driven them to London, but the attractions of far greater employment possibilities, as well as better wages, are enough to explain the move of the great majority.

For a London family seeking a maid servant, all that it was necessary to do was to meet the wagons coming into the capital from the countryside, or to frequent the inns at such coaching stations (1, 5). The obvious preference of such families for girls from the country suggests that London girls may have been less servile and submissive than their rural sisters.

At the beginning of the century Defoe suggested that the shortage of good servants necessitated legislation, both to limit the ability of servants to leave employment without good reason and to ensure the better treatment of servants by employers (7). Defoe's plea suggests that maltreatment of servants was not uncommon. The diary entry of Abigail Gawthern for 16 March 1776 reported no exceptional occurrence (20). For those that became common knowledge there must have been many that did not. Defoe blamed such treatment not only for the scarcity of servant maids, but also for the increase in prostitution in London.

Writings are full of the danger threatening any female servant especially in London, that great corrupter of youth (11). 'Notorious procuresses' waited the arrival of young girls from the country in search of a position. If they were so unfortunate as to lose a position for a period, there were many all too anxious to exploit the situation (12).

Of course, nearly all such advice comes not from the servants themselves but from those who employed them. Inevitably, they are prejudiced in favour of good, hardworking, humble and docile servants who know their place and recognise their betters. Yet all of them suggest that the life of the female servant was a difficult one) While pointing out the importance of preserving their chastity against all threats to it from both masters and men servants in the same household, the only hope of preserving it was by trusting in God (**9**). In an effort to avoid the most obvious pitfalls girls are advised to choose a place only after very careful checking of the credentials of the family (**12**).

One of the main attractions domestic service offered was the hope of social advancement. That few achieved it is certain, but foreign travellers were always remarking on the difficulty of distinguishing maid from mistress (**15, 16**). That they were usually referring to the upper ranks of domestic service seems likely. It was ladies' maids and companions who were recruited from the genteelly educated but impecunious daughters of the middle class who filled such positions and who accompanied their mistresses wherever they went. It is for such upper servants that Lady Pennington demands special treatment from their mistresses (**10**).

The work expected of female domestic servants varied enormously from ladies' maids to housekeepers to chambermaids and maids of all work (**17, 18, 19**). It also varied as between town and country servants. Common to all, however, was the board, and often the clothes, provided by their employers. The wages of female servants varied according to their status, their particular responsibilities and whether they worked in London or the countryside. Under-servants could earn from £2 to £6 a year while cooks averaged between £6 and £10 and a lady's maid about £10. Extra allowances, either in money or kind, were given to enable servants to drink tea twice a day (**21**).

Parson Woodforde seems to have gone through a remarkable number of servants (**21**). His experience suggests that female domestic servants rarely stayed in the same household for their working lifetime. Sarah Ball's nine years' experience at Pepper Street was, it would seem, exceptional (**20**). Servants moved on either for reasons of marriage (**21**) or because of bad relations with their employers. Far more frequent than reports of female servants leaving their place voluntarily are cases of dismissal by employers.

Many of the extracts included here, particularly in the final section, are mere snippets. Apart from the impressions of a handful of foreign travellers and the readily available advice and warnings offered to female servants, the main source for the actual experience of such servants is diaries. Such entries tend to be brief. On the whole, the experience of their servants did not occupy the thoughts of their employers, except when they died or were dismissed and they were thus forced to find a replacement.

(a) Sources of Supply of Female Domestic Servants

1

[The scene that may have inspired Hogarth's *A Harlot's Progress* (Plate 2)]
The last week I went to an inn in the city, to enquire for some provisions which were sent by a wagon out of the country; and as I waited in one of the boxes till the chamberlain had looked over his parcels, I heard an old maid and a young voice repeating the Questions and Responses of the church Catechism. I thought it no breach of good manners to peer at a crevice, and look therein at people so well employed; but who should I see there but the most artful procuress in town, examining a most beautiful country girl, who had come up in the same wagon with my things . . . Her innocent *forsooth's, yes's, and't please you's, and she would do her endeavour*, moved the good old lady to take her out of the hands of a country bumpkin her brother, and hire her for her own maid. (Richard Steele, *The Spectator*, 4 January 1712)

2

. . . nothing is more natural than the common jest we put upon the country girls, when we see them come up to London in the carriers' wagons, and on the pack horses, viz. to ask them if they have been church'd before they came from home; . . . for who would come away to London to go to service, if things were all well at home? (Daniel Defoe, *The Great Law of Subordination Consider'd*, 1724, p. 86)

3

We were very merry at passing thro' a village call'd Bloxham, on the occasion of a meeting of servants for hire, which the people there call a Mop; 'tis generally in other places call'd a Statute, because founded upon a statute law in Q. Elizabeth's time for regulating of servants. This I christn'd by the name of a Jade-Fair, at which some of the poor girls began to be angry, but we appeas'd them with better words.

I have observ'd at some of these fairs, that the poor servants distinguish themselves by holding something in their hands, to intimate what labour they are particularly qualify'd to undertake;

as the carters a whip, the labourers a shovel, the wood men a bill, the manufacturers a wool comb, and the like. But since the ways and manners of servants are advanc'd as we now find them to be, those Jade Fairs are not so much frequented as formerly, tho' we have them at several towns near London; as at Enfield, Waltham, Epping, etc. (Daniel Defoe, *A Tour through England and Wales*, 1724–7, Everyman's Library, Vol. 2, p. 31)

4

. . . small farmers were the people that used to stock the country with the best of servants: those were the nurseries for breeding up industrious and virtuous young men and women; whereas the generality of servants, now-a-days, are such as have had but little opportunity of learning how to do business so as to be fit to make good servants; for the labourer cannot be expected to be able to give his children that learning which is proper to fit them for good places; whilst those who rent small farms have generally where-withal to give and to know how to behave in a proper and decent manner. Besides, the girls have opportunities of learning at home how to brew, bake, cook, knit, sew, and get up linen, etc., whereas poor people's children have not such advantages. (Anon., *An Address to the P——t on Behalf of the Starving Multitude*, 1766, p. 39)

5

Yesterday, a decent looking girl about thirteen, whom some *humane* Churchwardens at Bristol had given the coachman a trifling fee to drop in London, came into the Bell in Bell Savage Yard, and inquired for a place; on being interrogated, she said, that her father . . . and her mother were both dead, and that fearing she would become chargeable to the parish, this cruel scheme had been taken as a preventative. (*London Chronicle*, Vol. 31, 1772, 472)

6

The idea of the pleasures to be enjoyed in the capital inspires the girls in the country with the most longing desire to participate in them. Imagination inflames their little heads, and presents every object under an exaggerated appearance. The young people of both sexes, who have been educated at a distance from town, imagine the metropolis to resemble that paradise promised to the mahometans by their prophet. (J. W. von Archenholz, *A Picture of England*, 1791, p. 191)

(b) Advice to Servants and their Mistresses

7

No servant should quit a place where they are well fed and paid, without assigning a good reason before a magistrate. On the other hand they should receive no abuse which should not be redressed; for we ought to treat them as servants, not slaves; and a medium ought to be observed on both sides. But if they are not restrained from quitting service on every vagary, they will throw themselves on the town, and not only ruin themselves, but others; for example, a girl quits a place and turns whore . . .

And unless we prevent our maid-servants being harboured by wicked persons when out of a place, or living too long on their own hands, our streets will swarm with impudent shameless strumpets; the good will be molested; those prone to evil will be made yet more wicked, by having temptations thrown in their way; and, to crown all, we shall have scarce a servant left, but our wives, etc., must do the household work themselves . . . If this be not worthy the consideration of a legislature, I would fain to know what is. Is it not time to limit their wages, when they are grown so wanton they know not what to ask? Is it not time to fix them when they stroll from place to place, and we are hardly sure of a servant a month together? Is it not time to prevent the increase of harlots, by making it penal for servants to be harboured in idleness, and tempted to theft, whoredom, murder, etc., by living too long out of place? (Daniel Defoe, *Augusta Triumphans*, 1728, pp. 18–20)

8

If you are in the house of a person of condition where there are many men servants, it requires a great deal of circumspection how to behave. As these fellows live high, and have little to do, they are for the most part very pert and saucy where they dare, and apt to take liberties on the least encouragement; you ought therefore to carry yourself at a distance towards them . . . you must behave with an extreme civility mixt with seriousness, but never be too free. To suffer them to toy or romp with you, will embolden them, perhaps to actions unbecoming modesty to bear, and the least rebuff provoke them to use you ill; whereas a cold reserve at first will prevent both the one and the other. (Anon., *A Present for a Servant-Maid*, 1743, p. 35)

9

. . . for as, whilst they are in service, they cannot avoid conversing with the men servants, and too frequently with such as are lewd and debauched; they ought to look upon themselves as greatly exposed to temptations to immodesty, and therefore should think it their duty to guard against such dangerous snares.

Let me then earnestly beg of you to think no pains and care too much to preserve your modesty and virtue, which are the chief honours of a woman. In order to do this, do not trust in your own strength, but beg of God to bestow on you the gift of chastity.

Avoid idleness. Apply yourself diligently to the duties of your service: and when you have any leisure time, employ it in reading good books, in examining your behaviour, in conversing with God in prayer, and sometimes in such amusements as are entirely innocent.

There is no harm in inoffensive cheerfulness, but there may be danger in excessive and immoderate mirth; for it raiseth the spirits above their usual pitch, and at the same time putteth reason off its guard, so that indecency of some kind or other will be very apt to surprise you.

Intemperance in drinking, you have heard, is odious in the other sex, but in woman it is still more abominable, and particularly because it robbeth them of shame and reason, which are the guardians of their chastity. Beware of dressing above your rank or station. Shun herein that foolish affectation of imitating your superiors, whom providence hath placed in a higher state of life, and what is allowable to them will in you be the subject of laughter and ridicule. Appear always as neat and clean as possible, but avoid the use of gawdy or fantastical ornaments; or putting on your clothes, which are made for a decent covering, in such a manner as to expose your person; for this will be wearing the attire of a harlot, and all sober people will suppose you do it with a design to allure and entrap the men.

Let no evil communication proceed 'out of your mouth'. Avoid all loose discourse. Never use an immodest word, or any that will bear a double meaning.

Show not yourselves over-fond of the company of men, and always behave before them with a proper reserve. Never listen to any of their flattering speeches. Be cautious in accepting from them either presents or treats, lest in return they should expect you to indulge them in greater freedoms, and such liberties, which, tho' they call them innocent, may in the end lead to the overthrow of your virtue. And above all things, be not prevailed upon, by promises of marriage, to do what you may for ever repent of; few men choosing afterwards to make wives of such who have before wedlock suffered themselves to be debauched by them. (Thomas Broughton, *Serious Advice and Warning to Servants*, (1746), 4th edn., 1763, pp. 20–3)

10

Should you at any time have an upper servant, whose family and education were superior to that state of subjection, to which succeeding misfortunes may have reduced her, she ought to be treated with peculiar indulgence:- if she has understanding enough to be conversable, and humility enough always to keep her proper distance, lessen, as much as possible, every painful remembrance of former prospects, by looking on her as an humble friend, and making her an occasional companion – but never descend to converse with those whose birth, education, and early views in life, were not superior to a state of servitude – their minds being in general suited to their station, they are apt to be intoxicated by any degree of familiarity, and to become useless and impertinent.

. . . treat all your domestics with such mildness and affability, that you may be served rather out of affection than fear; – let them live happily under you; – give them leisure for their own business, time for innocent recreation, and more especially for attending the public service of the church, to be instructed in their duty to God – without which you have no right to expect the discharge of that owing to yourself. – When wrong, tell them calmly of their faults; – and if they amend not after two or three such rebukes, dismiss them – but never descend to passion and scolding, which is inconsistent with a good understanding, and beneath the dignity of a gentlewoman. (Lady Sarah Pennington, *An Unfortunate Mother's Advice to her Absent Daughters* (1761), 1770, pp. 53–6)

11

. . .I think no lady can appear in a point of view more charming, than being divested of that insolence of levity which tempts so many to look down on others, she shows a maternal care of young female servants. The protection of one, who from her inexperience and poverty is most exposed to danger, adds honour and dignity to the most accomplished character.

. . . the mistress who is best taught, will be most attentive that her domestics shall know their duty . . . Much depends on your care! The larger your fortune and connections, and the higher your talents, the greater your charge.

[Thomas Trueman advises his daughter on the dangers for female servants in London]
Too well do I remember some of my good neighbours daughters, whom nothing would please but going up to London, as if they were sure of making their fortunes! Some of them have lived virtuously, single; others have succeeded in the world, by marriage; but it hath fared ill with several of the most distinguished for comeliness. They soon fell into the snares of those abandoned procuresses, who trade in sin, and under a pretence of getting them good places, brought them like birds to the net, or lambs to the slaughter . . . No country lass can suspect half the wicked arts which are played off to seduce young females, in that sink of iniquity, London . . .
. . . great caution is necessary in going to what they call public register offices, where those who want service, or servants, apply: and it is particularly necessary for a young woman to inform herself exactly of the character of the person who proposes to take her as a servant, which is sometimes difficult to be done; for you may be recommended for information, to persons of the same stamp. (Jonas Hanway, *Virtue in Humble Life*, 1774, Vol 1, pp. xix, lvi; Vol. 2, p. 223)

12

[Of seeking a place]
If you are in want of a place, inquire only of such persons as are respectable, and on whom you can depend. If you hear of such a place where a servant is wanted, and none of your friends know the parties, the best place to inquire about them is at some large grocers or linen draper's shop in the neighbourhood. Ask for the master or the mistress of the shop and beg of them the favour to tell you whether the house to which you have been directed is a place fit for a modest and respectable young woman to go to. For want of care in this particular, some girls, especially in London, have been drawn into very bad and improper places. . . . Servants cannot be too careful as to where they lodge when out of place; many young females have been corrupted by the companionship of the dissolute, with whom they have been thrown into contact during a temporary abode in low lodgings, principally chosen on account of their cheapness . . .
It is very often the case, that improper lodgings are chosen

through ignorance and inexperience; since a servant may have no knowledge of a city she has newly entered, and consequently can have no idea of the danger she incurs in entering an unknown lodging-house. (Anon., *A Present for Servants*, 1799, p. 161)

(c) Maid or Mistress?

13

Women servants are now so scarce, that from thirty and forty shillings a year their wages are increased of late to six, seven, and eight pounds per annum, and upwards; in so much that an ordinary tradesman cannot well keep one; but his wife, who might be useful in his shop, or business, must do the drudgery of household affairs. And all this, because our servant wenches are so puff'd up with pride now a days that they never think they go fine enough: it is a hard matter to know the mistress from the maid by their dress; nay, very often the maid shall be much the finer of the two: Our woollen manufacture suffers much by this, for nothing but silks and satins will go down with our kitchen wenches: . . .

Her neat's leathern shoes are now transformed into lac'd ones with high heels; her yarn stockings are turn'd into fine worsted ones, with silk clocks; and her high wooden pattens are kickt away for leathern clogs; she must have a hoop too, as well as her mistress; and her poor scanty linsey-woolsey petticoat is changed into a good silk one, four or five yards wide at the least. Not to carry the description farther, in short, plain country-Joan is now turn'd into a fine London-madam, can drink tea, take snuff, and carry her self as high as the best.

By their extravagance in dress they put our wives and daughters upon yet greater excesses, because they will (as indeed they ought) go finer than the maid. Thus the maid striving to out-do the mistress, or the tradesman's wife to out-do the gentleman's wife, the gentleman's wife emulating the lady, and the ladies one another, it seems as if the whole business of the female sex were nothing but excess of pride, and extravagance in dress. (Daniel Defoe, *Everybody's Business Is Nobody's Business* (1725) 1840–1, pp. 357, 361)

14

Many tradesmens' wives in London give their maids £8 a year, and enable them, with their vails, to gain as good silks and as fine linen, as their mistresses; which is not the condition of servants, whose wearing and living ought to be at a much greater distance: This makes them saucy and negligent. People were much better served formerly, when a maid in a good family had but 40s. a year, and wore a serge gown and a plain round-ear'd cap; a gown that with the neatness then in use, would last half a dozen years, and often much longer, and kept them in a state of humility, as servants ought to be kept. (Anon., *The Laws relating to Masters and Servants*, 1755, p. 11 fn.)

15

The servant-maids of citizens' wives, the waiting women of ladies of the first quality, and of the middling gentry, attend their ladies in the streets and in the public walks, in such a dress, that, if the mistress be not known, it is no easy matter to distinguish her from her maid. (P. J. Grosley, *A Tour to London*, (1765), 1772, p. 75)

16

The appearances of the female domestics will perhaps astonish a foreigner more than anything in London. They are in general handsome and well clothed: their dress has the appearance of some taste, and their conversation such as if they had kept the best company. A stranger is apt to be embarrassed at first, and can scarce imagine that they are not gentlewomen. They are usually clad in gowns well adjusted to their shapes, and hats adorned with ribbands. There are some who even wear silk and sattin, when they are dressed. All their work consists in keeping the house neat and dusting the furniture. To this employment they attend for a few hours in the morning; and after that, all the rest of the day is entirely at their own disposal.

As to the lady's maid, the eye of the most skilful *connoisseur* can scarcely distinguish her from her mistress. The appearance of a waiting-woman is that of an opulent and a fashionable person; she usually accompanies her lady in public, expects particular attention to be paid to her, and, after some years of service, generally receives a small annuity which makes her comfortable for life.

When out of place, servants of all denominations apply to a register office; a singular institution, known only in that country, by means of which they are immediately provided with employment. (J. W. von Archenholz, *A Picture of England*, 1791, pp. 207–8)

(d) Hiring, Firing and Conditions of Service

17

[A letter to the mother of a prospective servant maid in 1744 outlines the duties she will be expected to perform]
She must milk 3 or 4 cows & understand how to manage that Dairy, & know how to boyll & roast ffowlls & butcher's meatt. Wee wash once a month, she & the washerwoman wash the Buck [a large wash of coarser kinds of clothing]. She helps the other maid wash the rooms when they are done, she makes the Garrett beds & cleans them, & cleans ye great stairs & scours all the Irons & scours the Pewter in use, & wee have an woman to help when't is all done. There is very good time to do all this provided she is a servant, & when she has done her worke she sits down to spin. (*The Purefoy Letters, 1735–53*, ed. G. Eland, 1931, Vol. 1, p. 147)

18

[His landlord informed him of] a fat Welsh girl, who was just come out of the country, scarce understood a word of English, and was capable of nothing but washing, scouring and sweeping the rooms, and had no inclination to learn anything more. The wages of the girl were six guineas a year, besides a guinea a year for her tea, which all servant-maids either take in money, or have it found for them twice a day. The wages of a cook-maid, who knows how to roast and boil, amount to twenty guineas a year. (P. J. Grosley, *A Tour to London* (1765), 1772, p. 75)

19

[On the work expected of a housekeeper]
. . . a very capable Person to undertake the Management of a large Family of Fashion; she must thoroughly understand in what Manner to supply a Table in Town and Country; she must be neat and orderly, a good economist, and have authority to oblige the other Servants to be so; she must understand Pickling, Preserving, Potting, Salting Meat, and keeping all sorts of Provisions, to order and keep a proper Supply of them, buying in, paying for and keeping a regular Account thereof, and every Thing under her . . .
(*Daily Advertiser*, no. 12534, 1771, 26 February

20

[13 March 1773]
Ann Maltby went to live at my father's as cook, her wages £5 per year; she came from Lord Middleton's . . .

[16 March 1776]
At the assizes at the county hall, Mrs. Burnell of Winkburn had a trial for beating her maid servant; she was in court and sat close to the judge . . . she was hissed at going out of court.

[December 1789]
Sarah Ball went to live as cook in Pepper Street, Sep. 24; wages £4:14:6 per year; she was an excellent cook but a drunken woman.

Thomas Taylor, my father's servant, was taken ill, Thursday, Jan. 4, his disorder a fever; he was delirious and died Tuesday the 9th . . . he had lived sixteen years at my fathers, last 2nd of Nov, 1797; I fear he lost his life through intemperance.

[1798]
Sarah Ball left Pepper Street, Feb. 6, an excellent servant but fond of drinking; she was to have married Thomas Taylor if he had lived.

[1794]
Molly Ashmore, our housemaid, died suddenly in this house, Saturday, Sep. 27, aged 21; she was a widow and left a boy not four years old . . . she had lived with us near seven months. (A. Gawthern, *The Diary of Abigail Gawthern of Nottingham 1751–1810*, ed. Adrian Henstock, 1978–9, pp. 20, 31, 50, 73, 61)

21

[3 June 1776]
Two servant maids came to me this morning and offered their services to me. One of them is to be an upper servant and she lived very lately with Mr. Howes. A very pretty woman she is and understands cookery and working at her needle well. I am to give her per annum and tea twice a day – 5.5.0. She was well recommended to me by Mrs. Howes and the reason she was turned away from Mrs. Howes's was her not getting up early enough, as Mrs. Howes told me. The other maid was recommended to me by Mrs. Howes, she is a Tenant's daughter of Mr. Howes's, she is wooled. I agreed to give her per annum – 3.10.0. She is to come at Midsummer also. She is to milk, etc.

[14 October 1778]
I sent Cary's cart . . . to Little Melton . . . after my new maid this afternoon, and she returned about 6 o'clock. Her name is Eliz. Caxton about 40 yrs of age, but how she will do I know not as yet but her wages are £5. 15. 6d. per annum, but out of that she is to find herself in tea and sugar. She is not the most engaging I must confess by her first appearance that she makes. My other maid came to me also this evening. Her name is Anne Lillistone . . . about 18 years of age but very plain, however I like her better than the other at the first sight. I am to give her £2.0.0 per annum and to make her an allowance to find herself in tea and sugar.

[5 January 1779]
. . . My maid, Nanny Lillistone left my service this morning having had proper notice before given to her.
I paid her a Qrs wages due now 0.10.0. To her also for Qrs allowance for tea – 0.2.6. I gave to her also a free gift of 0.2.6. I had no other fault to find with her, but that she did not chuse to be under the other Maid. In every other respect a very good Servant I believe. Betty Greaves a girl of about 15 came to my house in the room of Nanny Lillistone. She is a neat girl and I hope will do – tho she is small . . .

[13 January 1783]
. . . This evening paid all my Servants their Years Wages – due January 6, 1783.

    To my Head Maid, Betty Claxton pd. 5. 15. 6
    To my Lower Lizzy Greaves pd. . . . . . 2. 0. 6.

[5 Jan. 1784]
. . .Paid my Servants their Wages this Day as follows:

    To Betty 1 Yrs Wages due this Day and for Tea also pd.
    . . . . . 5. 15. 6.
    To Lizzy 1 Yrs Wages due this Day and for Tea also pd. . . . . . .
    2. 12. 6.

[8 August, 1784]
. . . My head maid Eliz. Claxton this afternoon immediately after tea (gave notice) that she should go at Michaelmas in these abrupt and ungracious words 'Sir, I shall leave your service at Michaelmas next'! I told her that I thought the notice short. She gave no reason whatever for leaving.

[11 October 1784]
. . . After breakfast paid my maid Eliz. Claxton who leaves me today, three Qrs wages – being 4.7.0. She breakfasted here and left us about 11 this morn.

[12 October 1784]
. . . At 11 this morning . . . married my old maid Eliz. Claxton to Charles Cary of this parish by banns – recd for marrying them – 0.5.0. and which I gave to the bride after. (Rev James Woodforde, *Diary of a Country Parson, 1758–1802*, ed. John Beresford, 1924–31, Vol. 1, pp. 182–3, 236–7, 271–2, Vol. 2, pp. 55, 114, 147, 156)

22

Wanted in a Gentleman's Family, a middle-aged woman as cook; she must perfectly understand plain cooking, and have lived in a genteel family some time, from whence an unexceptionable character will be expected. Any person fully answering the above, may apply to Mr. Geary, in Salisbury. (*Salisbury and Winchester Journal*, 2 March 1789)

23

[Hester Piozzi writes to Mrs. Pennington, 18 December 1795]
You must enquire me a Housekeeper such as you *know* will suit us; a good country housewife, who can salt Bacon, cure Ham, see also to the baking, etc., and be an active manager of and for a dozen troublesome servants . . . (Hester Piozzi, *The Intimate Letters of Hester Piozzi and Penelope Pennington, 1788–1821*, ed. Oswald G. Knapp, 1914, pp. 132–3)

24

[The work of housemaids]
. . . to keep the whole house in a state of cleanliness, by carefully washing the rooms, stair cases, etc., cleaning the fire-grates, irons, and hearths, dusting carpets, and rubbing the furniture, as well as the locks, knockers, glasses, chimney ornaments, picture frames, etc. (Anon., *Every Woman her Own House-Keeper*, 1796, Vol. 2, 73)

25

This abuse ['the inequality of the reward of their labour, compared with that of men'] is in no instance more conspicuous than in the wages of domestic servants. A footman, especially of the higher kind, whose most laborious task is to wait at table, gains, including clothes, vails, and other perquisites, at least £50 per annum; whilst a cook-maid, who is mistress of her profession, does not obtain £20, though her office is laborious, unwholesome, and requires a much greater degree of skill than that of a valet. A similar disproportion is observable among the inferior servants of the establishment. (Priscilla Wakefield, *Reflections on the Present Condition of the Female Sex* (1798), 1817, p. 114 fn.)

Part   Women Protest
13

... if any histories were anciently written by
women, time and the malice of men have effectually
conspir'd to suppress 'em; and it is not reasonable to
think that men shou'd transmit, or suffer to be
transmitted to posterity, anything that might show
the weakness and illegality of their title to a power
they still exercise so arbitrarily, and are so fond of.
(Mary Astell (sometimes attributed), *An Essay in
Defence of the Female Sex*, 1696, p. 23)

Introduction

In some ways 1800 is a bad date at which to end this study of
women. It represents a time, however short-lived, when
opportunities for productive labour among women were at a
low ebb. Looking back over the century, it is difficult to avoid
the conclusion that for women the effects of developments
had been almost entirely divisive. Increasing awareness of
class differences constantly intrude into any attempt at simple analysis of events in feminist terms. Most women of the
labouring class, denied employment opportunities, were
preoccupied with fighting poverty and avoiding dependence
on the poor rates. The continued existence of a vast body of
women desperately anxious for any means of staving off
pauperism, meant that they remained vulnerable to the worst
of economic exploitation, representing a ready pool of cheap
labour with wages always well below those of the opposite
sex. Partly for the same reason, trade union organisation of
women in industry came slowly and late.

Women aspiring to the middle class, divorced from labour,
had little in common with their labouring sisters. Indeed, their
very aspirations demanded a sharp separation from those
women below them in the social hierarchy.

The way in which class-consciousness bedevils any
attempt to see women's history over the century as simply
one of male exploitation, is nowhere more evident than in
domestic service. The role of women of the respectable

classes might be one of total submission to their husbands, but they, in turn, expected the same humility and submission from their servants. One cannot avoid concluding that the role played by domestic service in women's history has been divisive and inhibiting of progress. Is it accidental that only when female domestic service began to decline was there a real breakthrough to a more militant women's movement?

Was there, then, no progress made by women in the eighteenth century? Are there no signs of forces making for change by the final years? Certainly, attitudes towards daughters and wives were slowly being modified towards greater freedom of choice and a recognition of a more positive role of companionship for the wife. Certainly, the new leisure that many women enjoyed, and the advent of the lending library, gave some of them new ideas that challenged existing conventions about relations between the sexes. Very slowly improvement was occurring in educational standards for daughters of the middle class. Yet, in some other respects, the situation for women worsened; employment opportunities for all women actually narrowed, the possibilities of working partnerships with husbands declined, the confidence that wives of labourers enjoyed from their ability to contribute to the family income was eroded. The inhibitions felt by some women writers and authors seem actually to increase in the early nineteenth century. At the very end of the eighteenth century the ideas of Mary Wollstonecraft were ignored because women saw her as unwomanly, as flouting the rigid sexual conventions of the time. It was to be decades before those ideas were to have any real influence among women.

The importance of unmarried women of the middle class in the developments of the nineteenth-century women's movement has been perhaps too little regarded. We have seen how they tend to remain outside the sphere of the worst male domination of the period. The urgent necessity of finding employments that were both genteel and enabled them to make a living, combined with an articulateness that came from a rather better education than that of the female poor, led to a growing demand for better training as governesses and school teachers and, indeed, as housekeepers. That the provision of such training was a major concern of the women's movement from the middle of the nineteenth century, and that single women played a leading role in that movement, seems more than accidental.

Throughout the century, nevertheless, the voices of women

are heard raised in protest at the role assigned to them, and the implications that role had for any claim to equality with men. The voices were mainly those of upper-class women. For those who lacked the ability to make an articulate protest one of a different kind was being made. Sometimes it was at the high prices of food-stuffs, sometimes at the effect of enclosures, sometimes against the introduction of machinery into a hitherto home-based trade, and sometimes such acts of protest were a response to the tyranny of male domination.

(a) Women Challenge their Allotted Role

1

Far be it from her to stir up sedition of any sort: none can abhor it more; and she heartily wishes, that our masters wou'd pay their civil and ecclesiastical governors the same submission, which they themselves exact from their domestic subjects. Nor can she imagine how she any way undermines the masculine empire, or blows the trumpet of rebellion to the moiety of mankind. Is it by exhorting women, not to expect to have their own will in anything, but to be entirely submissive, when once they have made choice of a lord and master, tho' he happens not to be so wise, so kind, or even so just a governor as was expected? She did not indeed advise them to think his folly wisdom, nor his brutality that love and worship he promised in his matrimonial oath, for this required a flight of wit and sense much above her poor ability, and proper only to masculine under-standings. However she did not in any manner prompt them to resist, or to abdicate the perjur'd spouse, tho' the laws of God and the land make special provision for it, in a case wherein, as is to be fear'd few men can truly plead Not Guilty.

'Tis true, thro' want of learning and of that superior genius which men lay claim to, she was ignorant of the Natural Inferiority of our sex, which our masters lay down as a self-evident and fundamental truth. She saw nothing in the reason of things to make this either a principle or a conclusion, but much to the contrary; it being sedition at least, if not treason to assert it in this reign. For if by the natural superiority of their sex, they mean that every man is by nature superior to every woman, which is the obvious meaning, and that which must be stuck to if they would speak sense, it wou'd be a sin in any woman to have dominion over any man, and the greatest Queen ought not to command her footman . . .

If they mean that some men are superior to some women, this is no great discovery; had they turn'd the tables they might have seen that some women are superior to some men.

. . . That the custom of the world has put women, generally speaking, into a state of subjection, is not deny'd; but the right can no more be prov'd from the fact, than the predominancy of vice can justify it.

. . . if absolute sovereignty be not necessary in a state, how comes it to be so in a family? or if in a family why not in a state; since no reason can be alledg'd for the one that will not hold more strongly for the other? If the authority of the husband so far as it extends, is sacred and inalienable, why not of the Prince? The domestic sovereign is without dispute elected, and the stipulations and contract are mutual, is it not then partial in men to the last degree, to contend for, and practice that arbitrary dominion in their own families, which they abhor and exclaim against in the state? For if arbitrary power is evil in itself, and an improper method of governing rational and free agents, it ought not to be practis'd anywhere; Nor is it less, but rather more mischievous in families than in kingdoms, by how much 100,000 tyrants are worse than one. What tho' a husband can't deprive a wife of life without being responsible to the law, he may however do what is much more grievous to a generous mind, render life miserable, for which she has no redress, scarce pity which is afforded to every other complainant, it being thought a wife's duty to suffer everything without complaint. If all men are born free, how is it that all women are born slaves? (Mary Astell, *Some Reflections upon Marriage*, (1700), 1706, preface)

2

Of all things in nature, I most wonder why men should be severe in the censures of our sex, for a failure in point of chastity: Is it not monstrous that our seducers should be our accusers? Will they not employ fraud, nay, often force, to gain us? What various arts, what stratagems, what wiles will they use for our destruction? but that once accomplished, every opprobrious term with which our language so plentifully abounds, shall be bestowed on us, even by the very villains who have wronged us. (Laetitia Pilkington, *Memoirs of Mrs Laetitia Pilkington*, 3 vols, (1749–54), 1770, p. 167)

3

Corporal distinction may at first, perhaps, have the greatest weight in the argument against us. This must relate to strength, and the inconvenience of child-bearing: With respect to the first every one knows it is greatly increased by exercise, and that if the women used as much as the men, though they might not in general be able to carry such great burdens as them, they would, at least be strong enough to undergo all the fatigues of business, or war.

. . . those who are brought up to labour, or take great exercise, are more robust than the delicate ladies who handle nothing but their needle. Hence it may be concluded, that if both sexes equally laboured, and took the same exercise, they would, perhaps, be equally vigorous.

Ask a man his opinion of the women in general, and he readily answers, (if he speaks from the heart) we were made for his use and convenience; appropriated to the bringing up of children in their tender years, and the regulation of household economy. Some of a more enlivened turn may, perhaps, add 'there are women who have sense and conduct, but if one critically examines either, the woman is always discovered; that they have neither prudence or resolution, devoid of the genuine sensibility with which men are endowed; and that the will of heaven is wisely executed by the men in preventing their dabbling in the sciences, having any share in the government of states, or employments of any real importance; that it would be a fine thing indeed to hear a woman speak in the House, or plead at the Bar; or how amply ridiculous would it be to see a lady actually upon the Bench, summing up the principal points of argumentation to clear the intellects of a jury; or turning to the hostile field, behold a female general conducting an army, giving battle to the enemy, or regulating a siege.

. . . Their general ignorance, which is ascribed to the difference of sex, should be attributed to the difference of education; to the prejudice and error they so early imbibe, and which no pains are scarce ever taken to eradicate; to the example set before them by their sex; to the custom of what is so absurdly called, Good Breeding; to the restraint, subjection and timidity, which are imposed upon them. (Anon., *Female Rights Vindicated*, 1758, preface, pp. 91, 28–9, 98)

4

. . . How many nervous diseases have been contracted? How much feebleness of constitution has been acquired, by forming a false idea of female excellence, and endeavouring, by our art, to bring nature to the ply of our imagination. Our sons are suffered to enjoy with freedom that time which is not devoted to study, and may follow, unmolested, the strong impulses which nature has wisely given . . . but if, before her natural vivacity is entirely subdued by habit, little Miss is inclined to show her locomotive tricks in a manner not entirely agreeable to the trammels of custom, she is reproved with a sharpness which gives her a consciousness of having highly transgressed the laws of decorum: and what with the vigilance of those who are appointed to superintend her conduct, and the false bias they have imposed on her mind, every vigorous exertion is suppressed, the mind and body yield to the tyranny of error, and nature is charged with all those imperfections which we alone owe to the blunders of art. (Catherine Macaulay, *Letters on Education*, 1790, pp. 46–7)

5

I wish to persuade women to endeavour to acquire strength, both of mind and body, and to convince them that soft phrases, susceptibility of heart, delicacy of sentiment, and refinement of taste, are almost synonymous with epithets of weakness, and that those beings who are only objects of pity, and that kind of love which has been termed its sister, will soon become objects of contempt.

Dismissing, then, those pretty feminine phrases, which the men condescendingly use to soften our slavish dependence, and despising that weak elegancy of mind, exquisite sensibility, and sweet docility of manners, supposed to be the sexual characteristics of the weaker vessel, I wish to show that elegance is inferior to virtue, that the first object of laudable ambition is to obtain a character as a human being, regardless of the distinction of sex and that secondary views should be brought to this simple touchstone.

. . . sedentary employments render the majority of women sickly – and false notions of female excellence make them proud of this delicacy, though it be another fetter, that by calling the attention continually to the body, cramps the activity of the mind.

Men have superior strength of body; but were it not for the mistaken notions of beauty, women would acquire sufficient to enable them to earn their own subsistence, the true definition of independence; and to bear those bodily inconveniences and exertions that are requisite to strengthen the mind. Let us then, by being allowed to take the same exercise as boys, not only during infancy, but youth, arrive at perfection of body, that we may know how far the natural superiority of man extends.

Why are girls to be told that they resemble angels; but to sink them below women? Or, that a gentle innocent female is an object that comes nearer to the idea that we have formed of angels than any other. Yet they are told, at the same time, that they are only like angels when they are young and beautiful; consequently it is their persons, not their virtues, that procure them this homage. (Mary Wollstonecraft, *Vindication of the Rights of Woman* (1792), Miriam Kramnick, 1978, introduction, pp. 171, 182–3, 194)

6

. . . to call much less than absolute and unlimited power, that which men may, and often do, exercise over their wives; is only deceiving ourselves, and prevents us perhaps from searching to the bottom an evil, which can never be remedied, till that is faithfully done.

To point out the frequent and melancholy abuses of this authority, would be to draw a picture, of what many an amiable woman suffers from it; and many an unamiable one too. For though men are apt, and perhaps naturally enough, to suppose, that these two characteristics merit very different treatments; yet they should consider, that all have the feelings of right and wrong, – all are equally entitled to justice, – though all have not an equal claim to love and admiration. (Mary Hays, *Appeal to the Men of Great Britain in Behalf of Women* 1798, p. 264)

(b) Women Claim Equality

7

In short let her own sex, at least, do her justice; lay aside diabolical envy, and its brother malice, with all their accursed company, sly whispering, cruel backbiting, spiteful detraction, and the rest of that hideous crew, which, I hope, are very falsely said to attend the tea table, being more apt to think they attend those public places where virtuous women never come. Let the men malign one another, if they think fit, and strive to pull down merit, when they cannot equal it. Let us be better-natured, than to give way to any kind of disrespectful thought of so bright an ornament of our sex merely because she has better sense; for I doubt not that our hearts will tell us, that this is the real and unpardonable offence, whatever may be pretended . . . let us freely own the superiority of this sublime genius, as I do in the sincerity of my soul, pleased that a woman triumphs, and proud to follow in her train. Let us offer her the palm which is so justly her due; and if we pretend to any laurels, lay them willingly at her feet. (Mary Astell in the preface to the manuscript diary of Lady Mary Wortley Montagu (1725), quoted from Myra Reynolds, *The Learned Lady in England, 1650–1760*, 1920, p. 200)

8

. . . Men, by thinking us incapable of improving our intellects, have entirely thrown us out of the advantages of education, and thereby contributed as much as possible to make us the senseless creatures they imagine us. So that for want of education, we are rendered subject to all the follies they dislike in us . . .

. . . And as our sex, when it applies to learning, may be said at least to keep pace with the men, so are they more to be esteemed for their learning than the latter: Since they are under a necessity of surmounting the softness they were educated in; of renouncing the pleasure and indolence to which cruel custom seem'd to condemn them to overcome the external impediments in their way of study; and to conquer the disadvantageous notions, which the vulgar of both sexes entertain of learning in women. And whether it be these difficulties add any keenness to a female understanding, or that nature has given women, a quicker more penetrating genius than to men, it is self-evident that many of our sex have far out-stript the men. Why then are we not as fit to learn and teach the sciences, at least to our own sex, as they fancy themselves to be . . .?

We may easily conclude then, that if our sex, as it hitherto appears, have all the talents requisite to learn and teach those sciences, which qualify men for power and dignity, they are equally capable of applying their knowledge to practice in exercising that power and dignity. (Anon., *Woman Not Inferior to Man*, from the Sophia Pamphlets, 1739–40, pp. 56, 38, 48)

9

If under the oppressive tyranny of the men, we have been able to give such striking instances of our fortitude, chastity, and abilities for learning; how much more conspicuous might we have expected to find the glorious actions of the sex had we been in everything upon a footing with them; – opportunities equally favourable to acquire . . . and occasions equally frequent to testify our knowledge and our skill! In all that is immediately dependent upon ourselves, how greatly superior do we appear even under our disadvantages.

. . . women in general are as fit for the offices of state, as those who most commonly fill them. All women are not born with great capacities any more than the men; but balance the account, and it will not, at least, poise against us. (Anon., *Female Rights Vindicated*, 1758, preface and p. 43)

10

She was even ashamed to proclaim her own great genius, probably because the custom of the times discountenanced poetical excellence in a female. The gentlemen of the quill published it not, perhaps envying her superior talents; and her bookseller, complying with national prejudices, put a fictitious name to her Love's Contrivance, thro' fear that the work shou'd be condemned if known to be feminine. With modest diffidences she sent her performances, like orphans, into the world, without so much as a nobleman to protect them; but they did not need to be supported by interest, they were admired as soon as known, their real standard, merit, brought crowding spectators to the playhouses, and the female author, tho' unknown, heard applauses, such as have since been heaped on the great author and actor, Colley Cibber . . .

This convinces me that . . . that foolish assertion, that female minds are not capable of producing literary works equal even to those of Pope, now loses ground, and probably the next age may be taught by our pens that our geniuses have been hitherto cramped and smothered, but not extinguished, and that the sovereignty which the male part of our creation have, until now usurped over us, is unreasonably arbitrary: And, further, that our natural abilities entitle us to larger share, not only in literary decisions, but that, with the present directors, we are equally entitled to power both in church and state . . . ('To the World', the preliminary address by an anonymous female author to *The Work of the Celebrated Mrs. Centlivre*, 1761)

11

While men pursue interest, honour, pleasure, as accords with their several dispositions, women, who have too much delicacy, sense and spirit, to degrade themselves by the vilest of interchanges, remain insulated beings, and must be content tamely to look on without taking any part in the great, though often absurd and tragical drama of life. Hence the eccentricities of conduct, with which women of superior minds have been accused – the struggles, the despairing though generous struggles, of an ardent spirit, denied scope for its exertions! The strong feelings, and strong energies, which properly directed, in a field sufficiently wide, might – ah! what might they not have aided? – forced back, and pent up, ravage and destroy the mind which gave them birth. (Mary Hays, *Memoirs of Emma Courtney* [1796], quoted from Claire Tomalin, *The Life and Death of Mary Wollstonecraft*, 1974, p. 197)

12

. . . did women receive equal advantage of education, there is every reason to suppose, they would equal men in the sublime science of politics; which as it includes the whole art of governing the multitude well in the most liberal sense of the word, requires not only such talents as the one sex is allowed to possess in common with the other, but includes likewise strength of mind – extensive foresight, – genius to plan schemes of importance – and resolution and stability to put them in execution. (Mary Hays, *Appeal to the Men of Great Britain in Behalf of Women*, 1798, p. 36)

(c) Women Act

13

Taunton, Somersetshire, June 25. Several hundred women and a great number of men, assembled in this town, in a tumultuous manner, and proceeded to a large weir, call'd French Weir, near a set of grist-mills call'd the Town-mills, when the women went briskly to work demolishing it, and that so as to prevent any corn being ground at the mills. The men all the while stood lookers on, giving the women many huzzas and commendations for their dexterity in the work. Their reason for it was a dislike they had to the manager of the mills, whom they charge with sending flour to other parts, whereby they apprehend corn was advanced to a higher price than otherwise it would have been. (*Gentleman's Magazine*, 1753, p. 343)

14

Newcastle, Sept 6. We are advised from Penrith, that lately a young girl in Kendal being with child and near her time, sent for a physician in town to do her the office of a midwife, which he refused, and giving her hard names, left her: She in return for this usage, and willing to do good for evil, dignified the man by declaring him the father of the child. (*Norwich Mercury*, 13 September 1755, quoted from the *Newcastle Journal*)

15

Thursday, 16th June . . . A mob (chiefly of women) assembled on the 15th at Cambridge, broke open a storehouse in which were lodged about 15 quarters of wheat, the property of a farmer, who had that day refused 9s. 6d. a bushel for it, and carry'd it all off. The mayor caused the proclamation to be read, but before the hour was expired, the mischief was done, and the mob dispersed. This day the mob assembled again, having intelligence of 27 sacks of flour being lodged at Small-bridges, and notwithstanding the constables attended, about ten they began to assault the place; and after a vigorous resistance in which seven or eight of them were dangerously wounded, they carried it, forced the mayor to release one of their number that had been made prisoner, and then went off in triumph. (*Gentleman's Magazine*, 1757, p. 286)

16

Last Saturday a female mob assembled in the market place at Hereford, upon information that one of the badgers had offered to buy grain above the market price; and, after seizing the badger, and beating him in a very severe manner, they broke all the windows in his house. (*London Chronicle*, 1757, p. 430)

17

On Saturday the market at Bewdley was put in great confusion by the assembling of a number of women, who cut open some bags of wheat, and insisted on their being sold at 7s. per strike, the price wheat sold at the Thursday before at Kidderminster. (*London Chronicle*, 1757, vol. 1, p. 527)

18

London, Sept. 26 . . . one day last week as the Jury of Annoyance were going through the markets of Salisbury, in order to examine the weights and measures, they came to a woman that sold butter, who thrust a half-crown into half a pound of butter, in order that it might be full weight, which being observed by a poor woman, she purchased the butter, and got the half crown, the woman not daring to complain for fear of discovery. (*Jackson's Oxford Journal*, 27 September, 1766)

19

On Saturday last a disturbance happened in the butter-market at Ashby-de-la-zouch; occasioned by a farmer asking two-pence per pound extraordinary for butter; when an old woman clapping one hand in the nape of his neck, with the other rubbed a pound of butter all over his face. (*Jackson's Oxford Journal*, 18 October, 1766)

20

A letter from Burton-on-Trent, in Staffordshire, informs us that on Friday the 31st of last month, several women were taken up for destroying the fences for enclosing the Rewhay, a common near that place, and brought to Burton, where they were examined before the Justices, and warrants made out for their commitment to Stafford gaol, but the populace getting information of the affair, immediately called to arms, and after a few broadsides of stones, dirt, etc. being discharged at the persons who were conducting the prisoners to confinement, they rescued the women from the hands of the officers, and took them away in triumph. (*Northampton Mercury*, 10 June 1771)

21

A certain manufacturer of worsted threatened a sister of ours, whom he employed, that he would send all his jersey to be spun at the mill; and further insulted her with the pretended superiority of that work. She having more spirit than discretion, stirred up the sisterhood and they stirred up all the men they could influence (not a few) to go and destroy the mills erected in and near Leicester, and this is the origin of the late riots there. (From the 'Humble Petition of the Poor Spinners', Leicester, 1788, British Museum Tracts, B. 544(10), quoted from B. L. Hutchins, *Women in Modern Industry*, 1915, app., p. 271)

22

[From a letter found on a weaver from Middleton Cheney describing events in Nottingham in September 1800]

. . . the bakers and flour sellers had a private meeting on Sunday and had agreed to raise the price of flour up to six shillings a stone on Monday and there having been but a very scanty supply all the week before exasperated the inhabitants to that degree that they begun with them on the Sunday night . . .

Your hearts would have ached to have seen the women calling for bread and declaring they would fight till they died before they would be used so any longer however the gentlemen began to be frightened and a meeting of the sheriff and county gentlemen has been held at the County Hall and they have agreed to compel their tenants to bring corn to market and to sell it in small quantities to the poor thus has the price been lowered almost four pounds a quarter by nothing but the courage of the people in declaring against oppression . . . (Home Office Papers, Public Record Office, HO 42/51, Whitmore to Portland (letter enclosed), 17 September 1800, quoted from *Popular Protest and Public Order*, ed. John Stevenson and Roland Quinault, 1974, p. 58)

23

A number of women . . . proceeded to Gosden wind-mill, where, abusing the miller for having served them with brown flour, they seized on the cloth with which he was then dressing meal according to the directions of the Bread Act, and cut it into a thousand pieces; threatening at the same time to serve all similar utensils he might in future attempt to use in the same manner. The amazonian leader of the petticoated cavalcade afterwards regaled her associates with a guinea's worth of liquor at the Crab Tree public house. (Quoted from E. P. Thompson, 'The moral economy of the English crowd in the eighteenth century', *Past and Present*, no. 50, February 1971)

Bibliography

Unless otherwise stated, the place of publication is London.

Books

Aikin, J., *A Description of the Country from Thirty to Forty Miles round Manchester* (1795).

Alexander, William, *The History of Women*, 2 vols (1779).

Anon., *An Address to the P——t on Behalf of the Starving Multitude* (1766).

Anon., *Cursory Remarks on Enclosure . . . by a Country Farmer* (1786).

Anon., *Every Woman Her Own House-Keeper*, 2 vols (1796).

Anon., *Female Rights Vindicated, or The Equality of the Sexes Morally and Physically Proved. By a Lady* (1758).

Anon., *Genuine Memoirs of the Celebrated Miss Maria Brown*, 2 vols (1766).

Anon., *Laws Relating to Masters and Servants* (1755).

Anon., *The Laws Respecting Women* (1777).

Anon., *A Political Enquiry into the Consequences of Enclosing Waste Lands* (1785).

Anon., *A Present for a Servant-Maid* (1743).

Anon., *A Present for Servants* (1799).

Anon., *Remarks upon Mr Webber's Scheme and the Drapers' Pamphlet* (1741).

Anon., *Thoughts on the Use of Machines in the Cotton Manufacture. By a Friend of the Poor* (1780).

Anon., *Woman Not Inferior to Man, or A Short and Modest Vindication of the Natural Rights of the Fair Sex to a Perfect Equality of Power, Dignity and Esteem with Men*, from the Sophia Pamphlets (1739–40).

Anon., *Women Triumphant, or The Excellency of the Female Sex Asserted in Opposition to the Male* (1721).

Archenholz, J. W. von, *A Picture of England Translated from the French* (1791).

Ariès, Philip, *Centuries of Childhood* (1962).

Arnold, Ralph, *A Yeoman of Kent: An Account of Richard Hayes (1725–1790) of Cobham* (1949).

Astell, Mary (sometimes attributed), *An Essay in Defence of the Female Sex* (1696).

Astell, Mary, *A Serious Proposal to the Ladies for the Advancement of Their True and Greatest Interest*, Pt 1 (1696).

Astell, Mary, *Some Reflections upon Marriage*, (1700), 3rd edn (1706).

Ayton, Richard, *A Voyage round Great Britain Undertaken in the Summer of the Year 1813*, 2 vols (1814).

Bailey, J., and Culley, G., *General View of the County of Northumberland* (1797).

Baird, Thomas, *General View of the Agriculture of the County of Middlesex* (1793).

Bald, R., *General View of the Coal Trade of Scotland* (1812).

Barker, Jane, 'A Virgin Life', from *Poetical Recreations*, Pt 1 (1688).

Bennett, Rev. John, *Letters to a Young Lady on a Variety of Useful and Interesting Subjects*, 2 vols (1795).

Blackstone, Sir William, *Commentaries on the Laws of England in Four Books* (1753), 12th edn, ed. Edward Christian (1793).

Boswell, James, *Boswell's Life of Johnson* (1776), ed. G. B. Hill and L. F. Powell (1934–50).

Brand, John, *Observations on Popular Antiquities*, 2 vols ([1777], 1813).

Broughton, Thomas, *Serious Advice and Warning to Servants* (1746), 4th edn (1763).

Burgess, Marion Ardern, *A History of Burlington School* (1937).

Burton, John, *An Essay towards a Complete New System of Midwifery* (1751).

Cadogan, W., *An Essay upon Nursing and the Management of Children* (1748).

Campbell, R., *The London Tradesman* (1747).

Cappe, Catherine, *An Account of Two Charity Schools for the Education of Girls etc.* (1800).

Cappe, Catherine, *Memoirs of the Life of the Late Mrs Catherine Cappe* (1824).

The Case of the Poor Cotton Spinners (1780).

The Case of the Poor Straw Hat Makers in the Counties of Hertford, Bedford, Buckingham, etc. (1719).

Centlivre, Mrs, *The Work of the Celebrated Mrs Centlivre* (1761).

Chapone, Hester, *Posthumous Works*, 4 vols ([1773], 1807).

Charke, Mrs Charlotte, *A Narrative of the Life of Mrs Charlotte Charke* (1775).

Collections towards the History and Antiquities of Bedfordshire (1783).

Collier, Jeremy, *Essays upon Several Moral Subjects* (1705).

Cowper, William, *Correspondence of William Cowper*, ed. Thomas Wright (1904).

Cowper, William, *Verse and Letters of William Cowper*, ed. Brian Spiller (1968).

Davies, David *The Case of Labourers in Husbandry* (1795).

Day, Thomas, *Sandford and Merton* (1786).

Deering, Charles, *Nottinghamia Vetus et Nova* (1751).

Defoe, Daniel, *Augusta Triumphans, or The Way to Make London the Most Flourishing City in the Universe* ([1728], 1841).

Defoe, Daniel, *The Complete English Tradesman* (1725–7), from *The Novels and Miscellaneous Works of Daniel Defoe* (1840–1).

Defoe, Daniel, *Conjugal Lewdness, or Matrimonial Whoredom* (1727).

Defoe, Daniel, *Everybody's Business Is Nobody's Business* ([1725], 1840–1).

Defoe, Daniel, *The Great Law of Subordination Consider'd, or The Insolence and Unsufferable Behaviour of Servants in England* (1724).

Defoe, Daniel, *Moll Flanders* (1721), Abbey Classics, Vol. 21 (1924).

Defoe, Daniel, *A Plan of the English Commerce* (1728).

Defoe, Daniel, *Religious Courtship: Being Historical Discourses on the Necessity for Marrying Religious Husbands and Wives Only* ([1722], 1840–1).

Defoe, Daniel, *Roxana, or The Fortunate Mistress* ([1724], 1840–1).

Defoe, Daniel, *A Tour through England and Wales*, Everyman's Library, 2 vols ([1724–7], 1948).

Defoe, Daniel, *A Weekly Review of the Affairs of France (1704–13)*, ed. Arthur Wellesley Secord (New York, 1938).

Doran, Dr, *A Lady of the Last Century (Mrs Elizabeth Montagu)* (1873).

Dossie, Robert, *Memoirs of Agriculture and Other Commercial Arts*, 3 vols (1768).

Duck, Stephen, *Poems on Several Occasions* (1736).

Dyer, George, *The Complaints of the Poor People of England*, 2nd edn (1793).

Dyer, George, *Poems* (1792).

Eden, F. M., *The State of the Poor*, 3 vols (1797).

Edgeworth, Maria, *Letters from Literary Ladies* (1795).

Edgeworth, Maria, *Practical Education* (1798).

Ellis, William, *The Country Housewife's Family Companion* (1750).

Ellis, William, *The Modern Husbandman*, 4 vols (1744).

Fielding, Henry, *The History of Tom Jones*, Everyman's Library, 2 vols ([1749], 1908–9).

Fielding, Henry, *Love in Several Masques: A Play* (1728).

Fielding, Henry, *An Old Man Taught Wisdom, or The Virgin Unmask'd: A Play* (1734).

Fielding, Sir John, *A Plan for a Preservatory and Reformatory for the Benefit of Deserted Girls, and Penitent Prostitutes* (1758).

Fordyce, Dr James, *The Character and Conduct of the Female Sex* (1776).

Fordyce, Dr James, *Sermons to Young Women* (1766).

French, Gilbert J., *The Life and Times of Samuel Crompton* (1868).

Gardiner, William, *Music and Friends*, 3 vols (1838–53).

Gawthern, Abigail, *The Diary of Abigail Gawthern of Nottingham, 1751–1810*, ed. Adrian Henstock, Thoroton Society of Nottinghamshire Record Series (1978–9).

Gay, John, *The Beggar's Opera* (1728).

Girdler, J. S., *Observations on the Pernicious Consequences of Forstalling, Regrating and Engrossing* (1800).

Gisborne, Thomas, *An Enquiry into the Duties of the Female Sex*, (1797) 3rd edn (1798).

Goldsmith, Oliver, *The Works of Oliver Goldsmith* (1845).

Gregory, John, *A Father's Legacy to His Daughters* (1774).

Grosley, P. J., *A Tour to London, or New Observations on England and Its Inhabitants*, trans. from the French by Thomas Nugent ([1765], 1772).

The Grub-Street Opera (July 1731), air XXXV.

Hanway, Jonas, *An Earnest Appeal for Mercy to the Children of the Poor* (1766).

Hanway, Jonas, *A Journal of Eight Days' Journey* (1757).

Hanway, Jonas, *A Plan for Establishing a Charity House, or Charity Houses for the Reception of Repenting Prostitutes, etc.* (1758).

Hanway, Jonas, *Virtue in Humble Life*, 2 vols (1774).

Hardy, W. J., and Page, W., *Bedfordshire County Records* (1907).

Harris, Walter, *Treatise on the Acute Diseases of Infants* (1742).

Hayley, William, *A Philosophical, Historical and Moral Essay on Old Maids*, 3 vols (1786).

Hays, Mary, *Appeal to the Men of Great Britain in Behalf of Women* (1798). See the *Analytical Review* (July 1798), where it was reviewed.

Holcroft, Thomas, *Anna St Ives*, 5 vols (1792).

Hone, William, *The Everyday Book of Popular Amusements* (1826–7).

Howard, John, *An Account of the Principal Lazarettos in Europe, etc.* (1789).

Howard, John, *The State of the Prisons* (1777).

Hutton, William, *A History of Birmingham* (1781), 3rd edn (1806).

Hutton, William, *The History of Derby* (1791).

Hutton, William, *A Journey to London* (1785).

Inchbald, Elizabeth, *Nature and Art* (1796), from Mrs Barbauld (ed.), *The British Novelists*, Vol. 27 (1820).

Kalm, Pehr, *Account of His Visit to England on His Way to America in 1748*, trans. Joseph Lucas (1892).

Kennedy, Joseph, *History of Leyton* (1894).

Lackington, James, *Memoirs of the Forty-Five First Years of the Life of James Lackington*, 7th edn (1794).

Lee, William, *Daniel Defoe: His Life and Recently Discovered Writings*, 3 vols (1869).

Lillo, George, *The London Merchant: A Play* (1731).

Lysons, Daniel, *The Environs of London*, 4 vols (1796).

Macaulay, Catherine, *Letters on Education* (1790).

Malcolm, J. P., *Anecdotes of the Manners and Customs of London during the 18th Century* (1807).

Malthus, Thomas, *An Essay on the Principle of Population*, ed. T. H. Hollingsworth ([1798], 1973).

Mandeville, Bernard de, *The Fable of the Bees* (1714), 3rd edn, 2 vols (1724).

Mandeville, Bernard de, *A Modest Defence of Public Stews* (1724).

Mandeville, Bernard de, *The Virgin Unmask'd, or Female Dialogues, etc.* (1714), 2nd edn. (1724).

Manley, Mary de la Rivière, *The New Atlantis*, 2 vols (1709).

Marshall, William, *Minutes of Agriculture Made on a Farm of 300 Acres . . . Near Croydon, Surrey* (1778).

Marshall, William, *The Rural Economy of Gloucestershire*, 2 vols (1796).

Marshall, William, *The Rural Economy of the Midland Counties*, 2 vols (1790).

Marshall, William, *The Rural Economy of Norfolk*, 2 vols (1787).

Massie, J., *An Account of a Plan for Charity Houses* (1758).

Merchants' Miscellany and Travellers' Complete Compendium (1785).

Misson, M., *Memoirs and Observations in His Travels over England, etc.*, trans. from the French by Mr Ozell (1719).

Mitcham Settlement Examinations, 1784–1814, ed. Blanche Berryman, Surrey Record Society, Vol. 27 (1973).

Montagu, Lady Mary Wortley, *Letters and Works of Lady Mary Wortley Montagu*, ed. Lord Wharncliffe, 3 vols (1837).

Moore, Francis, *The Exhorbitant Price of Provisions* (1773).

More, Hannah, *Essays on Various Subjects, Principally Designed for Young Ladies* (1791).

More, Hannah, *Strictures on the Modern System of Female Education* (1799), 5th edn (1800).

Moritz, Carl Philip, *Journeys of a German in England in 1782*, trans. and ed. Reginald Nettel (1965).

Paine, Thomas, *The Writings of Thomas Paine, 1774–1779*, ed. M. D. Conway, 2 vols (1894).

Palmer, Charlotte, *It Is and It Is Not a Novel*, 2 vols (1792).

Pargeter, W., *Observations on Maniacal Disorders* (1792).

Paulson, R., *Hogarth: His Life, Art and Times*, 2 vols (1931).

Pennant, Thomas, *Tour in the North of Scotland* (1774).

Pennington, Lady Sarah, *An Unfortunate Mother's Advice to Her Absent Daughters in a Letter to Miss Pennington* (1761), 5th edn (1770).

Petition of Lace Manufacturers to House of Commons (1698).

Pettigrew, Thomas Joseph, *Memoirs of the Life and Writings of the Late John Cockley Lettsom*, 3 vols (1817).

Phillips, Sir R., *A Morning Walk from London to Kew* (1817).

Pilkington, Laetitia, *Memoirs of Mrs Laetitia Pilkington, Wife of the Revd Mr Matthew Pilkington, Written by Herself*, 3 vols (Dublin [1749], 1770).

Pinchbeck, Ivy, and Hewitt, Margaret, *Children in English Society*, 2 vols (1969–73).

Piozzi, Hester, *The Intimate Letters of Hester Piozzi and Penelope Pennington, 1788–1821*, ed. Oswald G. Knapp (1914).

Place, Francis, *The Autobiography of Francis Place (1771–1854)*, ed. Mary Thale (1972).

Plumb, J. H., 'The new world of children in eighteenth-century England', *Past and Present*, no. 67 (May 1975).

Pococke, Dr Richard, *The Travels through England of Dr Richard Pococke*, ed. J. J. Cartwright, 2 vols, Camden Society (1888–9).

Pringle, A., *General View of the County of Westmoreland* (1794).

The Purefoy Letters, 1735–53, ed. G. Eland, 2 vols (1931).

Richardson, Samuel, *Correspondence of Samuel Richardson*, ed. A. L. Barbauld (1804).

Richardson, Samuel, *The History of Clarissa Harlowe in a Series of Letters* (1748), from *The Works of Samuel Richardson*, ed. Rev. E. Mangin, 8 vols (1811).

Richardson, Samuel, *Letters from Particular Friends on the Most Important Occasions* (1741).

Richardson, Samuel, *Pamela, or Virtue Rewarded*, 4 vols (1740).

Richardson, Samuel, *Sir Charles Grandison* (1753–4), from *The Works of Samuel Richardson*, ed. Rev. E. Mangin, 8 vols (1811).

Rudder, Samuel, *A New History of Gloucestershire* (1779).

Ryder, Dudley, *The Diary of Dudley Ryder, 1715–1716*, ed. William Matthews (1939).
Smeaton, John, *A Narrative of the Building and a Description of the Construction of the Eddystone Lighthouse with Stone* (1791).
Smith, Adam, *The Wealth of Nations*, Everyman's Library ([1776], 1921).
Smith, William, *The State of the Gaols in London, Westminster, and the Borough of Southwark* (1776).
Steele, Richard, *The Tender Husband: A Play* (1705).
Sterne, Laurence, *Letters of Laurence Sterne*, ed. Lewis P. Curtis (1935).
Stevenson, John, and Quinault, Roland (eds), *Popular Protest and Public Order* (1974).
Stock, J. E., *Memoirs of the Life of Thomas Beddoes* (1811).
Stone, Lawrence, *The Family, Sex and Marriage in England, 1500–1800* (1977).
Stout, William, *The Autobiography of William Stout of Lancaster, 1665–1752*, ed. J. D. Marshall (1967).
Stringer, M., *English and Welsh Mines and Minerals* (1699).
Swift, Jonathan, *The Furniture of a Woman's Mind* (1727).
Swift, Jonathan, *The Works of Jonathan Swift, DD*, ed. Sir Walter Scott, 19 vols (1814).
Thompson, E. P. 'The moral economy of the English crowd in the 18th century', *Past and Present*, no. 50 (February 1971).
Turner, Thomas, *The Diary of a Georgian Shopkeeper, 1754–65*, ed. G. H. Jennings (1979).
Vancouver, Charles, *General View of the Agriculture of the County of Devon* (1808).
Wakefield, Priscilla, *Reflections on the Present Condition of the Female Sex with Suggestions for Its Improvement*, (1798), 2nd edn (1817).
Watts, Isaac, *An Esssay towards the Encouragement of Charity Schools* (1728).
Watts, Isaac, *The Improvement of the Mind, to Which Is Added a Discourse on the Education of Children and Youth* ([1725], 1819).
White, C., *Treatise on the Management of Pregnant and Lying-In Women* (1777).
Wilkes, Rev. Mr Wettenhall, *A Letter of Genteel and Moral Advice to a Young Lady* (1740), 8th edn (1766).
Wollstonecraft, Mary, *Collected Letters of Mary Wollstonecraft*, ed. Ralph M. Wardle (1979).
Wollstonecraft, Mary, *Thoughts on the Education of Daughters* (1787).
Wollstonecraft, Mary, *Vindication of the Rights of Woman* (1792), ed. Miriam Kramnick (1978).
Wollstonecraft, Mary, *The Wrongs of Woman*, from *Mary and The Wrongs of Woman*, ed. Gary Kelly (1980), Vol. 2.
Woodforde, Rev. James, *Diary of a Country Parson: the Reverend James Woodforde, 1758–1802*, ed. John Beresford, 5 vols (1924–31).
Young, Arthur, *The Autobiography of Arthur Young with Selections from His Correspondence*, ed. M. Betham-Edwards (1898).
Young, Arthur, *The Farmer's Tour through the East of England*, 4 vols (1771).

Young, Arthur, *A General View of the Agriculture of the County of Suffolk* (1797).

Young, Arthur, *A Six Months' Tour through the North of England*, 3 vols (1770).

Young, Arthur, *A Six Weeks' Tour through the Southern Counties of England and Wales*, ([1768], 1772).

Journals and Newspapers

Annals of Agriculture, vol. 17.
Annual Register
Bath Chronicle
British Chronicle, or Pugh's Hereford Journal
British Merchant
Daily Advertiser
Daily Courant
Daily Post-Boy
Gentleman's Magazine
The Guardian
Ipswich Journal
Jackson's Oxford Journal
Kentish Gazette
Ladies Magazine
London Chronicle
London Evening Post
Newcastle Journal
Newgate Calendar
Northampton Mercury
Norwich Mercury
Public Advertiser
Reading Mercury
Salisbury and Winchester Journal
Sarah Farley's Bristol Journal
The Spectator
Whitehall Evening Post

Index

Subjects which occur frequently throughout the volume, and where the Contents List gives sufficient indication of the area in which they are considered, have not been indexed here; nor have the names of those obscure characters who occur only once.